'This book shows how econometrics can be of real value to understanding major global problems such as violent conflict and poverty. With an easily readable style, the book encourages everyone to try their hand at running regressions.'

Professor Anthony Addison
Executive Director, Brooks World Poverty Institute, University of Manchester

'*Running Regressions* ... combines statistical analysis with the relevant theories and their economic policy implications. [It] encourages the reader to see the relevance and importance of empirical analysis, and also allows the reader to see the links between theory and empirical analysis in a clear and consistent way. The writing and presentation style is very user-friendly and accessible.'

Professor Philip Arestis
University of Cambridge

'Michelle Baddeley and Diana Barrowclough have written an outstanding book for undergraduate economists. It offers a well-structured introduction to econometric models via a series of illuminating applications. Readers see not only the statistical tools themselves, but also how they can be *used* to address important questions in economics. Students will welcome the seamless integration of economic and statistical theory in an accessible manner, and teachers will appreciate how effectively the book shows the relevance of econometrics to economics.'

Dr Nicholas Fawcett
University of Oxford

'This is an exceptionally readable and interesting book. Students now have an econometrics text that they will enjoy. It shows, by way of example, the power and usefulness of econometric analysis.'

Professor Bernard Fingleton
University of Strathclyde

'For students of politics and international relations, *Running Regressions* demystifies an often daunting set of analytical tools and provides practical, critical advice on how to use them.'

Dr Carolyn Deere
Global Economic Governance Programme, University College, Oxford

Running Regressions

A Practical Guide to Quantitative Research in Economics, Finance and Development Studies

Running Regressions introduces social science undergraduates, particularly those studying economics and business, to the practical aspects of regression analysis, without adopting an esoteric, mathematical approach. It shows that statistical analysis can be simultaneously straightforward, useful and interesting, and can deal with topical, real-world issues. Each chapter introduces an economic theory or idea by relating it to an issue of topical interest, and explains how data and econometric analysis can be used to test it. The book can be used as a self-standing text or to supplement conventional econometric texts. It is also ideally suited as a guide to essays and project work.

Michelle Baddeley is Director of Studies (Economics), Fellow and College Lecturer at Gonville and Caius College, Cambridge. She is the author of *Investment: Theories and Analysis* (2003).

Diana Barrowclough is a senior economist, Office of the Secretary General, United Nations Conference for Trade and Development (UNCTAD). She formerly lectured economics at the University of Cambridge, where she was a fellow of St John's College.

Running Regressions

A Practical Guide to Quantitative Research in
Economics, Finance and Development Studies

Michelle Baddeley
Gonville and Caius College, Cambridge

Diana Barrowclough
United Nations Conference for Trade and Development (UNCTAD)

CAMBRIDGE
UNIVERSITY PRESS

CAMBRIDGE
UNIVERSITY PRESS

University Printing House, Cambridge CB2 8BS, United Kingdom

One Liberty Plaza, 20th Floor, New York, NY 10006, USA

477 Williamstown Road, Port Melbourne, VIC 3207, Australia

314-321, 3rd Floor, Plot 3, Splendor Forum, Jasola District Centre, New Delhi - 110025, India

103 Penang Road, #05-06/07, Visioncrest Commercial, Singapore 238467

Cambridge University Press is part of the University of Cambridge.

It furthers the University's mission by disseminating knowledge in the pursuit of education, learning and research at the highest international levels of excellence.

www.cambridge.org
Information on this title: www.cambridge.org/9780521603089

First published 2009

A catalogue record for this publication is available from the British Library

Library of Congress Cataloging in Publication data
Baddeley, Michelle, 1962–
Running regressions : a practical introduction to OLS in economics, finance and development studies / by Michelle Baddeley & Diane Barrowclough
    p. cm.
Includes index.
ISBN 978-0-521-84211-2 (hdbk.) – ISBN 978-0-521-60308-9 (pbk.)
1. Econometrics. 2. Least squares   3. Regression analysis.   I. Barrowclough, Diana.   II. Title.
HB139.B34   2009
330.01'519536–dc22

                                                                                2009007332

ISBN 978-0-521-84211-2 Hardback
ISBN 978-0-521-60308-9 Paperback

To my parents (M.C.B.)

To my family (D.V.B.)

Contents

Figures

Tables

Boxes

Acknowledgements

Any imprecision and all mistakes/omissions remain our own. However, we do gratefully acknowledge the help of numerous people from Cambridge University Press: including Liz Davey, Lynn Dunlop, Phil Good, Chris Harrison and Pat Maurice. Thank you also to Fran Robinson for compiling the index, and to our copy editor – Jon Billam. We have also benefited from helpful substantive comments from various readers including Peter Batchelor (UNDP), Tony Addison and Charles Gore (UNCTAD) as well as anonymous reviewers. We would like to thank Chez Hall (Department of Engineering, Cambridge University) for his invaluable advice in our research into aircraft emissions, and the International Civil Aviation Authority for data on airline passengers and revenues.

We also thank the generations of Cambridge University undergraduates whom we have had the pleasure to know and to teach; and whose curiosity and enthusiasm inspired us to write this book. The 'toolbox' outlined in *Running Regressions* offers a fascinating and increasingly relevant way to improve our understanding of topical world issues, and we hope that these pages will continue to spark our students' (and graduates') interest. Some who helped directly by commenting on early drafts of chapters included Arun Advani, Philomena Aw, Bruce Chen, Nicholas Fawcett, Oliver de Groot, Heather Katsonga Phiri, Dominique Lam, Nathan Lang, Raymond Lung, Adrian McMullan, Sarah Miller, Sarah Murphy, Natasha Prasad, Stefanie Stantchev, Daniel Thomas, Jon Waters, Hai Li Wu and Sophie Yu.

Finally, warm gratitude is owed also to our families and friends for their patient and seemingly endless support and encouragement during the long (and sometimes arduous!) process of writing and producing this book.

Acronyms

ADF	Augmented Dickey Fuller test
APC	Average Propensity to Consume
BEA	Bureau of Economic Analysis (US)
BG	Breusch–Godfrey LM test for Serial Correlation
CI	Confidence Interval
CIA	Central Intelligence Agency
CLT	Central Limit Theorem
CML	Council of Mortgage Lenders (UK)
df	Degrees of freedom
DF	Dickey–Fuller Test
DGP	Data generating process
DW	Durbin–Watson test
ESS	Explained sum of squares
GDP	Gross Domestic Product
GLS	Generalised Least Squares
GM	Gauss–Markov
GQ	Goldfeld–Quandt test
HDI	Human Development Index
HPI	Human Poverty Index
IBRD	International Bank for Reconstruction and Development
ICT	Information and Communication Technologies
IDA	International Development Association
IEA	International Energy Agency
IMF	International Monetary Fund
IPCC	Intergovernmental Panel on Climate Change
IT	Information Technology
LDC	Least Developed Country
LPM	Linear Probability Model
LRE	Long Run Elasticity
MDG	Millennium Development Goal

MLE	Maximum Likelihood Estimation
MPC	Marginal Propensity to Consume
MPC-UK	Monetary Policy Committee (UK)
MRA	Multiple Regression Analysis
NCHS	US National Center for Health Statistics
NGO	Non Governmental Organisation
OLS	Ordinary Least Squares
ONS	Office of National Statistics (UK)
PDI	Personal Disposable Income
QLI	Quality of Life Index
R&D	Research and Development
RSS	Residual sum of squares
SME	Small/Medium Sized Enterprise
SML	Survey of Mortgage Lenders
SRA	Simple Regression Analysis
SRF	Sample Regression function
TSS	Total Sum of Squares
UNCTAD	United Nations Conference for Trade and Development
UNDP	United Nations Development Program
UNWTO	United Nations World Tourism Organisation
WLS	Weighted Least Squares

How to use this book ...

A minority of students relish the prospect of studying econometrics, as many are deterred perhaps by the technical jargon e.g. 'autocorrelated disturbances', 'heteroscedasticity' and 'identification problems'. The aim of *Running Regressions* is to apply the practical aspects of elementary regression analysis to some interesting issues and without adopting an excessively esoteric and/or mathematical approach. *Running Regressions* shows that statistics and econometrics can be straightforward, useful and interesting.

A view to the real world

Running Regressions focuses on some topical, real-world issues. Econometric analyses may not seem to be the focus of articles in *The Economist*, the front page of the *Financial Times, New York Times* or in OXFAM's latest newsletter. But the professional application of econometric techniques underlies the insights expressed in the business press. Applied econometrics can earn you a living and win you arguments; it gives empirical 'flesh' to what might otherwise be dismissed as subjective opinion or abstract theory. Econometric analysis is used by policy-makers in deciding how much of the budget to devote to health or education, and/or what the tax rate should be. It is used by central bankers deciding whether to raise or lower interest rates. It is used by non-governmental organisations (NGOs) in illustrating the benefits of debt relief and/or how world trade rules can be designed better to advance the interests of developing countries. And it is used by hedge fund analysts to forecast stock market movements and currency fluctuations. Applied econometrics is relevant to every part of economics, finance and development studies and the topics selected for analysis in *Running Regressions* are chosen accordingly; for example, we have including chapters on international relations (world poverty and armed conflict), local and personal issues (housing, divorce) and cutting-edge fields such as behavioural economics.

Use it simply

The book is not about excessively complex econometric techniques. Our present goal is to explain economic phenomenon using elementary econometric techniques of the 'plain vanilla' variety – one at a time to highlight the key aspects. Good econometricians will focus on parsimony: they will attempt to abstract from the complexity to strip theoretical models to their bare essentials. In selecting techniques, the best techniques will be the most straightforward and intuitive as long as these techniques are also relatively reliable and accurate. Adopting a relatively simple approach does not reduce the power of the analysis. Simplicity is often very effective. So the aim of *Running Regressions* is to present analyses in which there is clear connection between the phenomenon observed, the underlying theory, the raw data and the econometric techniques.

Use it with versatility: econometrics for the social sciences

The econometric tools outlined in *Running Regressions* can be used to analyse a wide range of issues from economics, finance, business studies and the other social sciences. Social scientists examine complex aspects of human decision-making and so the methods of pure science cannot be adopted without adaptation. Good applied econometrics requires a judicious mix of sound economic theory, reliable data and correctly applied statistical techniques. These ingredients do not always readily combine. Finding the data with which to examine theory is usually the hardest part, in practical terms. Social scientists do not deal with a purely physical world and we rarely have laboratories in which we can run controlled, replicable experiments to generate reliable data sets. We may not have data that is directly related to the phenomenon we want to study. It is so often as if we had started off with the plan to make *duck à l'orange* for dinner, only to discover that there is no duck and we must substitute chicken; that we have only lemon rind when orange is called for; parsley in place of *fines herbes* and so on. This does not mean that the analysis is going to be a flop – indeed, if we select our techniques carefully we will come up with useful insights as long as we realise that we may be able only roughly to approximate the reality we want to understand.

It follows from this that applied econometrics involves some subjective judgements. Which elements of the real world should we include and highlight? Which should we subdue or leave out entirely? This decision will be influenced by preference and perception. Just as Monet's representation of exactly the same tree would be different from, say, Vincent van Gogh's, so two econometricians can differ in their representation of social science. Different features of reality can be emphasised or downplayed according to the perspective that seems most relevant, topical or exciting – or which best fits a view of the world. It is this aspect of discretion and personal choice that contributes to making econometrics as much an art as it is a science. It is useful to remember, when carrying out one's own analysis or interpreting the work of others, that there are many different ways of approaching the same question.

Use it frequently

We toyed with the idea of calling this book *An Econometrician's Toolbox* because the methods presented in this book are used regularly by social scientists using applied econometric techniques. Whether one works in business (estimating the demand curve for airline ticket sales), in development (estimating the effectiveness of various policies on poverty reduction), in law (fighting a monopoly pricing suit, or trying to prove unfair business practices) … the applications are as infinite as the questions that social scientists set out to answer. Of course it is rare that one would run regressions every single day of the week, but the point remains that researchers are required most days to give empirical evidence to back up their arguments and to persuade colleagues as well as critics. Not least, applied econometrics is about providing empirical examples that support (or refute) hypotheses, illustrate trends and allow us to draw inferences about relationships between phenomena. Even if working life consists more of reading the results of studies conducted by others, we must nonetheless understand the implications of what went into the models (and what was left out) and be able to judge whether or not the conclusions are robust. Why was one theory chosen over another? Why those variables selected and not others? Does the data used adequately represent the problem at hand? Has the appropriate yardstick been chosen to assess statistical significance? We need to understand the mechanics and implications of all these elements.

Use it as a complement to other texts, or by itself

The advantage of *Running Regressions* is that it blends a practical approach with a holistic perspective. So *Running Regressions* is an ideal complement to mainstream econometrics texts because it illustrates a wide range of commonly taught techniques using topical and thought-provoking examples soundly based in elementary economic theory. Alternatively, it does cover all the basic econometric techniques and so it could be used as the main text for introductory applied econometrics and/or research methods courses.

The structure of *Running Regressions* and its chapters

You can read *Running Regressions* from start-to-finish, or take the *à la carte* approach, selecting each chapter from the menu of contents, according to particular need or interest. *Running Regressions* is unusual in that it incorporates two titles for each chapter: a main title referring to an econometric technique and a sub-title referring to an economic issue or theory. This division of the titles reflects *Running Regressions'* marriage of theory and applied econometrics. Both titles are listed in the table of contents. So if you are selecting on a chapter-by-chapter basis, you need to decide whether to select either from the list of econometric techniques or from the list of theoretical concepts. This might depend on whether your goal is to prepare for project work/class assignments, to refresh your understanding of a particular theory, to find out more about a particular data issue or to learn about an econometric technique via an interesting illustration of how it works. This unconventional combination of the disparate elements of econometrics into a cohesive whole was one of the book's primary goals, based on the numerous requests from students for a 'roadmap' of econometrics.

If your aim is to read a general overview of econometrics, we recommend starting at the beginning and working your way through. The book opens with fundamental principles of econometrics and concludes with more complex examples. (The last few chapters, for example would not usually be covered in first-year undergraduate courses.) *Running Regressions* covers a variety of methods – starting at the most basic (running a regression by hand using a hand-held calculator), moving through the statistical tools available via Excel and then focussing on a widely used tailor-made econometrics package – *EViews*. In early chapters, data sets are available to allow our readers to try the techniques themselves; in later chapters website links are provided. If you use our data then there may be slight variations in the estimates you get – reflecting rounding differences or specific features of the various programmes but your results should be much the same as the ones we got ourselves.

If you are reading *Running Regressions* for guidance about how to do a research report or project in an area covered by this book then follow the 'Table of Contents' for guidance about the relevant theories and models. Core theories and their contenders are described, along with a reading list for further and more specialised reading.

How to get started

Each of the chapters in *Running Regressions* goes through a systematic series of steps to show how data and econometric analysis can be used to test a theory. So each chapter is roughly set out in the format that is conventionally expected in applied economic analysis: a theoretical model is developed, the data is presented and analysed and models are estimated and assessed. (Alternatively, one could say that each chapter introduces a different theoretical issue, and then uses an econometric analysis to illustrate it.) For each chapter, the argument will be built up as follows:

1. *The issue*

   In this preliminary section, the basic theoretical ideas, data and econometric approaches are briefly introduced.

2. *The theory*

   We set out the underlying theory or hypothesis, on the basis of existing literature. We then analyse the theory using econometrics but modifying the theory if the econometric evidence suggests that the real world does not conform to the theory. We express this theory as an econometric model. This means simplifying the hypothesis into a simple testable assertion and then re-working it into a form that can be analysed using the available data.

3. *Data*

   Each chapter will go into important details about using data. One can learn a great deal simply by evaluating and describing the empirical landscape that a dataset presents. Descriptive analysis is an oft under-estimated, critical step in the whole exercise. So data plots should be examined carefully: chart variables over time and against each other. Look for obvious trends and patterns.

4. *Empirical results and interpretation*

The next step is to obtain numerical values, or estimates, of the relationships between the variables in the model, from the data available. In this book, we do this through regression analysis, usually using Ordinary Least Squares (OLS), as explained in Chapter 1. In explaining the detail of OLS techniques, we have kept things simple by concentrating on one set of econometric issues per chapter. But in real-world analysis, it is important to remember that we will usually have more than one step in our estimation procedure and so for your own investigations you may have to combine econometric techniques from two or more chapters. Usually a model will need improving. So it is important to consider what could be done to make the model better. Sometimes this means additional work to extend the theoretical model. Sometimes it will involve finding more appropriate or precise data. At other times it may be a matter of using more reliable and accurate econometric techniques.

It is also important to interpret our results in the light of theoretical issues. Do the findings confirm our theoretical hypotheses or not? What do our econometric results tell us about the relationship between the variables of our model? Are the relationships between variables positive or negative; are the impacts large or small? In order to assess this we test the statistical significance of our estimates using hypothesis tests such as Student's t-test and/or F tests. What do the tests mean in terms of the underlying phenomena studied, and in terms of our understanding of the theory? Do they allow us to make some forecasts about the future? Of course, just as a defendant in a courtroom can only be declared 'not guilty' rather than 'innocent', the results can only provide support (or not) to a hypothesis. We can never 'prove' a hypothesis. This is why econometricians are cautious with their language, sometimes the statistical linguistic style is necessarily unwieldy: hypotheses are not 'accepted'; at best they are 'not rejected'. This is because the empirical findings are by their nature probabilistic: unlikely outcomes are always possible and evidence appearing to support a hypothesis may just be a coincidence.

5. *Policy implications and conclusions*

It is not enough just to present results and state whether or not they confirm a theory. Good applied econometrics provides practical answers and policy guidance. So we need to set out our conclusions clearly but also to think about the policy implications suggested by our results. This may be where advocacy comes in, for example if an NGO wants to support arguments for policy change; or if Treasury or central bank officials see a case for financial reform during a credit crunch; or funds managers see a warning to overhaul their corporate policy on portfolio allocations.

6. *Further reading*

We have included further reading for readers who would like to follow-up on the intricacies of the issues we explore. We have referred to a range of readings from textbooks, journal articles and policy reports but these references are just a taster of the range of readings available. We have selected the ones that are relatively straightforward, particularly relevant and/or readily accessible. Intentionally, we have kept these further reading lists relatively brief and we haven't been able to discuss in detail every relevant reference or reading. For further ideas on readings, don't forget to do further searches using JSTOR, Google and/or Wikipedia, or just by browsing through economics collections in libraries. The *Journal of Economic Literature* can be a good source of summary articles. Many topical economic and financial issues are the focus of articles and/or surveys in *The Economist* and so this magazine is also a useful starting point in a quest to understand topical world issues.

7. *Chapter exercises*

For most chapters, we have provided some exercises for students who would like to explore the data and/or test and techniques in more detail.

Going on from here ...

Where possible, each chapter gives references to institutions that are associated with the topic examined or to ongoing research programmes. Our goal is to stimulate readers to realise that applied econometrics can be relevant, fun, and an essential beginning in a journey of understanding the economic, financial and social world around us ...

Part I

Simple regression and data analysis

In this part we outline some basic econometric techniques, including running regressions by hand using Ordinary Least Squares (OLS) estimation techniques. We focus on simple regressions, i.e. regressions on models with just one explanatory variable.

We also introduce Microsoft's Excel as a user-friendly spreadsheet package for running simple regressions.

Running regressions on models with more than one explanatory variable – Multiple Regression Analysis (MRA), will be analysed from Part II onwards.

An introduction to Ordinary Least Squares

This chapter provides a brief and intuitive summary of the econometric theory that underlies OLS estimation, including:

- The data generating process and sample regression functions
- Types of data
- Ordinary Least Squares (OLS) estimation
- Measuring correlation and goodness of fit
- The Gauss–Markov theorem
- Properties of estimators
- Hypothesis testing

1.1   Introduction

Running Regressions is about the quantitative analysis of observed behaviours and phenomena using economic theory, probability and statistics. By bringing these different elements together we can improve our understanding of people, firms and countries – in the past, the present and the future. For those readers who approach the subject with trepidation, it may be worth remembering this practical goal.

The skills that are required are not intrinsically difficult if a systematic approach is followed. Not least, our intention in *Running Regressions* is to illustrate commonly used techniques in an imaginative and interesting way. This chapter provides a brief introduction to concepts and techniques that are then worked through as practical examples in the following chapters.

Finally, whilst we focus on economics, finance and development studies in our selection of topics, the approach can be used in analysing a wide range of all real-world situations. The techniques can be, and are, used in all the social and natural sciences.

1.2   Models and data

The aim of econometric analysis is to understand the **data generating processes** (DGPs) that underlie economic systems and human behaviour. These DGPs are like the engines in a car and they propel socio-economic actions and events. For example, the interaction between income and consumption is determined by a DGP. This DGP causes consumption and income to rise together and these rises will be transmitted into the recorded data on income and consumption. Unfortunately, an econometrician rarely has direct knowledge of DGPs and so he/she has to draw inferences about it from samples of data. For a brief analysis of the types of data used in econometric analyses, see Box 1.1.

To capture how DGPs operate an econometrician will use socio-economic and/or financial theory as an initial guide, building up a testable **model** from previous knowledge about a process or system. Once a testable empirical model has been devised, the econometrician will proceed to estimate the **parameters** of their model. As explained below, estimating parameters is one of the aims in applied econometrics because the parameters of a model capture the magnitude and direction of interactions between the variables of the model. Another aim is to use econometric evidence for forecasting the future and parameter estimates are used in constructing these forecasts. Either way, estimating parameters accurately and reliably is the essence of an applied econometrician's task.

1.3   Constructing empirical models

Theoretical ideas are translated into empirical hypotheses via some assumptions about the DGP. The DGP is expressed as a mathematical function linking a **dependent variable** – the variable that the econometrician is trying to 'explain' (sometimes called the **regressand**); and the explanatory variables (sometimes called **regressors** or **independent variables**). For a lot of econometrics, the selection of a variable as the independent variable is complicated by the fact that causality may not be unidirectional, e.g. for the example used in this chapter: poverty might cause low growth; low growth might cause poverty; they may both affect each other (i.e. there may be a **simultaneous** relationship between them) and/or a third factor may be generating changes in both.

Box 1.1 Types of data

When gathering data we should try to ensure that our data sample is representative of the data generating process (DGP). We do not gather data on average height by measuring only world-class basketball players and we do not conduct household surveys at times of the day when people in formal employment are out and so those at home are a biased subset of the total.

Data dimensions

Three types of datasets are used in this book: time series; cross-sectional and pooled/panel datasets.

Time-series data are data collected over the temporal dimension to capture the evolution of variables over time. For example, we might be tracking national GDP trends, analysing one country's performance over time. Time-series data can be collected at any sort of frequency, e.g. monthly, quarterly, weekly, daily or more frequently; for example, **high-frequency data** (available at intervals as short as every minute or every second) is sometimes useful in the analysis of financial markets.

Cross-sectional data are collected over the spatial dimension and they provide a snapshot of a cross-sectional pattern at one point in time. Cross-sectional data can be captured at many levels of disaggregation. For example, the Population Census in the UK surveys a sample of households at one point in time. In microeconometric analyses household or employer/worker survey data is used; in macroeconometric analyses, international, national and regional data is used.

Pooled and panel data sets combine cross-sectional and time-series data, for example by gathering data on the same sample of families, firms or countries, every year over a number of years. Special techniques may be needed in analysing these types of data, as is explained in Chapter 11.

The nature of data

Broadly speaking, the nature of data collected can be categorised according to how the phenomena under investigation are measured.

Quantitative data capture things that are measurable using an objective, **cardinal** scale. Cardinal measurement involves calculating 'how many' and requires clear units of measurement. For example, to measure unemployment we count how many people are without a job; to measure GDP we count how many currency units of output have been produced. Other quantitative data are calculated using indices based around units of measurement, for example price indices are calculated from prices of goods measured in currency units.

Qualitative data cannot be counted. There are no objective units of measurement for qualitative data and so assigning these data numbers must necessarily embed some sort of subjective judgement. This subjective judgement will emerge either in the method of measurement or in the system of weighting different components of a phenomena. For example the United Nations Development Programme (UNDP) Human Development Indicator (HDI) is calculated using infant mortality rates, GDP per capita and literacy rates. Each of these components is captured using different units of measurement and to sum them together is like counting apples and eggs. In practice, the HDI index is constructed giving indices of these components an equal weighting; but even the decision to assign different components equal weights is in essence a subjective judgement. Why should literacy be as important as infant mortality? Why should GDP per capita be as important as literacy? For business confidence surveys, respondents are asked to give subjective scores using an ordinal system of measurement, i.e. they are asked to rank alternatives according to their subjective assessments and individual preferences.

We have divided quantitative and qualitative data starkly but it is important to remember that there is fuzziness at the boundary between them. For example, defining and measuring variables such as prices, unemployment and GDP is rarely completely straightforward; **information uncertainty** (the uncertainty associated with data constraints and measure-ment problems) and potential for **measurement error** should always be acknowledged in empirical analysis. Also, in many areas of social sciences, e.g. psychology and behavioural economics, data are collected based on observed behaviour, often in a binary form as **dummy variables** (e.g. $D = 1$ if the experimental subject did perform a specific action; $D = 0$ if they didn't). So it is possible to count the number of people performing an action even though the data is reflecting a subjective decision-making process.

In practice, many studies will use both quantitative and qualitative data. In Britain for example, the UK's Monetary Policy Committee (MPC-UK) sets central bank interest rates to moderate inflationary pressures using a variety of indicators. Given the uncertainties surrounding accurate measurement and forecasting of the variables affecting inflation etc. these procedures cannot be mechanical; the final decision of the MPC will, inevitably, have qualitative/subjective elements. Nonetheless statistical information will be very useful to the members of the MPC-UK in forming their judgements.

In devising a model, it is important to remember that econometrics is about using, testing and developing economic theories. It is not about the mindless churning of data. For research to be useful as well as interesting, socio-economic and financial theories should always be the starting point.

In this discussion we are confining our discussion to linear models.[1] In a linear world the dependent variable is a linear (i.e. additive) function of

---

[1] A linear world is relatively simple but the basic procedure outlined here can be adapted to estimating non-linear relationships though different estimation techniques would be required. Non-linear estimation is introduced in Chapter 12.

explanatory variables and can be represented as a simple linear equation. For example, if an econometrician hypothesises that a linear relationship exists between poverty and GDP growth per capita then he/she will formulate the following:

$$Y_i = \alpha + \beta X_i + \varepsilon_i \tag{1.1}$$

where Y_i represents the average change in the poverty rate in the ith country and X_i represents the growth in GDP per capita in the ith country.

There are two main components to this model: a deterministic component and a random or 'stochastic' component.

The deterministic component is represented by $\alpha + \beta X_i$, which is an amalgam of **parameters** (α and βs) and explanatory variables. We hypothesise that these parameters represent properties inherent to a 'population' of data. But what is α? What is β? The parameters α and β are the unknowns of the system and the essence of the applied econometrician's task is to identify them. A good econometrician is looking for reliable and accurate information about the magnitude and sign of these parameters.

The stochastic component is represented by ε, which is commonly called the **error term** or **disturbance term**. The error term captures all the excluded (and by assumption unimportant) influences on the dependent variable. It also captures the inherent randomness within the DGP. The existence of this randomness means that there will always be a probabilistic element within econometric analysis. The world of statistics and econometrics is a world of probability and chance; anything can happen. So the econometrician must (usually) concentrate on what is **most likely** to be true rather than what is **exactly** true.

1.4 The sample regression function (SRF)

Econometricians cannot usually see the DGP (unless they artificially create one for themselves using **Monte Carlo experiments**) and so they have to make inferences about the population from a **sample** of data. The model estimated using sample data is sometimes referred to as the **sample regression function (SRF)**. This is because even if an econometrician knows what population they should be using to get their data sample (in a cross-sectional context for example, it might be the population of the US) it will be infeasible and/or too costly for them to collect and analyse information on all US citizens. It is even more complicated in a time series context where it is not intuitively clear what the population of data actually is. All the data used in *Running*

Regressions is sample data; we don't have observations for every member of the population under investigation. But because we're not using whole populations we rarely know the true values of the parameters α and β. We have to make educated guesses and for this to work well we have to select our sample carefully to ensure that it is representative and to avoid **sample selection bias**. A biased sample will not be representative of a population; for example an internet survey of favourite foods/drinks conducted via facebook will give a sample of data biased in favour of younger age groups and/or those who are relatively technically literate; this sample would not be representative of people of all age groups,

For the poverty example above, we could collect a sample of cross-sectional data on Y and X for i different countries. Then we would construct the following SRF:

$$Y_i = \hat{\alpha} + \hat{\beta}X_i + \hat{\varepsilon}_i \tag{1.2}$$

You will notice that this SRF looks very similar to (1.1) except $\hat{\alpha}$ and $\hat{\beta}$ are the sample **estimates** of α and β not the population values. The term $\hat{\varepsilon}_i$ is the sample **residual**, which is the estimate of the error term. As is explained below, we assume that the **expected value** or mean of this error is zero, i.e. we assume that $E(\varepsilon_i) = 0$.

Using an example that is explained more fully in Chapter 2, our working hypothesis is that changes in poverty vary as growth rates vary. To assess this hypothesis we derive estimates of changes in poverty for a given growth rate, i.e. our expected value of Y_i conditional upon a given $X_i - E(Y_i|X_i)$, using parameter estimates and observations on Y and X as follows:

$$\hat{Y}_i = \hat{\alpha} + \hat{\beta}X_i \tag{1.3}$$

where $\hat{Y}_i$ is an **estimate** of Y given X. The estimate of Y may also be referred to as the **predicted value** or **fitted value** of Y.

Linking these ideas into our example from above, if $\hat{\beta}$ is negative and 'significantly' different from zero (i.e. relatively large) then it may suggest that countries with higher growth rates have reduced poverty more rapidly than countries with lower growth rates. So if we want a more equitable world, then one policy possibility is to encourage GDP growth.

But in order to make these inferences, we need some accurate and reliable information about the parameter estimates $\hat{\alpha}$ and $\hat{\beta}$. How can we get this information? A simple and (often) reliable method is Ordinary Least Squares (OLS).

1.5   Ordinary Least Squares (OLS)

In the previous section we explained that estimates of the parameters describing a DGP are derived from sample data and that these parameter estimates can be used to derive an estimate of dependent variable conditional upon each value of an explanatory variable. But how do we calculate parameter estimates? There are a large number of different estimation techniques, many of which can give reliable answers. But in this book we are concentrating on the simplest of them – Ordinary Least Squares (OLS).

OLS involves estimating the **line of best fit** or **regression line** through the observations on Y and X. For our example of poverty and GDP growth, Figure 1.1 depicts the line of best fit. With GDP growth on the horizontal axis and average change in poverty on the vertical axis, the pairs of observations on Y and X for each country are represented as dots. The line that fits these observed values best will pass through the means for both the dependent and the explanatory variable and it will minimise the spread of observations around the line.

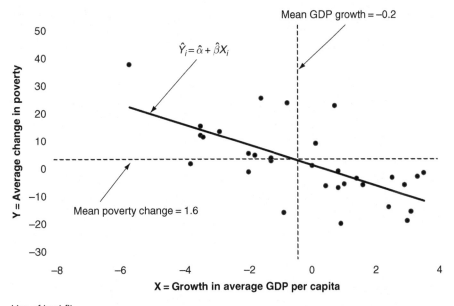

Figure 1.1   Line of best fit

What do we mean by minimising the spread of observations? For OLS, we are minimising the spread of sample residuals ($\hat{\varepsilon}_i$), where the residuals are the vertical distances between the observed value and the predicted value:

$$\hat{\varepsilon}_i = Y_i - \hat{Y}_i = Y_i - \hat{\alpha} - \hat{\beta}X_i \tag{1.4}$$

Spread is captured statistically as squared deviations from means and, because the mean of residuals is zero, the residual spread is measured as the sum of squared residuals (RSS).

In practice, OLS involves using differential calculus to identify the parameter estimates that minimise this sum of squared residuals:

$$RSS = \sum_{i=1}^{n} \hat{\varepsilon}_i^2 = \sum (Y_i - \hat{Y}_i)^2 \tag{1.5}$$

When we minimise RSS, we get the **normal equations** and solve to give the following formulae for the parameter estimates:

$$\hat{\beta} = \frac{\text{cov}(X, Y)}{\text{var}(X)} = \frac{\sum (X_i - \bar{X})(Y_i - \bar{Y})}{\sum (X_i - \bar{X})^2} \tag{1.6}$$

$$\hat{\alpha} = \bar{Y} - \hat{\beta}\bar{X} \tag{1.7}$$

where cov(X, Y) is the covariance between our explanatory variable, and $\bar{X}$ and $\bar{Y}$ are the sample means for the variables X and Y respectively.

Covariance captures the extent to which two variables 'co-vary'. To explain **covariance**: it is measured using the products of deviations from means; if two variables (in this case X and Y) are deviating from their means in a similar way, then the covariance between them will be large in absolute terms. So if we have a large covariance then (all things being equal) this will generate a β that is large in absolute terms – we will be picking up a strong association between the variables. In the denominator of (1.6) we have var(X) – the **variance** of X. The variance of a variable is measured by summing the squared deviations of a variable from its mean, giving a measure of spread or dispersion. If a variable has a tendency to deviate widely from its mean, then the variance will be large.

Measures of variance and spread are also important in assessing the accuracy of our estimation procedure. Minimising the RSS in OLS is equivalent to minimising the **residual variance**. (The definitions and formulae for residual variance and the variances of our parameter estimates are explained in Box 1.2.) With OLS, the expected value (i.e. the mean) of residuals will be

---

Box 1.2 Calculating variances and standard errors

As explained above, OLS involves minimising the spread of observations around the line of best fit. For OLS, we are minimising this spread by minimising RSS so we will also be minimising the **residual variance**, defined as:

$$\hat{\sigma}_i^2 = \frac{1}{n-k-1} \sum_i^n \hat{\varepsilon}_i^2 = \frac{RSS}{n-k-1} \tag{1.8}$$

where k is the number of explanatory variables in our model (in this chapter's example, we have one explanatory variable and so we would have $n-2$ in our denominator).

We can use this information to calculate the variances and standard errors of each parameter estimate as follows:

$$\text{var}(\hat{\beta}) = \frac{\sigma^2}{\sum(X_i - \bar{X})^2}$$

$$se(\hat{\beta}) = \sqrt{\frac{\hat{\sigma}^2}{\sum(X_i - \bar{X})^2}} \tag{1.9}$$

where $se(\hat{\beta})$ is the standard error of $\hat{\beta}$.

Similarly the variance and standard error of the intercept parameter are:

$$\text{var}(\hat{a}) = \left\{ \frac{\sum X_i^2}{n \sum (X_i - \bar{X})^2} \right\} \times \sigma^2$$

$$se(\hat{a}) = \sqrt{\left\{ \frac{\sum X_i^2}{n \sum (X_i - \bar{X})^2} \times \hat{\sigma}^2 \right\}} \tag{1.10}$$

Note that in the above formulae for the variances of the parameter estimates $\hat{a}$ and $\hat{\beta}$, the true error variance (σ^2) is used; in the real world, however, we will not know this true error variance and so in calculating the standard errors for our parameter estimates we must use the sample estimate of the error variance i.e. the residual variance $\hat{\sigma}^2$. Also, it is important to note that these variances and standard errors are calculated assuming **homoscedasticity**, i.e. that the error variance is constant across all observations. If this assumption is violated, i.e. if there is **heteroscedasticity**, then heteroscedasticity robust variances and standard errors should be used. The homoscedasticity assumption is explained below and the heteroscedasticity problem is explored in detail in Chapter 6.

zero, i.e. $E(\varepsilon_i|X_i) = 0$ but the spread of the residuals (the **residual variance**) may still be large. A model with a relatively large residual variance will not fit the observed data very well and our next step will be to assess how well our estimated model is fitting the observed data.

Goodness of fit and the coefficient of determination

The correlation coefficient

Econometric analysis often starts with an investigation of **correlation**, which is the degree of *linear* association between two variables; OLS estimation is essentially a sophisticated form of correlation analysis. In assessing the results from an OLS regression we will need an objective measure of the nature of clustering in a scatter plot of Y against X; this is captured in its simplest form by the **correlation coefficient** which captures the relative magnitude of the linear association between two variables and thus is a simple measure of statistical 'dependence'.

The first step in calculating the correlation coefficient involves measuring the extent to which the two series co-vary using covariance (as explained above). The extent to which one variable covaries with another gives a useful clue about correlation because if variables are correlated then the covariance between them will be relatively large in comparison with the variances. The correlation coefficient is calculated from the covariances and variances as follows:

$$r_{XY} = \frac{\sum (X_i - \bar{X})(Y_i - \bar{Y})}{\sqrt{\sum (X_i - \bar{X})^2 \sum (Y_i - \bar{Y})^2}} = \frac{\mathrm{cov}(X, Y)}{\sqrt{\mathrm{var}(X) \times \mathrm{var}(Y)}} \qquad (1.11)$$

where r_{XY} is the correlation coefficient between X and Y.

This correlation coefficient is a 'normalised' covariance: the association between deviations from means for Y and X is normalised to lie between ± 1. A correlation coefficient of $+1$ implies that the variables are moving together completely. A correlation coefficient of -1 implies that they are mirroring each other (i.e. moving in opposite directions but completely in tandem). A correlation coefficient of 0 implies that there is no systematic (linear) association between the variables.

Note that in calculating the correlation coefficient, no distinction is made between a dependent and an explanatory variable. This is because the correlation coefficient is just a measure of linear association. It tells us nothing about which variable causes the other; in fact, some third variable might be causing both. It is very important to remember that a statistical correlation does not necessarily imply an underlying causal mechanism.

Goodness of fit

As explained above, Figure 1.1 presents a visual impression of how well our estimated line fits the observations. But we can capture how neatly our estimated line for Y fits the spread of observed values on Y more precisely by measuring the **goodness of fit**. The goodness of fit captures the extent to which our line of best fit neatly fits the pairs of observations on Y and X. This can be measured by calculating the ratio of 'explained' variance to unexplained variance as follows:

1. For each observation we calculate the difference between the estimate of Y (calculated using Equation (1.3)) and the sample mean $\bar{Y}$. We sum these deviations together across all our observations to give the explained sum of squares (ESS).
2. Similarly, we calculate the sum of deviations of each observed value of Y from the sample mean $\bar{Y}$. This is the total sum of squares (TSS).
3. We take the ratio of the ESS to the TSS. This ratio is R^2 – the **coefficient of determination**:

$$R^2 = \frac{ESS}{TSS} = \frac{\sum (\hat{Y} - \bar{Y})^2}{\sum (Y_i - \bar{Y})^2} \tag{1.12}$$

The intuition underlying R^2 is that it gives a relative measure of the proportion of the total variability in Y that is 'explained' by the model, i.e. that is captured by the line of best fit.

In the two-dimensional world of **simple regression analysis (SRA)**, i.e. for regressions on just one explanatory variable, there is no essential difference between the correlation coefficient (r) and the goodness of fit. In SRA, $R^2 = r^2$; the **coefficient of determination** is just the square of the correlation coefficient. But, as explained in Chapter 5, the relationship becomes more complex in multiple regression analysis (MRA).

1.6   The Gauss–Markov Theorem

Now that we've explained the mechanics of OLS we need to explain why OLS is so commonly used. OLS is a popular technique because, given some assumptions (as explained below), OLS estimators will reliable and accurate. This justification for the OLS method is captured by the **Gauss–Markov Theorem**, which states that if the **Gauss–Markov assumptions** are satisfied then the OLS parameter estimators will be **BLUE (Best Linear Unbiased Estimators)**. BLUEness is associated with reliability and accuracy and the technical definitions of these terms are explained in Box 1.3.

Box 1.3 Statistical indicators of reliability

In assessing how well an estimation technique such as OLS is working, performance is judged in terms of the desirable properties of estimators. Desirability reflects the fact that we would like our estimators to be as simple, accurate and reliable as possible. BLUEness is about these desirable properties of estimators. The main desirable small sample properties are **unbiasedness** (= accuracy), **minimum variance** (= reliability) and **linearity** (associated with simplicity).

Unbiasedness is associated with accuracy. For example, if an estimate of the slope parameter β is unbiased, this means that if lots of samples of data are taken and each is used to get an estimate $\hat{\beta}$, then the average $\hat{\beta}$ from all the samples will be equal to the true value in the population β. In mathematical notation: $E(\hat{\beta}) = \beta$, where $E(\hat{\beta})$ is the expected value (i.e. average) of $\hat{\beta}$. The property of unbiasedness is shown visually in Figure 1.2. Each panel of this diagram shows sampling distributions for two estimation procedures A and B, and captures the probability of getting each value of $\hat{\beta}$. If we were to take repeated samples and estimate the parameter β from all these samples of data, then the sample parameter estimate $\hat{\beta}$ will take a range of values because it is a random variable. If our estimator is unbiased then the average of these values will be the correct value. For example, Figure 1.2 shows that the sampling distribution for A is centred around the true value β. Over many samples, on average $\hat{\beta}_A$ is equal to the true value β i.e. $E(\hat{\beta}_A) = \beta$ so A is an unbiased estimator of β. For estimator B, over many samples the most likely estimate is not centred around the true value β so $E(\hat{\beta}_B) \neq \beta$ and $\hat{\beta}_B$ is a biased estimator of β

Minimum variance is associated with reliability. The minimum variance estimator will be the estimator with the smallest variance of its sampling distribution for $\hat{\beta}$. From Figure 1.3, you can see that both sampling distributions for $\hat{\beta}$ are symmetrically distributed around the true value β and both have the same area of 1.[2] But the left-hand sampling distribution for $\hat{\beta}_A$ is taller and narrower than that for $\hat{\beta}_B$ showing that the spread of estimates around the true value β is smaller for the $\hat{\beta}_A$ sampling distribution than for the $\hat{\beta}_B$ sampling distribution. So A is the minimum variance estimator in this case.

Linearity is associated with linear (i.e. additive) calculation rather than multiplicative, non-linear calculation. OLS estimators are derived from the linear summing of random variables and this means that OLS estimates can be calculated relatively easily. In some cases, if a model is just non-linear in the variables but linear in the parameters, then OLS techniques can still be used on a transformed model. For example, a production function of form $Y = AK^\gamma L^\beta$ is a non-linear, multiplicative combination of the variables

---

[2] This is because they are probability distributions and the sum of the probabilities of a set of mutually exclusive and exhaustive possibilities must necessarily equal 1.

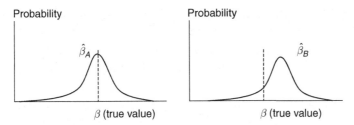

Figure 1.2   Sampling distributions for unbiased estimator A and biased estimator B

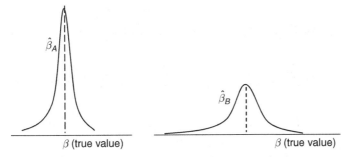

Figure 1.3   Sampling distributions showing minimum variance estimator $\hat{\beta}_A$

K and *L*; but it can be simplified to a form in which it is an additive function of the logged variables as follows: $\ln Y = \ln A + y \ln K + \beta \ln L$. OLS can be used to estimate this logged function because this function is **linear in the parameters** (which in this case are y, β and $\ln A$).

This property is important in justifying the use of OLS because OLS is not the only accurate and/or reliable estimation technique; there are many others, for example Maximum Likelihood Estimation (MLE)[3]. Whilst MLE is not always unbiased it is efficient in large samples (i.e. it is 'asymptotically efficient' and 'consistent', properties that are explained below). But calculating MLE parameter estimates involves complicated non-linear techniques. The linearity property of OLS gives it an advantage over MLE in terms of relative simplicity. With modern econometrics software however this ease of OLS estimation is of less importance than when the churning of numbers necessary to running a regression was a relatively laborious, human-error prone process.

Asymptotic properties and the Central Limit Theorem (CLT)

As you will see in the chapters that follow, common violations of the Gauss–Markov assumptions mean that we rarely see a full set of desirable properties in small samples.

---

[3] MLE is briefly introduced in Chapter 12.

But if an econometrician has a large sample of data with a large number of observations then they may not need to worry if their estimators are not BLUE as long as they have other desirable properties. One of the advantages of large samples is that estimators that do not work well in small samples may possess desirable **asymptotic (large sample) properties** instead and these asymptotic properties emerge as $n \to \infty$. So provided your sample is large enough, then lack of BLUEness does not necessarily create insurmountable problems.

This is because, for very large samples of data, we can invoke the **law of large numbers**: when large numbers of variables are averaged, errors will cancel out and estimates are more likely to be unbiased. More specifically, given the **Central Limit Theorem** (CLT), random variables will approximate the standard normal distribution in large samples. (The **standard normal distribution** is a probability distribution used widely in statistics; it is a symmetric distribution with a mean of zero and a variance of 1.)

Most of the asymptotic properties are corollaries of the properties associated with BLUEness, e.g. two important asymptotic properties are **asymptotic unbiasedness** and **asymptotic efficiency**. For example, an estimator may be biased in small samples but as the sample size increases, i.e. as $n \to \infty$, the bias is eliminated and we can therefore say that the estimator is asymptotically unbiased. One of the most important asymptotic properties is **consistency**. For a consistent estimator, its sampling distribution shrinks in spread as n increases until 'at the limit', i.e. as $n \to \infty$, bias and variance go to zero. As illustrated in Figure 1.4, the sampling distribution for the parameter estimate collapses to an infinitely tall vertical line (the variance around a line is zero) at the true value of the population parameter.

Consistency is an important property in practice because, as explained below, OLS is only BLUE given certain assumptions (i.e. the Gauss Markov assumptions). For some violations of these assumptions BLUEness is lost, but consistency remains. So, as long as our sample size is large enough, OLS will still giving reliable and accurate estimates.

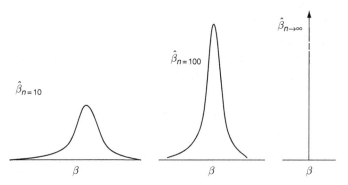

Figure 1.4   Sampling distributions for a consistent estimator

> In claiming on these asymptotic properties we need a large sample of data. But when is our sample big enough for us to start claiming on asymptotic properties? Asking this question is a bit like asking 'How long is a piece of string?' For some models very large sample sizes are needed for asymptotic statistics to be a reasonable approximation. It depends on the size of the population of data and a range of other factors, e.g. the complexity of the model. As a minimum, you should generally aim to have sample sizes of 50 observations or so.

As explained above, OLS will only work well if the Gauss Markov assumptions are satisfied.

We will focus on some key assumptions including the following:

1. The **mean of the error terms is zero**.
2. No **autocorrelation** – the covariance between error terms is zero.
3. **Homoscedasticity**: the variance of the error is constant across all observations.
4. The **model is correctly specified**, including all relevant explanatory variables, no unnecessary ones and represented using the correct **functional form**.
5. **Exogeneity**: the error term and explanatory variables are independently distributed, i.e. are not correlated with each other.
6. **Linearity in the parameters**: The model capturing the DGP must be linear in the parameters because OLS is a linear estimation technique.

Some of the Gauss–Markov assumptions can be represented more quickly and easily in mathematical notation, as shown in Box 1.4.

Different textbooks present Gauss–Markov assumptions (also known as **Gaussian assumptions**) in different ways. For example, some textbooks also include assumptions such as perfect multicollinearity (no perfect linear association between explanatory variables) and non-zero variance of explanatory variables; violating these assumptions will prevent the mathematical identification of the parameters. We are not focussing on these assumptions here because if a model is properly formulated and based on a sensible interpretation of underlying theories, then these problems will not occur.

As will be explained in the subsequent chapters, from estimating an SRF we can infer whether or not our hypotheses about the DGP are accurately capturing reality. From looking at the sample parameter estimates, the econometrician can make inferences about the parameters underlying the DGP. But if we want specifically to test whether or not these inferences are accurate, then we have to add in the **normality assumption** i.e. we have to assume that our error terms are normally distributed. As explained above, in large samples the normality assumption is justified by the CLT and the law of large numbers.

Box 1.4 Gauss–Markov assumptions – mathematical notation

1. The mean or **expected value** of ε_i, the error term is zero: $E(\varepsilon_i) = 0$.
2. No autocorrelation, i.e. a zero covariance between error term for observation i and the error term for observation j: $cov(\varepsilon_i, \varepsilon_j) = 0$
3. Homoscedasticity, the variance of the error term, i.e. $var(\varepsilon_i)$, is a constant: $var(\varepsilon_i) = \sigma^2$, where σ^2 is a constant.
4. Exogeneity: $cov(\varepsilon_i, X_i) = 0$ where X is the explanatory variable.

It is important to remember that the Gauss–Markov assumptions are neither independent nor mutually exclusive and just because one assumption is violated does not mean that another assumption can't be violated too. In fact, sometimes the violations of groups of assumptions can give a clue as to what might be wrong with a model – for example any sort of systematic pattern in residuals may be a sign that the model econometric is misspecified.

The problem for OLS estimation is that whilst it is a simple technique, its underlying assumptions **are** often violated. So the popularity of OLS as an estimation technique is not always justified. In order to establish whether or not OLS is working, **diagnostic tests** must be used to test the Gauss–Markov (GM) assumptions. If these tests are failed, then the techniques can sometimes be adapted to resolve the problem. Alternatively, other estimation techniques may be needed.

In some of the subsequent chapters of this book, we examine the key GM assumptions and illustrate some of the diagnostic tests used to test whether or not these GM assumptions are satisfied. We explain the consequences of violating these Gauss Markov assumptions and we outline some of the corrective procedures designed to allow the econometrician to return to a BLUE(ish) world.

1.7   Drawing inferences and hypothesis tests

What is the difference between our parameter estimates $\hat{\alpha}$ and $\hat{\beta}$ and the underlying 'true' values of α and β? If we want specifically to test whether or not these inferences are accurate, we will use **hypothesis tests**: hypothesis tests are a way to draw statistical inferences from our results. Of course we do not know the true value for the coefficients because we have a random sample and there is always a probability that our random sample is not at all representative of the DGP and/or population as a whole. Unless we have created our own dataset we will never know whether or not our parameter estimates match the true values. But, using a statistical/probability distribution as a benchmark, we can investigate the statistical significance of the difference between our parameter estimates and a null hypothesis about the true value(s).

Hypothesis tests: General principles

The first step in hypothesis testing is to set-up the null hypothesis (H_0) and alternative hypothesis (H_1). Null hypotheses are usually constructed around a 'conventional wisdom' representing the consensus of opinion on an issue. As will be seen below, this ensures that the null is relatively difficult to reject. In principle at least, we should be prepared to reject the null (and disregard existing information and/or judgements about a phenomenon) only if we have results that are extremely different from our null.

The next step is to use our sample data to construct a test statistic. Test statistics are constructed around estimates from a sample of data. Remembering that sample estimates are random variables, test statistics will also be random variables following some statistical distribution. The test statistics used in this book (i.e. the t and F tests) are relatively simple and widely known; statisticians have established that they will fall within well-known probability distributions, i.e. the t and F distributions (variants of the standard normal distribution). Essentially we investigate whether or not our test statistics fall in the tails of these distributions; if they do, then we will infer that our null is relatively unlikely and we reject it. If our test statistic falls in the middle of the relevant distribution then we 'do not reject' the null. This rather unwieldy and pedantic language reflects the fact that, for statistical analysis, we are in a world of induction (not deduction) and so we can never 'prove' anything. Statisticians/econometricians are cautious people. They are very aware of the distinction between extremely unlikely and impossible. Statisticians do not 'accept' anything; they prefer to say that they 'do not reject' it.

In deciding whether or not to reject a null hypothesis, we use a **decision rule**. We will discuss decision rules based around critical values and decision rules based around probability values (p values).

The **critical value** of a test statistic marks the boundary between rejection and non-rejection of our null and, using significance levels and degrees of freedom, we can find critical values in the statistical tables for t and F distributions.

But what do we mean by a **significance level**? Significance levels determine critical values and thus what we do with our null hypothesis. For example, if a critical value of a test statistic is selected using a 5% significance level, this means that we would expect to see a test statistic more extreme than the critical value in only 5% of samples. We go on to infer that it is unlikely that we would see such extreme values if our null were true and so we reject our null. This doesn't mean that our null is wrong; it just means that it doesn't seem very probable given the results from our sample of data.

It is important to remember that the selection of the significance level does introduce some arbitrariness into hypothesis testing. Also, selection of significance levels will affect the chances of making a **Type I error** (the error of incorrectly rejecting a true H_0) versus a **Type II error** (the error of not rejecting a false null). For most econometric analysis we won't know whether or not we are making these mistakes because the whole point is that we don't know what's true. If we did then perhaps we wouldn't have to bother with running regressions! Significance levels will directly determine the probability of Type I error, i.e. a significance level of 5% implies that the probability of a Type I error is 5%. Significance levels will also affect the **power** of hypothesis tests (the power of a test is 1 minus the probability of Type II error). The trade-offs between Type I and Type II errors raise a whole range of interesting issues beyond the scope of this text but addressed in detail in any good text on statistical theory. We abstract from these complexities by using conventional significance levels, i.e. 1%, 5% and 10%.

The critical values for the t and F tests used in this book will also be determined by the degrees of freedom in our model. Degrees of freedom give us statistical 'room for manoeuvre'; if we have many degrees of freedom then we can more accurately estimate the parameters of an empirical model. In running a regression, we lose one degree of freedom for each parameter estimated. In SRA we will lose one degree of freedom (df) in estimating the slope and another in estimating the intercept. This gives $df = n - k - 1 = n - 2$. In multiple regression, more parameters must be estimated and so more degrees of freedom will be lost in calculating these parameters, e.g. the degrees of freedom in a model with $k = 5$, i.e. with five explanatory variables is $df = n - 5 - 1 = n - 6$.

An alternative to using critical values is to use p **values (probability values)**. These give an **exact significance level**, i.e. the significance level at which we would reject our null. So a relatively low p value would suggest that we should reject our null and a relatively high p value would suggest that we should retain it. If we are using a 5% significance level, then our p value decision rule would be:

If $p > 0.05$ (i.e. 5%), then do not reject H_0; if $p < 0.05$ then reject H_0.

These p values can be used for any sort of hypothesis test, including t tests, F tests (and other hypothesis tests) and are now widely reported in most statistical and econometrics packages (including Excel and EViews). Using p values saves the time and trouble involved in looking up statistical tables.

Tests of individual significance – Student's t test

For our tests of the individual significance of specific parameter estimates, we use **Student's t test**. The H_0 and H_1 for the t tests can be constructed in two ways depending on whether we are using a one-tailed test or a two-tailed test. With **one-tailed tests** we construct an asymmetric H_1 implying that the parameter of interest will deviate from the null in one direction only. We use a one-tailed test when we have some prior information about the sign of our parameters. One-tailed tests are more powerful because the rejection region is concentrated in one tail of the t distribution. One-tailed t tests are illustrated in Chapter 3.

For **two-tailed tests**, the H_1 is constructed to allow deviations from the null in either direction. To illustrate the procedures for a two-tailed t test on a slope parameter of our model in Equation (1.1), our null and alternatives would be

$H_0 : \beta = 0$

$H_1 : \beta \neq 0$

The test statistic for the Student's t test is:

$$\hat{t} = \frac{\hat{\beta} - \beta_{H_0}}{se(\hat{\beta})} \tag{1.13}$$

where β_{H_0} is the value of β hypothesized within our null, $\hat{\beta}$ is our estimate of β and $se(\hat{\beta})$ is the standard error of our estimate of β.

Our decision rule will be to reject H_0 if the absolute value of the t statistic is 'significantly greater' than 0 with a 5% significance level and constructing this decision rule around critical values gives:

If $-t_{\text{crit}} < \hat{t} < +t_{\text{crit}}$ then do not reject H_0, but if $|\hat{t}| < t_{\text{crit}}$, then reject H_0

where t_{crit} is the critical value of our test statistic.

A rejection of H_0 implies that the slope parameter is significantly different from zero and therefore suggests a systematic association between Y and X.

Confidence intervals

We can turn the t testing procedure on its head to give an alternative way of drawing inferences about our H_0 by constructing a **confidence interval** (CI). CIs give the numerical region in which we would have some degree of confidence that our null is true, i.e. they capture the region in which our null would not be rejected. The formula for the confidence interval is given by:

$$\left|\hat{\beta}\right| \pm se(\hat{\beta}) \times t_{\text{crit}} \tag{1.14}$$

If H_0 falls within the CI then we would not reject H_0 but if H_0 falls outside the CI we would conclude that it is relatively unlikely and so would reject H_0. An example of the construction of confidence intervals is illustrated in Chapter 2.

Tests of joint significance – The *F* test of explanatory power

For simple regression analysis (SRA) we are interested in testing hypotheses about a single slope parameter. In MRA we have more than one explanatory variable and so we will need to use joint tests of significance if we want to draw inferences about parameters on groups of variables. For example if we want to establish whether or not *all* the explanatory variables in our model are statistically associated with our dependent variable, then we can test whether or not the slope parameter(s) are jointly equal to 0 using an **F test of explanatory power**. To conduct this test on a model with k explanatory variables (and so with k slope parameters), our hypotheses will be:

$H_0 : \beta_1 = \beta_2 = \cdots = \beta_k = 0$

H_1: at least one of these parameters is not equal to zero

The formula for the F test of explanatory power is:

$$F_{k,n-k-1} = \frac{R^2/k}{(1-R^2)/n-k-1} \tag{1.15}$$

Decision rule: If $F > F_{\text{crit}}$, then reject H_0.

In essence, the F test of explanatory power captures the relative magnitude of R^2; if R^2 is relatively large, then F is more likely to exceed F_{crit} and the null of parameter values of zero on all the explanatory variables (i.e. of no association between the dependent variable and explanatory variables) will be rejected.

In SRA, this F test statistic will be equal to the square of a Student's t test statistic on $H_0 : \beta_1 = 0$. But in MRA, the relationship becomes more complex and this relationship between t and F will break down.

This section has illustrated the basic principles of hypothesis testing but we will use many other hypothesis tests in *Running Regressions*, for example another F test – the F test of restrictions (explained in detail in Chapter 5).

1.8   What's next?

Now that we have introduced the basic concepts underlying OLS regression analysis, we are ready to apply the principles to a range of real-world examples. To ensure that the econometric analysis is 'digestibile', we will introduce the tests and techniques one-by-one. For quick reference, the Gauss–Markov assumptions and basic formulae essential to running regressions are summarised in the Appendix to this chapter. For further details on the techniques, we have also suggested some relatively easy econometrics references in the section on further reading.

Some good news about applied econometrics – an econometrician rarely has to do all the computational work him/herself. There are a variety of econometrics packages on the market with various pros and cons. In addition, regressions can be run relatively easily using most popular spreadsheet packages, e.g. running regressions in Excel can be done using the option 'Data Analysis – Regression' (usually accessible via 'Tools' in the Excel toolbar). In Chapter 2 of this book we do illustrate how you could run a regression 'by hand' (i.e. using a handheld calculator) to estimate a simple line of best fit because this illustrates the principles and procedures underlying OLS. For the remainder of the book, the models will be estimated either using a spreadsheet package (we use Excel) or a specialised econometric package (we use EViews).

1.9   Further reading

This econometric introduction provides just a very brief and relatively intuitive summary of the econometric theory that underlies OLS because we want to concentrate on the interesting business of using the techniques to explain how socio-economic processes work. All of econometrics becomes a lot easier if you have a good understanding of the basic statistical concepts. The readings that follow represent good textbook introductions to various aspects of statistical and econometric theory. Most of these are printed in new editions every few years.

Introductory

Damodar N. Gujarati, *Essentials of Econometrics*, New York: McGraw-Hill.
Damodar N. Gujarati, *Basic Econometrics*, New York: McGraw-Hill.

Intuitive

Peter Kennedy, *Guide to Econometrics*, Oxford: Blackwell.

Good overall coverage

Christopher Dougherty, *Introduction to Econometrics*, Oxford: Oxford University Press.
William H. Greene, *Econometric Analysis*, Upper Saddle River, NJ: Prentice-Hall.
James H. Stock and Mark W. Watson, *Introduction to Econometrics*, Harlow: Pearson Education/Addison-Wesley.

Time series econometrics

R. L. Thomas, *Modern Econometrics – An Introduction*, Harlow: Addison-Wesley.

Cross-sectional analysis and 'microeconometrics'

Jeffrey M. Wooldridge, *Introductory Econometrics – A Modern Approach*, Thomson South-Western.

Appendix – Summary of assumptions and tests

A.1   The Gauss–Markov Theorem

For OLS to give the Best Linear Unbiased Estimators (BLUE) in small samples, the following Gauss–Markov assumptions must be true:

1. The mean or **expected value** of ε_i, the error term, is zero: $E(\varepsilon_i) = 0$.
2. No autocorrelation in the errors, i.e. a zero covariance between error term for observation i and the error term for observation j: $cov(\varepsilon_i, \varepsilon_j) = 0$.
3. Homoscedasticity, the variance of the error term, i.e. $var(\varepsilon_i)$, is a constant: $var(\varepsilon_i) = \sigma^2$, where σ^2 is a constant.
4. Exogeneity: $cov(\varepsilon_i, X_i) = 0$ where X is an explanatory variable.

A.2   Running regressions checklist

In general, the following steps should form the basis of any regression analysis:

1. In constructing an empirical model carefully investigate the relevant theory and previous empirical research and specify your model accordingly. For example: if you are estimating a demand function then you will need to take the natural logs of your variables (see Chapter 3); for binary dependent variables, you will be estimating probabilities so you will need to use logit or probit techniques (see Chapter 12).
2. Test hypotheses about individual significance (e.g. using Student's t test) and joint significance (e.g. using F tests) explicitly stating your null and alternative hypotheses and decision rules. Remember that decision rules can be constructed around critical values or p values (see Chapters 2–4).
3. Assess the goodness of fit as captured by R^2 in SRA (see Chapter 2) or $\bar{R}^2$ in MRA (see Chapter 5).
4. Use F tests of explanatory power statistically to test the goodness of fit (see Chapter 4).
5. Visually inspect residuals to check for heteroscedasticity and autocorrelation (see Chapters 6 and 7).
6. Conduct diagnostic tests for heteroscedasticity and autocorrelation (see Chapters 6 and 7).
7. Conduct diagnostic tests for model misspecification e.g. Ramsey's RESET test (see Chapter 8).
8. If you do not have many observations, consider combining cross-sectional and time-series data in conducting a panel estimation (see Chapter 11).

More specifically for time-series data, you will need to:

9. Identify an appropriate lag structure (see Chapter 10).
10. Check for structural breaks (see Chapter 9).
11. Check for deterministic and stochastic trends (see Chapter 9).
12. If variables are non-stationary, take differences until you identify a stationary form of the variables. Alternatively, check to see if non-stationary variables are cointegrated (see Chapters 9 and 10).

A.3 Essential formulae

A.3.1 Residual sum of squares (RSS) and residual variance

$$RSS = \sum \hat{\varepsilon}_i^2 = \sum (Y_i - \hat{Y}_i)^2$$

$$\hat{\sigma}_i^2 = \frac{RSS}{n - k - 1}$$

A.3.2   **Parameter estimates, variances and standard errors**
Slope

$$\hat{\beta} = \frac{\text{cov}(X, Y)}{\text{var}(X)} = \frac{\sum (X_i - \bar{X})(Y_i - \bar{Y})}{\sum (X_i - \bar{X})^2}$$

$$\text{var}(\hat{\beta}) = \frac{\sigma^2}{\sum (X_i - \bar{X})^2}$$

$$se(\hat{\beta}) = \sqrt{\frac{\hat{\sigma}^2}{\sum (X_i - \bar{X})^2}}$$

Intercept

$$\hat{\alpha} = \bar{Y} - \hat{\beta}\bar{X}$$

$$\text{var}(\hat{\alpha}) = \left\{ \frac{\sum X_i^2}{n \sum (X_i - \bar{X})^2} \right\} \times \sigma^2$$

$$\hspace{6cm} (1.10)$$

$$se(\hat{\alpha}) = \sqrt{\left\{ \frac{\sum X_i^2}{n \sum (X_i - \bar{X})^2} \times \hat{\sigma}^2 \right\}}$$

A.3.3   **Hypothesis tests and confidence intervals**
Student's t test (two-tailed)

$$H_0 : \beta_1 = 0$$

$$H_1 : \beta_1 \neq 0$$

$$\hat{t} = \frac{\hat{\beta} - 0}{se(\hat{\beta})}, \text{ using Equation (1.14)}$$

Decision rule: if $|\hat{t}| < |t_{\text{crit}}|$, then reject H_0. If $-t_{\text{crit}} < \hat{t} < +t_{\text{crit}}$ then do not reject H_0

Confidence interval
The confidence interval is given by:

$$\left| \hat{\beta} \right| \pm se(\hat{\beta}) \times t_{\text{crit}}$$

A.3.4 **Correlation and goodness of fit**

$$r_{xy} = \frac{\sum (X_i - \bar{X})(Y_i - \bar{Y})}{\sqrt{\sum (X_i - \bar{X})^2 \sum (Y_i - \bar{Y})^2}} = \frac{\text{cov}(X, Y)}{\sqrt{\text{var}(X) \times \text{var}(Y)}}$$

$$R^2 = \frac{ESS}{TSS} = \frac{\sum (\hat{Y} - \bar{Y})^2}{\sum (Y_i - \bar{Y})^2}$$

Adjusted R^2

$$\bar{R}^2 = 1 - \left[(1 - R^2) \times \frac{n-1}{n-k-1} \right]$$

F test of explanatory power

$$H_0 : \beta_1 = \beta_2 = \cdots = \beta_k = 0$$

$$F_{k,n-k-1} = \frac{R^2/k}{(1 - R^2)/n - k - 1}$$

Decision rule: If $F > F_{\text{crit}}$, then reject H_0.

Running simple regressions

Global poverty and economic growth

The test of our progress is not whether we add to the abundance of those who have much; it is whether we provide enough for those who have too little.

US President Franklin D. Roosevelt, 2nd inaugural address, 1937.

Economic issues include:
- Poverty reduction – the role of investment and trade
- Millennium Development Goals (MDGs)
- Development economics and development institutions

Econometric issues include:
- Correlation coefficients
- Running OLS regressions 'by hand'
- Single hypothesis tests: Student's *t* test
- Point estimates and confidence intervals
- Goodness of fit and the coefficient of determination

Data issues include:
- Quantitative indicators of development
- A qualitative indicator – the Human Poverty Index

2.1 The issue

How can we reduce poverty and improve living standards for the poor? There are no easy answers and in addressing the problems of global poverty, the world's heads of state met in September 2000 to discuss a universal framework for development, agreeing on targets to promote development. The then 189 UN member states agreed to the eight Millennium Development Goals (MDGs) listed in Box 2.1. Poverty reduction was one of these primary goals and the UN member states pledged to halve world poverty by 2015. These goals were

---

Box 2.1 The Millennium Development Goals (MDGs)

- Eradicate extreme poverty and hunger
- Achieve universal primary education
- Promote gender equality and empower women
- Reduce child mortality
- Improve maternal health
- Combat HIV/AIDS, malaria and other diseases
- Ensure environmental sustainability
- Develop a global partnership for development

Source: www.un.org/millenniumgoals/

---

reaffirmed at the World Summit held in September 2005, and the issue has been kept alive ever since by a number of high-profile awareness-raising and fund-raising events, backed by a diverse range of people – rockstars included.

There is therefore a clear consensus on the importance of the MDGs themselves but little agreement about how to achieve them. The target date of 2015 is now not far away and there is a lot left to do. Many fear that the first decade of the new millennium will be marked down as one of lost opportunities, rather than improvements. In devising strategies, policies and initiatives to achieve the MDG of poverty reduction it is important for policy makers to have a good understanding of how poverty evolves in the first place. In this chapter, we make a start in analysing poverty by examining some simple statistical evidence about the relationship between poverty and economic growth.

The problem of poverty amidst wealth and abundance has long concerned economists in both the developing and the developed world. There are many competing views and prescriptions about what to do about it and analysis of these is the focus of development economics, an area of economics that is of enormous interest to national governments, international organisations (such as the UN and its sister organisations), as well as to non-governmental organisations. In Box 2.2 there is a quick summary of the practical aspects of development economics as well as a list of some of the organisations particularly interested in analysing the process of development.

Defining poverty

In this chapter we explain the distinction between relative poverty and absolute poverty. **Relative poverty** is manifested in inequalities of income

Box 2.2 'Doing' development economics

In one sense, almost all economists are interested in the topic of development, in that we strive for ways to better understand and to improve human welfare and economic life. However a number of individuals and institutions focus in particular on these challenges in the more extreme context of developing countries, or in the pockets of under-development that exist within countries that are otherwise rich and 'developed'. The topic is increasing in popularity, at both the theoretical and the practical level, perhaps as a response to concerns that so much remains to be done but also with the increasing recognition that problems that do not initially appear to be economic in nature often have underlying economic causes and solutions. For example, the 1998 Nobel laureate, Amartya Sen, used the tools of economics to challenge the conventional assumption that starvation was caused by food shortages, droughts and famines. His 1981 book *Poverty and Famines* showed that many recent famines had occurred when there was no significant shortage of food arguing that institutional constraints and other economic features are the cause of starvation so institutional reform should be central to policy solutions. Increasingly development economists today are focussing on institutional features relating to poverty and under-development, including the role of 'good government'; failures of international and national capital markets; and the importance of international trade rules, rather than focussing on inherent features of the natural world.

Readers who are interested in learning more about the scale and scope of practical development economics can view the wide range of current initiatives being conducted by economists (and lawyers, social scientists, health professionals etc.) in the small selection of websites of development organisations listed below. Many of the better-known agencies, institutions and non-governmental organisations (NGOs) also offer internships (paid or voluntary) and interesting full or part-time careers. Most universities also offer courses in development economics at the graduate level, in addition to introductory courses at the undergraduate level.

Some interesting websites

Governmental organisations

United Nations Development Programme	www.undp.org
World Health Organisation	www.who.org
International Monetary Fund	www.imf.org
UN Research Institute for Social Development	www.unrisd.org
Asian Development Bank	www.adb.org
African Development Bank	www.afdb.org
Inter-American Development Bank	www.iadb.org
UN Economic Commission for Europe	www.unece.org

UN Food and Agriculture Organisation	www.fao.org
UN Conference for Trade and Development	www.unctad.org
UN University World Institute for Economic Development Research	www.wider.un.edu
World Bank	www.worldbank.org
Organisation for Economic Cooperation and Development	www.oecd.org
International Labour Organisation	www.ilo.org
Australian Government Overseas Aid	www.ausaid.gov.au
International Development Research Centre (Canada)	www.idrc.ca
UK Department for International Development	www.dfid.gov.uk
US Agency for International Development	www.usaid.gov
International jobs in development economics	www.devnetjobs.org
Non-governmental organisations	
Oxfam	www.oxfam.org
World Vision	www.worldvision.org
Care	www.care.org

and wealth. Relative poverty is the focus of a particular and special intensity in the modern world but concerns about people's relative positions in an economy are not new. As early as 400 BC the Greek philosopher Plato had advised that the gap between the richest and the poorest citizens should never be greater than a factor of four – i.e. that the richest should be no more than four times wealthier than the poorest. Plato argued that this 4:1 ratio was necessary not only for ethical and moral reasons, but also for practical and pragmatic ones: greater inequality could fuel civil violence or even war. At the 2001 World Economic Forum meeting, held in New York in the aftermath of the September 11 tragedy, UN Secretary General, Kofi Annan likened the world's rich and poor to fellow passengers on an unstable boat:

None of us can afford to ignore the condition of our fellow passengers on this little boat. If they are sick, all of us risk infection. And if they are angry, all of us can easily get hurt.

How does the modern world match-up in terms of Plato's ideal? Table 2.1 shows the relationship between relative incomes in a selection of countries and reveals some stark differences. In Argentina for example, the richest **decile** (i.e. the richest 10% of the population) received an income that was on average 40 times higher than the country's poorest decile. In Brazil the gap

Table 2.1 Relative incomes of rich and poor[1]

On average, how many times as much income do the richest
10% earn relative to the poorest 10%?
Factor differences in income between richest and poorest deciles:

Argentina	40
Brazil	94
Japan	4.5
Switzerland	10
United States	16
The world	103

Source: UNDP 2005.

between the top and bottom decile was even greater. At the global level, the richest decile of the world's population (who live for the most part in North America, Europe and parts of Asia) had income levels that were more than 100 times higher than the poorest 10% – who live, for the most part, in the Least Developed Countries (LDCs). Table 2.1 also shows that richer, more developed countries can also have large gaps between their richest and poorest decile. In the United States, for example, the richest decile earned 16 times as much as the poorest decile . Plato's four-fold ratio clearly fails to hold today; in 2005, only Japan was close to Plato's ideal ratio. Furthermore, research by World Bank economists Ravallion, Chen and Sangraula (2008) suggests that relative poverty has been worsening in the developing world in recent years.

While inequality is clearly a major aspect of poverty, recent approaches to the subject have tended to focus less on relative poverty, and more on **absolute poverty**. This is reflected in the use of benchmarks, capturing a 'breadline' of decent living below which society should not allow households to slip. At the national level, different countries use different definitions of their breadline, depending on national income, and on national perceptions of what constitutes their society's minimum bundle of goods and capabilities. At the global level, this approach has culminated in a concrete, quantitative definition of poverty as the condition affecting people trying to live on less than $1 per day. This defines a global 'social floor' that makes it easy to see first, how countries perform relative to each other and second, if there have been improvements

---

[1] See also Chapters 4 and 12 for more on technical measures of poverty, viz. Lorenz curves and Gini coefficients.

Box 2.3 Poverty and development: the record so far

Development record of the last decade:

The positives	The negatives
130 million people were lifted out of extreme poverty	2.5 billion people still live on less than $2 a day
2 million fewer child deaths a year	10 million preventable child deaths a year
30 million more children are in school	115 million children are still out of school – especially girls
1.2 billion people gained access to clean water	More than 1 billion people still have no access to safe water
	2.6 billion lack access to sanitation

Source: United Nations Development Program (UNDP), *Human Development Report 2005.*

---

over time. It is easier to reduce absolute poverty (e.g. through cash transfer programmes) than to reduce inequality (redistribution of assets via land reform is problematic in countries where inequality has been embedded for centuries).

Box 2.3 summarises the development record from the last decade and illustrates that whilst much has been achieved, much remains to be done.

2.2   The theory

Abstracting from the complexity of issues relevant to development economics, the particular economic theory tested in this chapter is that the key to poverty reduction is *rapid and sustained economic growth*. The idea is that, if incomes and wealth are growing in one sector of the economy, then the benefits of growth will 'trickle down' to poorer groups. This is of course an extremely simplistic way to phrase **trickle-down theory**, and nobody thinks that growth is the only factor affecting poverty, but the core of this view is widely supported. Most undergraduate texts in economics take it as given that growth will moderate poverty – for example Lipsey and Chrystal (2007) summarise a vast literature on growth, development and poverty by concluding that '*economic growth is the economy's most powerful engine for generating long-term increases in living standards*'. Even those with opposing views are likely to agree that it is easier to slice and re-distribute an expanding cake, rather than a shrinking one. The real controversy lies in answering the prior question of how to achieve growth in the first place. There are many competing theories on this subject, some of which arise in subsequent chapters of this book. Keynesian models, for example, emphasise the role of household consumption; others have focused on the role of labour productivity. More recently writers have emphasised the role of factors such as savings and investment (e.g. Swan, 1956, Solow, 1956) and human capital effects gained through education and human capital formation (e.g. Mankiw, Romer and Weil, 1992). An excellent overview of the subject is given by Thirlwall (2005) in the introductory textbook *Growth and Development*.

As described more fully by United Nations Conference for Trade and Development in its *Least Developed Countries Report* 2002 (UNCTAD, 2002), economic growth enables LDCs to reduce domestic poverty because of its impact upon household income and consumption. UNCTAD's story is an extension of earlier arguments by Rodrik (1999), who asserted that countries that had had rapid growth alongside rapid poverty reductions had also directed more and more of their domestic production towards export markets. And this trend was particularly pronounced amongst low-income countries. The UNCTAD Report describes a cycle where LDCs experience a process of 'late industrialisation', brought about by increases in investment. This investment enables sectors of the economy that were previously marginal (e.g. subsistence agriculture) to become productive. New investment leads to the construction of factories, transport and communications networks, which allow modern industrial manufacturing processes to replace traditional agricultural and pre-industrial systems. Resources are gradually shifted away from the traditional activities and into higher technology and capital-intensive industries. New products are created which can be exported to global markets that pay higher prices than local markets. As the share of domestic production geared towards exports increases, wages rise and job opportunities are increased. Incomes rise, household consumption rises, and poverty levels fall through a series of trickle-down effects.

This chapter provides some data that can be used in testing some assertions from the UNCTAD report. There are two sets of simple and readily testable theories/assumptions that can be explored:

(a) economic growth affects poverty,

(b) increased investment and exports lead to economic growth.

Below, we test hypothesis (a) via a cross-sectional analysis comparing the relative performance of 31 LDCs over a period of twelve years. We predict that countries with higher levels of growth were more able to reduce poverty than countries with lower growth. For hypothesis (b) we would expect that countries with higher levels of investment and increased export orientation will have experienced faster growth than countries without increased investments or exports.[2]

2.3   The data

The data used in this chapter is taken from UNCTAD (2002) but comparable data is readily available elsewhere, including for example the IMF, World Bank, UN WIDER inequality and poverty database and national accounts. In all cases we look at the data in terms of the change in the indicators, over the years from 1987 to 1999. We do this primarily because our focus is on the extent to which poverty levels have worsened or improved rather than absolute poverty levels (which will be affected by many other factors in addition to economic growth). (see e.g. poverty studies network www.chronicpoverty.org.)

It is helpful in research analyses to present a detailed 'descriptive analysis' of the data before going on to regression analysis, to tease out the broad patterns. The data set presented in Annex 2.2 – Table 2.6 focusses on the following variables: change in absolute poverty, measured as the percentage change in the proportion of the population living on $1 per day or less; annual average GDP growth per capita; % change in exports as a share of GDP; and investment, measured as the growth in gross capital formation (GCF).

In column 1 of Table 2.6 we have our dependent variable – poverty. Over the period 1987–1999 this indicator ranged from an increase in poverty of 37.2% (Sierra Leone) to a decrease in poverty of 20.4% (Malawi). The mean or average for the sample reflected a slight increase in poverty (of + 1.63%) but there was considerable variance across the individual countries in the sample.

In column 2 we have our explanatory variable: *economic growth*. This is measured as the rate of change in *GDP per capita*. Over the years studied, this ranged from + 3.5% (Lao Peoples' Democratic Republic) to –5.7% (Sierra Leone). The average was slightly negative at –0.2%.

The change in *exports as a share of GDP* is in column 3. This also varied considerably from country to country, around an average increase of 4.7%. Angola scored particularly highly with an export growth rate of 23.6% per annum, reflecting sales of natural resources such as oil and diamonds;

---

[2] We don't explicitly analyse hypothesis (b) here but we have provided additional data on exports and investments (see Annex 2.2 – Table 2.6) and we suggest some empirical strategies for analysing this hypothesis in Section 2.6 – chapter exercises.

but incomes from these commodity sales were accrued by a small fraction of Angola's population and/or spent on imports and so would not necessarily foster improved living standards amongst Angola's poorest.

In column 4, we have *investment growth*, measured as the rate of change of *Gross Capital Formation* (GCF); GCF measures the change in the capital stock i.e. the accumulation of physical capital including factories, plant and machinery. This was slow – increasing by an average of only 1.6% over the sample period, perhaps reflecting the relatively stagnant rates of economic growth mentioned above.

Focussing just on the associations between poverty and GDP growth: of the 31 countries in our sample, 16 countries experienced rising GDP per capita. For most of these 16 countries this was associated with reduced poverty but the two exceptions were Lesotho and Mali. Of the declining growth countries, Sierra Leone quite spectacularly exhibited what we expected, with GDP falling by 5.7% and poverty levels rising sharply by 37.2%.

Empirical results and interpretation

We can test the accuracy of this verbal description of the data by using some simple techniques. We start with correlation analysis and by running a regression – statistically to capture the degree of association between changing poverty and growth in GDP per capita.

The following pages work through the hypothesis that growth in GDP is associated with reductions in poverty using the same data set and techniques introduced in Chapter 1. As explained in Chapter 1, the first step in statistical analysis is to start with an empirical hypothesis and construct an empirical model around it. This empirical model should capture the hypothesised data generating process (DGP). Our hypothesis is that GDP growth is negatively associated with changing poverty and that this association takes a linear form, so this hypothesis can be expressed mathematically as follows:

$$Y_i = \alpha + \beta X_i + \varepsilon_i \qquad \beta < 0 \qquad\qquad (2.1)$$

where Y_i = change in proportion of population living on $1/day for country for the 31 countries in our sample (from Lao PDR, $i = 1$, to Sierra Leone, $i = 31$)
X_i = change in average annual GDP per capita (also for each country i)
α = intercept parameter
β = slope parameter (capturing the change in Y for a unit change in X)
ε_i = stochastic (i.e. random) error term

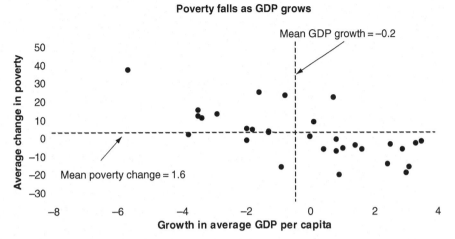

Figure 2.1   Poverty and growth

A good starting point in any empirical analysis is to have a look at some plots of the data. This sort of visual inspection can reveal some of the broad and/or stark patterns in the data. It's also a good way to check that there aren't any obvious problems with data.

Focussing on poverty and growth, we can have a look at the data to see if the inverse association between economic growth and poverty predicted by our theory is a realistic hypothesis. Figure 2.1 shows a simple **scatter plot** showing for each country the pairs of observations on the dependent variable Y (change in poverty) and the explanatory variable X (GDP growth per capita).

Our data sample of observations on changing poverty and GDP growth are presented in Figure 2.1. The two 'centres of gravity' created by the two sample averages or means are depicted by a dotted vertical line at the mean GDP growth rate change of −0.2; and a dotted horizontal line at the mean poverty change of 1.63.

Most countries are either in the SE quadrant with a (−,+) association between poverty changes and GDP growth, or in the NW quadrant with a (+,−) association for each pair of observations.

So there is a negatively sloped clustering running from the north-west (NW), top left-hand side of the graph to the south-east (SE) corner of the graph.

Specifically the north-west (NW) quadrant of Figure 2.1 contains countries whose poverty levels worsened and whose GDP growth slowed – i.e. $Y_i > \bar{Y}$ and $X_i < \bar{X}$. More specifically in the NW corner, Sierra Leone is a particularly extreme example of a country in which growth was low and poverty worsened.

The SE quadrant contains countries whose poverty levels were falling by more than the mean, and whose GDP was growing fast – i.e. $Y_i < \bar{Y}$ and $X_i > \bar{X}$. Uganda stands out as an example here.

Countries in the NE quadrant are characterised by a (+,+) relationship reflecting disproportionate rises in poverty in spite of relatively fast growth (i.e $Y_i > \bar{Y}$ and $X_i > \bar{X}$); only Mali and Lesotho appear in this quadrant. In the SW quadrant are the countries that experienced a (–,–) relationship with lower than average GDP growth but also a lower than average worsening of poverty – i.e. $Y_i < \bar{Y}$ and $X_i < \bar{X}$. Gambia, Togo and Angola are in this quadrant.

But these countries are in a clear minority. On balance the sample is dominated by countries which, one way or the other, are characterised by an inverse association between changing poverty and GDP growth. So our initial inspection of the data verifies the basic hypothesis: the scatter plot in Fig. 2.1. is consistent with our basic hypothesis that poverty reduction is associated with GDP growth. We further verify this pattern when we measure the correlation coefficient and run a regression.

Capturing correlation

In getting a more objective measure of the nature of clustering in the scatter plot we can measure the **correlation** between the two variables – i.e. the extent of linear association or statistical dependence between two variables. As explained in Chapter 1, the first step in assessing correlation involves measuring the extent to which the two series 'co-vary'. Mathematically, covariances are the product of deviations from means. The measure of movements between two variables relative to their respective means in a given sample of data is the **sample covariance**. Some of the data transformations needed to measure this covariance are summarised in Table 2.2.

As explained in Chapter 1, the correlation coefficient is a 'normalised' measure of the linear association between two variables and the range of possible values is $-1 \le r_{XY} \le +1$. Using variable transformations shown in columns 5, 6 and 8 of Table 2.2 and the method for calculating correlation coefficients outlined in Chapter 1 gives:

$$r_{XY} = \frac{\sum (X_i - \bar{X})(Y_i - \bar{Y})}{\sqrt{\sum (X_i - \bar{X})^2 \sum (Y_i - \bar{Y})^2}} = \frac{\text{cov}(X, Y)}{\sqrt{\text{var}(X) \times \text{var}(Y)}}$$

$$= \frac{-663.8}{\sqrt{179.3 \times 5540.5}} = -0.66 \tag{2.2}$$

Table 2.2 Changing poverty (Y) and GDP growth (X): regression by hand

	1	2	3	4	5	6	7	8
	Y_i	X_i	$X_i - \bar{X}$	$Y_i - \bar{Y}$	$(X_i - \bar{X})(Y - \bar{Y})$	$(X_i - \bar{X})^2$	X_i^2	$(Y_i - \bar{Y})^2$
Lao PDR	−2	3.5	3.7	−3.6	−13.4	13.7	12.3	13.2
Bangladesh	−3.4	3.3	3.5	−5.0	−17.6	12.3	10.9	25.3
Uganda	−16.1	3.1	3.30	−17.7	−58.5	10.9	9.6	314.4
Bhutan	−19.2	3	3.20	−20.8	−66.7	10.2	9.00	433.9
Cape Verde	−6.3	2.9	3.1	−7.9	−24.6	9.6	8.4	62.9
Mozambique	−3.6	2.5	2.7	−5.2	−14.1	7.3	6.3	27.4
Nepal	−14.3	2.4	2.6	−15.9	−41.4	6.8	5.8	253.8
Solomon Is	−4.1	1.4	1.6	−5.7	−9.2	2.6	2.0	32.8
Benin	−6.1	1	1.2	−7.7	−9.3	1.4	1.00	59.8
Malawi	−20.4	0.9	1.1	−22.0	−24.2	1.2	0.8	485.3
Ethiopia	−1.2	0.8	1.0	−2.83	−2.8	1.0	0.6	8.0
Lesotho	22.3	0.7	0.9	20.7	18.6	0.8	0.5	427.2
Burkina Faso	−6.5	0.4	0.6	−8.1	−4.9	0.4	0.2	66.1
Mali	8.7	0.1	0.3	7.1	2.1	0.1	0.0	50.0
Senegal	0.8	0	0.2	−0.8	−0.2	0.0	0.0	0.7
Central African Republic	23.3	−0.8	−0.6	21.7	−13.0	0.4	0.6	469.6
Chad	2.5	−1.3	−1.1	0.9	−1.0	1.2	1.7	0.8
Vanuatu	3.5	−1.3	−1.1	1.9	−2.1	1.2	1.7	3.5
Guinea-Bissau	25	−1.6	−1.4	23.4	−32.7	2.0	2.6	546.2
Madagascar	4.5	−1.8	−1.6	2.9	−4.6	2.6	3.2	8.2
Comoros	11.8	−3.5	−3.3	10.2	−33.6	10.9	12.3	103.4
Angola	1.5	−3.8	−3.6	−0.1	0.5	13.0	14.4	0.0
Mauritania	−6.2	1.6	1.8	−7.8	−14.1	3.2	2.6	61.3
Guinea	−7.4	0.8	1	−9.0	−9.0	1.0	0.6	81.5
Gambia	−16.3	−0.9	−0.7	−17.9	12.6	0.5	0.8	321.5
Togo	−1.7	−2	−1.8	−3.3	6.0	3.2	4.0	11.1
Niger	5.1	−2	−1.80	3.5	−6.2	3.2	4.0	12.0
Rwanda	13.1	−2.9	−2.7	11.5	−31.0	7.3	8.4	131.6
Burundi	11	−3.4	−3.20	9.4	−30.0	10.2	11.6	87.8
Haiti	14.9	−3.5	−3.3	13.3	−43.8	10.9	12.3	176.1
Sierra Leone	37.2	−5.7	−5.5	35.6	−195.6	30.3	32.5	1265.2
Mean		1.63	−0.20		−21.4			
Total					−663.8	179.3	180.5	5540.5

This indicates that there is a strongly negative statistical association between the variables Y and X of −0.66. Note that, in a two-variable context, the calculation of the correlation coefficient is not affected by which variable is the dependent variable and which variable is the explanatory variable. (It becomes

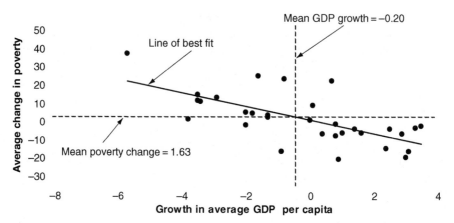

Figure 2.2   Line of best fit

more complex when there are more variables because there may be indirect effects.)

Overall $r = -0.66$ is consistent both with our initial hypothesis and with our visual inspection of the scatter plot. This high and negative correlation between changing poverty and GDP growth per capita is encouraging for our initial hypothesis.

Running a regression

From the correlation coefficient we have some information about the direction and magnitude of linear association between Y and X. To get more information about the form of the correlation, we can use OLS to estimate the parameters of a model. As explained in Chapter 1, econometric analysis often starts with an estimation of a **line of best fit** or a 'regression' line. In this section we will investigate **simple regression analysis** (i.e. a regression on just one explanatory variable). **Multiple regression analysis**, when more than one explanatory variable is used, is explored from Chapter 5 onwards.

The concept of a line of best fit can be understood visually by imagining how to place the line so that it fits the observations neatly with a small spread of observations around the line (see Figure 2.2).

When we run our regression, the extent to which the two series co-vary together will be manifested in estimates for coefficients α and β, their standard errors and the estimate of the sample variance $\hat{\sigma}^2$.

Parameter estimates

Using the formulae outlined in Chapter 1, the parameter estimates can be calculated by plugging the numbers from Table 2.2 into the following formulae:

$$\hat{\beta} = \frac{\text{cov}(X, Y)}{\text{var}(X)} = \frac{\sum(X_i - \bar{X})(Y_i - \bar{Y})}{\sum(X_i - \bar{X})^2} = \frac{-663.8}{179.3} = -3.70 \tag{2.3}$$

and

$$\hat{\alpha} = \bar{Y} - \hat{\beta}\bar{X} = 1.63 - (-3.70 \times -0.20) = 0.89 \tag{2.4}$$

So our estimated line of best fit is:

$$\hat{Y}_i = 0.89 - (3.70 \times X_i) \tag{2.5}$$

The result that $\hat{\beta} = -3.70$ confirms that the association between GDP growth and poverty change is negative, i.e. $\hat{\beta}$ has the negative sign expected by our theory and suggests that there is a strong negative association between changing poverty and GDP growth. For this sample of data, a 1% *increase* in GDP growth is associated with a 3.7% *decrease* in the proportion of people living on $1/day.

Drawing inferences and constructing hypothesis tests

There does seem to be an association but what can we infer from it? Perhaps the negative association is not a robust measure of a real association. We need a benchmark to decide how large or small our parameter estimates are relative to our initial hypothesis. To establish this we use a **hypothesis test** to test how statistically significant is the difference between our parameter estimates (which took the values 0.89 and –3.70 respectively) and the benchmark **null hypothesis**.

In this case we are testing a single hypothesis about the relationship between poverty and GDP growth. So the null and alternative hypotheses are as follows:

Null hypothesis H_0: $\beta = 0$
alternative hypothesis H_1: $\beta \neq 0$.

When the alternative hypothesis is true, i.e. when $\beta \neq 0$, GDP growth does have an impact on poverty.

If we wanted to be more precise we could test H_0 against H_1: $\beta < 0$ using a **one-tailed test** but, in the interests of simplicity, we are using a two-tailed test in this chapter; one-tailed hypothesis tests are illustrated in Chapter 3.

As explained in Chapter 1, to test this sort of **single hypothesis** we can use **Student's t test** to estimate a t statistic. As is shown below, to calculate Student's t test we need measures of the standard errors of the parameter estimates, and the procedure for calculating these is explained in Box 2.4.

Box 2.4 The standard errors of the parameter estimates

The starting point in calculating the standard error of the parameter estimates is to get an estimate of the variance of the sample estimate ($\hat{\sigma}^2$). This is found using the residual sum of squares (RSS) and dividing through by degrees of freedom, as explained in Chapter 1. The residual sum of squares has been calculated in column 7 of Table 2.3 using the following formula:

$$RSS = \Sigma \hat{\varepsilon}_i^2 = \sum (Y_i - \hat{Y}_i)^2 \tag{2.6}$$

Then the RSS is divided by the degrees of freedom ($= n - k - 1$) where k is the number of explanatory variables. We have 31 observations so $n = 31$; $k = 1$ so we lose one degree of freedom in estimating the slope parameter and another from estimating the intercept parameters. So the degrees of freedom are $31 - 2 = 29$.

Using the RSS and degrees of freedom (df) we can calculate the variance of the estimate as follows:

$$\hat{\sigma}^2 = \frac{\Sigma \hat{\varepsilon}_i^2}{(n - k - 1)} = \frac{3082.8}{31 - 2} = 106.3 \tag{2.7}$$

where $\Sigma \hat{\varepsilon}_i^2$ is the residual sum of squares (RSS) and $df = n - k - 1$.

We are now ready to find the standard errors of each of the two estimated coefficients using the method explained in Chapter 1.[3] All the information needed has already been calculated above and in Table 2.3 so plugging these numbers in gives:

$$se(\hat{\beta}) = \sqrt{\frac{\hat{\sigma}^2}{\sum (X_i - \bar{X})^2}} = \sqrt{\frac{106.3}{179.3}} = 0.77 \tag{2.8}$$

Similarly the standard error of the intercept parameter can be calculated following the procedure outlined in Chapter 1:

$$se(\hat{a}) = \sqrt{\frac{\sum X_i^2}{n \sum (X_i - \bar{X})^2} \times \hat{\sigma}^2} = \sqrt{\frac{180.5 \times 106.3}{31 \times 179.3}} = 1.86 \tag{2.9}$$

---

[3] As explained in Chapter 1, this will only provide an unbiased estimate of the standard error when the Gauss–Markov assumption of homoscedasticity is satisfied, i.e. when the error variance is constant across all observations. The violation of the homoscedasticity assumption creates a problem of heteroscedasticity, one of the consequences of which is that the OLS standard errors are calculated wrongly. These issues are explored in more detail in Chapter 6.

Using the parameter estimates and their associated standard errors, a Student's t test on our **point estimate** of $\hat{\beta}$ can be calculated as follows:

$$\hat{t} = \frac{\hat{\beta} - \beta_{H_0}}{se(\hat{\beta})} = \frac{-3.70}{0.77} = -4.81 \tag{2.10}$$

where β_{H_0} is the value of β hypothesised within our null, $\hat{\beta}$ is our point estimate of β and $se(\hat{\beta})$ is the standard error of $\hat{\beta}$.

Similarly the t test for the intercept parameter $\hat{\alpha}$ gives:

$$\hat{t} = \frac{\hat{\alpha} - \alpha_{H_0}}{se(\hat{\alpha})} = \frac{0.89}{1.86} = 0.48 \tag{2.11}$$

The next step is to find out whether or not these estimates of the t statistics are significantly different from the null hypothesis.

Concentrating on the slope parameter, the alternative hypothesis is that β is not equal to zero so we will be assessing whether or not the estimated t statistic is more extreme than the **critical value** using a **two-tailed t test**. The critical value of a test statistic marks the boundary between relatively likely and relatively unlikely, as we will illustrate below. Our decision rule will be to reject H_0 if the absolute value of the t statistic is 'significantly greater' than 0 at a 5% **significance level**.

But what do we mean by a significance level? As explained in Chapter 1, critical values are determined by the significance level. If a critical value of a test statistic (e.g. a t statistic) is selected using a 5% significance level, this means that we would expect to see an estimated t value more extreme than the critical value in only 5% of samples, i.e. it is quite unlikely that we would see such extreme t values if the null were true. Therefore, if our estimated t *is* more extreme than our critical value, then it follows that we will reject our null hypothesis. This doesn't mean that our null is wrong; it just means that it doesn't seem very probable for the sample of data that we're using.

It is important to remember that the selection of the significance level does introduce some arbitrariness into hypothesis testing. However, there are conventions – i.e. 1%, 5% and 10% significance levels are commonly used in statistical analysis.[4]

For our analysis of the relationship between poverty and GDP growth, we select a 5% significance level. With $df = 29$ and two-tailed test, the critical value of our t statistic will be $t_{crit} = 2.04$ where t_{crit} is the '*critical value*'. So our

---

[4] These issues are explored in more detail in Chapter 4.

decision rule is: if $|\hat{t}| > |t_{crit}|$, then reject H_0. If $-t_{crit} < \hat{t} < +t_{crit}$ then do not reject H_0.

So, with a 5% significance level, we reject our null and conclude that $\hat{\beta}$ is statistically '*significant*'. This is shorthand (in a two-tailed test context) for saying that $\hat{\beta}$ is statistically significantly different from the null (H_0: $\beta = 0$) so we can reject the null hypothesis and verify the alternative hypothesis. We have evidence confirming a significant association between falling poverty rates and rising GDP growth per capita. If we wanted a more powerful test of this, we could use a one-tailed test but, as noted above, we are using two-tailed tests to keep the analysis simple. But once you have read the illustration of one-tailed hypothesis tests, outlined in Chapter 3, you could try a one-tailed test on this example.

Comparing a point estimate of t statistic against the relevant critical value is just one way of assessing a hypothesis. But, as explained in Chapter 1, another way to assess hypotheses is to use **confidence intervals**. In this case we will use a 95% confidence interval; this should capture the true value of β in 95% of samples. It is important to remember first, that we are using just one sample of data; and second, that there is always a 5% probability that the true value of β is **not** captured within our confidence interval. For this reason, we cannot prove anything about the value of β; we can only make inferences about what is likely given our evidence.

That said, the formula for the confidence interval in this case is:

$$\left|\hat{\beta}\right| \pm se(\hat{\beta}) \times t_{crit} \tag{2.12}$$

So our confidence interval for β is:

$$-3.70 - (0.77 \times 2.04) < \beta < -3.70 + (0.77 \times 2.04)$$
$$\rightarrow -5.27 < \beta < -2.13$$

Our value of β postulated within our H_0, i.e. of $\beta = 0$, does not fall within our confidence interval and therefore we can reject H_0. This finding is completely consistent with the t test on the point estimate $\hat{\beta}$, outlined above.

To summarise our findings from estimating the line of best fit, the parameter estimates and associated standard errors can be summarised as follows:

$$\begin{array}{lll} Y_i = 0.89 & -3.70X_i & \\ \quad (1.86) & (0.77) & \tag{2.13} \\ \quad t = -0.48 & t = 4.81 & \end{array}$$

with the standard errors in brackets.

These results confirm the findings from our visual inspection of the scatter plot and from our estimate of the parameters of the line of best fit. There is an assocation between rising poverty and falling GDP growth which is statistically significantly different from zero at a 5% significance level.

R^2 and goodness of fit

In looking at the overall performance of our OLS estimation we need to ask: how well does our regression line fit the observed data? To capture this, we can calculate the **coefficient of determination** – a measure of the **goodness of fit** (i.e. the extent to which the estimated line neatly fits the pairs of observations on Y and X for each country). This is easy to do using the transformations summarised in Table 2.3.

The first step in finding R^2 is to calculate the difference between the observed values for each country (Y_i) and the **estimates** of $\hat{Y}_i$ (i.e. the **fitted** or **predicted** values for the poverty variable). This vertical distance between the observed and predicted values gives the **sample residual**. The sum of these residuals across the sample is the **residual sum of squares (RSS)**. We can get the predictions for Y for each country taking advantage of our new information that:

$$\hat{Y}_i = 0.89 - 3.70X_i \tag{2.14}$$

For example the predicted values of Y for various countries in the sample can be calculated as follows:

$$\hat{Y}_{Lao} = 0.89 + (-3.70 \times 3.5) = -12.1$$
$$\hat{Y}_{Bangladesh} = 0.89 + (-3.70 \times 3.3) = -11.3$$
$$\hat{Y}_{Uganda} = 0.89 + (-3.70 \times 3.1) = -10.6 \tag{2.15}$$

and so on.

The predicted values for all the countries in this sample are listed in column 1 of Table 2.3, and the extent to which they differ from the observed value of Y is shown in column 6. As we would expect from our initial graph, because our sample captures such a diverse range of experiences, our regression estimates are very different from the actual/observed Y_i in some countries. This was particularly apparent in the case of Sierra Leone, Malawi, Lesotho, Central African Republic and Gambia. But although these may seem like big errors, OLS methodology is already giving us the smallest error possible consistent with identifying a line that fits all the data points as neatly as possible.

To measure goodness of fit, we look at the total variability in Y and assess how much of this is 'explained' by the model and how much is caught in the residuals. This variability is measured using sums of squared deviations. To calculate the total sum of squares (TSS), we measure the deviation of the observed value from the mean $Y - \bar{Y}_i$, square these and then sum across all observations to give TSS = 5540.5. These calculations are shown in columns 2 and 3 of Table 2.3. Similarly, as shown in columns 4 and 5, for the explained sum of squares (ESS), we measure the deviations between the predicted values $\hat{Y}_i$ and the overall mean $\bar{Y}_i$; then we square these and sum across all observations to give ESS = 2454.2. Finally, as shown in columns 6 and 7, we measure the residual sum of squares (RSS) by calculating the residual $(Y_i - \hat{Y}_i)$ squaring and summing this to give RSS = 3082.8.

R^2 is measured by calculating the ratio of explained sum of squares (ESS) to total sum of squares (TSS). This formula can be applied here as follows:

$$R^2 = \frac{ESS}{TSS} = \frac{\sum(\hat{Y} - \bar{Y})^2}{\sum(Y_i - \bar{Y})^2} = \frac{2454.2}{5540.5} = 0.44 \qquad (2.16)$$

In simple regression analysis (SRA) the coefficient of determination is also easy to calculate using the correlation coefficient because it is just r^2, i.e. the square of the correlation coefficient. We've already calculated $r = -0.66$ so $r^2 = 0.44$. This verifies our calculation from above, i.e. R^2 is the square of the correlation coefficient ($r = -0.66$).

But this simple relationship between r^2 and R^2 holds only for SRA. In multiple regression analysis (MRA), i.e. when two or more explanatory variables are involved, measuring goodness of fit is more complicated than simply squaring the correlation coefficient. But the formula in Equation (2.16) can be applied in MRA too because it abstracts from the contribution of individual explanatory variables and instead focusses on the overall relationship between predicted and observed values of a single dependent variable. Measuring goodness of fit in MRA is explained in more detail in Chapter 5.

As shown above, our calculation of the coefficient of determination indicates that 44% of the variability in poverty changes can be captured by the variability in GDP growth. So the results suggest a good fit between growing GDP and falling poverty. But with econometrics it is important to think of caveats, conditions and qualifying factors. This result may be misleading if it indirectly reflects other factors relevant to poverty changes, such as whether the country is a democracy or not; whether it has social policies aimed at the poor, and so on. If we leave these factors out of our simple regression we could generate **omitted variable bias** (a problem explained in Chapter 8). Many economic factors are affected by more than one explanatory

Table 2.3 Measuring the sums of squares to estimate R^2

	1	2	3	4	5	6	7
	$\hat{Y}_i$	$(Y_i - \bar{Y})$	$(Y_i - \bar{Y})^2$	$(\hat{Y}_i - \bar{Y})$	$(\hat{Y}_i - \bar{Y})^2$	$(Y_i - \hat{Y}_i)$	$(Y_i - \hat{Y}_i)^2$
Lao PDR	−12.1	−3.6	13.2	−13.7	186.6	10.1	101.2
Bangladesh	−11.3	−5.0	25.3	−12.9	166.9	7.9	62.7
Uganda	−10.6	−17.7	314.4	−12.2	148.4	−5.5	30.5
Bhutan	−10.2	−20.8	433.9	−11.8	139.5	−9.0	80.8
Cape Verde	−9.8	−7.9	62.9	−11.4	130.9	3.5	12.5
Mozambique	−8.4	−5.2	27.4	−10.0	99.2	4.8	22.7
Nepal	−8.0	−15.9	253.8	−9.6	92.0	−6.3	39.8
Solomon Is	−4.3	−5.7	32.8	−5.9	34.7	0.2	0.0
Benin	−2.8	−7.7	59.8	−4.4	19.4	−3.3	10.8
Malawi	−2.4	−22.0	485.3	−4.0	16.3	−18.0	322.6
Ethiopia	−2.1	−2.8	8.0	−3.7	13.5	0.9	0.8
Lesotho	−1.7	20.7	427.2	−3.3	10.9	24.0	576.0
Burkina Faso	−0.6	−8.1	66.1	−2.2	4.8	−5.9	34.9
Mali	0.5	7.1	50.0	−1.1	1.2	8.2	66.9
Senegal	0.9	−0.8	0.7	−0.7	0.5	−0.1	0.0
Central African Republic	3.9	21.7	469.6	2.3	5.1	19.5	378.3
Chad	5.7	0.9	0.8	4.1	16.8	−3.2	10.2
Vanuatu	5.7	1.9	3.5	4.1	16.8	−2.2	4.8
Guinea-Bissau	6.8	23.4	546.2	5.2	27.1	18.2	330.9
Madagascar	7.6	2.9	8.2	6.0	35.4	−3.1	9.3
Comoros	13.8	10.2	103.4	12.2	149.8	−2.0	4.2
Angola	15.0	−0.1	0.0	13.4	178.2	−13.5	180.9
Mauritania	−5.0	−7.8	61.3	−6.6	44.0	−1.2	1.4
Guinea	−2.1	−9.0	81.5	−3.7	13.5	−5.3	28.4
Gambia	4.2	−17.9	321.5	2.6	6.9	−20.5	421.1
Togo	8.3	−3.3	11.1	6.7	44.8	−10.0	99.8
Niger	8.3	3.5	12.0	6.7	44.8	−3.2	10.2
Rwanda	11.6	11.5	131.6	10.0	100.4	1.5	2.2
Burundi	13.5	9.4	87.8	11.9	140.9	−2.5	6.1
Haiti	13.8	13.3	176.1	12.2	149.8	1.1	1.1
Sierra Leone	22.0	35.6	1265.2	20.4	415.3	15.2	231.6
Sums of Squares			**TSS = 5540.5**		**ESS = 2454.2**		**RSS = 3082.8**

variable and for this reason a lot of econometric analysis does tend to focus on MRA.

This chapter focusses on calculation by hand but most spreadsheet and econometric packages (including Excel and EViews) will perform the necessary calculations with a click of a mouse, as will be shown in the following chapters. Some of the output produced by these packages will include the predicted values for the dependent variable as well as the residuals. Both can also be generated in graphical form. Analysis of the residuals and/or predicted values is an important step in assessing whether or not OLS is working properly; this information can be used to test whether or not it is valid to make the assumptions about BLUEness outlined in Chapter 1. The practical aspects testing for BLUEness are analysed in subsequent chapters of this book.

Overall, we have shown some empirical support for the 'trickle-down' assertion that rapid growth is associated with poverty reduction. But our evidence does not prove that the relationship is robust and we'd be well advised to explore further. More detailed evidence could be found perhaps by examining a single country's experience over time, using time-series data for the last 20 years or more. (Not least, we might want to explore some of the confounding countries, such as Angola, which had extremely high increases in investment and exports, but negative growth and minimal improvement in poverty.) We might also develop richer measurements of poverty, for example incorporating qualitative aspects of inequality and participation, as well as daily consumption. (See Annex 2.1 for some ideas about alternative poverty measures.) Perhaps our sample is not representative in which case a larger sample set might prove to be more representative of LDCs as a whole. Most importantly, we should allow for the possibility that our theory is flawed, and go back to the drawing board!

2.4   Implications and conclusions

Our results have supported the trickle-down hypothesis: growth does seem to be associated with falling poverty. But what are the policy implications? One obvious way to reduce world poverty would be for the rich to make an immense lump-sum payment to the poor to enable them to invest and grow. Such a transfer would certainly change the income (and possibly wealth) distribution profile. However it is unlikely to be politically acceptable, to the rich at least; and moreover it would not necessarily guarantee sustainable improvements in the long run either. Philanthropy and aid is of course vital to developing countries, especially for health, education and other forms of public investment. But few, if any, would claim that aid alone will forge a lasting path out of poverty. Aid does not ensure that poor societies have the tools, the technologies and the resources that will help them to create sustainable economic futures (UNCTAD, 2008); and there is no guarantee that the rich will continue to feel philanthropic, or even to be as productive, in the long run.

As you might expect, there is no monopoly of prescriptions to reduce poverty and in fact there are a myriad of theories from which to choose. This is not surprising, given that poverty is a multi-faceted problem and there will be more than one way of contributing to its reduction. However, one widely held view is that sustainable poverty reduction requires a combination of massive public investment alongside private sector investment, in order to create jobs and income-generating opportunities that can help the poor to become masters of their own destinies. These arguments became more pressing in 2008, in debates about how to cope with global recession. Enabling all countries easy access to global export markets can be encouraged via fair trade rules. These points are for the most part widely accepted. The contention lies rather in the details: what is the sequencing of events required to get economies moving? How can public and private investment be harnessed most effectively together? What priorities are most important; what constitutes fair trade? Econometric analysis can give us small clues about past patterns and whilst statistical evidence cannot provide answers to these complex questions, it can at least give us a starting point in enhancing our understanding of the links between variables.

2.5 Further reading

Books

Addison, A., Hulme, D. and Kanbur, R. (2008) *Poverty Dynamics*, Oxford: Oxford University Press.

Lipsey, R. and Chrystal, A. (2007) *Economics* (11th edition), Oxford: Oxford University Press. Chapters 33–34.

Sen, A. (1981) *Poverty and Famines*, Oxford: Oxford University Press.

Thirlwall, A. P. (2005) *Growth and development* (8th edition), London: Macmillan. Chapters 1, 2 and 16.

Academic articles and working papers

Asian Development Bank (ADB) (2008), 'Special chapter: Comparing poverty across countries: the role of purchasing power parities', in *Key Indicators for Asia and the Pacific 2008*, Manila: ADB, pp. 3–54.

Atkinson, A. B. (1987) 'On the measurement of poverty', *Econometrica* vol. 55, no. 4, 749–64.

Chen, S. and Ravallion, M. (2000) *How Did the World's Poor Fare in the 1990s*, Washington: World Bank.

Collier, P. and Dollar, D. (2001) 'Can the world cut poverty in half? How policy reform and effective aid can meet International Development Goals, *World Development*, vol. 29, no. 11, 1727–802.

Mankiw, G., Romer, D. and Weil, D. (1992) *A Contribution to the Empirics of Economic Growth*, NBER Working Paper, No. 3541.

Ravallion, M., Chen, S. and Sangraula, P. (2008), *A Dollar a Day Revisited*, World Bank Policy Research Working Paper No. 4620, Washington: World Bank.

Rodrik, D. (1999) *The New Global Economy, Making Openness Work*, Policy Essay No. 24, Overseas Development Council, Washington D.C.

Solow, R. (1956) 'A contribution to the theory of economic growth', *Quarterly Journal of Economics*, vol. 70, 65–94.

Swan, T. (1956) 'Economic growth and capital accumulation', *Economic Record*, vol. 32, no. 2, 334–61.

Policy reports

UN *Millennium Development Goals Report* 2007, Geneva: United Nations.

UNCTAD (2008) *Least Developed Countries Report*, Geneva and New York: United Nations.

UNDP (annual), *Human Development Report*, Geneva: United Nations Development Program.

World Bank (annual), *World Development Report*, Washington: World Bank Group.

2.6   Chapter exercises

1. Using the data provided in Annex 2.2 – Table 2.6:
   (a) Assess the impact on GDP growth of export orientation by analysing the statistical associations between these variables.
   (b) Using your calculator, estimate a line of best fit and discuss your findings.
   (c) What are the implications of your findings for economic development policies?
2. Using the data provided in Annex 2.2 – Table 2.6:
   (a) Construct scatter plots of the change in poverty against
      i. growth in GDP per capita
      ii. share of exports in GDP
      iii. rate of growth in gross capital formation.
   (b) Construct a matrix of correlation coefficients to show the associations between change in poverty, growth in GDP per capita, share of exports in GDP and rate of growth in gross capital formation.
   (c) What are some theoretical and statistical implications of the correlations between these variables that should be kept in mind when devising policies to reduce poverty?

Annex 2.1 – Data focus: Quantitative and qualitative measurements of poverty

Sound measurements of poverty are important if we care about *who* is poor, for example whether the incidence is mostly in the young or the old; in racial minorities; women more than men; or those living in particular regions. We may be concerned that poverty is path-dependent in the sense that poor children are more likely to become poor adults, and so on. Another reason is to assess the progress of anti-poverty strategies and on these grounds alone poverty measurement is likely to become a particularly topical subject over the next decade, given the targets contained in the MDGs. As explained at the beginning of this chapter, the first of the eight MDGs is to eradicate extreme poverty. Other goals and targets, which are also for the most part poverty related, include reducing hunger, achieving universal primary education, and improving health. As donor countries and NGOs are committing billions of dollars and effort to achieving these goals – not to mention being genuinely concerned about human suffering – the way poverty is measured will become increasingly important. Table 2.4 shows an example of a MDG for which the target can be measured using both monetary and qualitative/non-monetary indicators of poverty.

Each type of indicator will have advantages and disadvantages, some of which are described below.

Monetary indicators

Monetary indicators of poverty are usually based around a **poverty line**, expressed in US dollars or national currency. This describes a critical threshold

Table 2.4 A development target and its indicators

MDG Target 1 → Eradicate extreme poverty and hunger	Indicators of progress
Between 1990 and 2015, halve the proportion of people whose income is less than $1/day.	1. Proportion of population below $1 (PPP) a day. 2. Poverty gap ratio (incidence × depth of poverty). 3. Share of poorest quintile (20%) in national consumption.

below which one cannot have a minimum nutritionally adequate diet, or essential non-food requirements (such as housing). In developing countries, the bundle of goods and services that comprises these minimum requirements is derived using a variety of methods, including an approach based on defining **basic human needs**, or an approach based on a minimum level of 'food energy'. Once the bundle has been established, it is given a monetary value.

The $1 a day per person poverty line used in this chapter is a commonly used international indicator introduced by the World Bank in 1990. Some researchers have adjusted this benchmark upwards e.g. a new international poverty line at $1.25 has been advocated by Ravallion, Chen and Sangraula (2008); and the Asian Development Bank has suggested a special Asian Poverty Line at about $1.35 a day (ADB, 2008) after surveys in a number of countries indicated that it was an appropriate level for both national and inter-country comparisons. (Later, an additional $2 benchmark line was also introduced; and typically in developed countries significantly higher bench-marks are used.) In order to know how many people live below the benchmark, household surveys are conducted in each country, asking questions about sources of income and spending patterns. (This is of course a simplification of issues. Readers interested in the properties and criteria that income-based poverty indices should meet could start with Atkinson (1987), for an excellent overview, and Chen and Ravallion (2000), Ravallion, Chen and Sangraula (2008) for the World Bank view.)

Limitations to this approach include the following:

- Different households may have different preferences, so necessities for one household may be less important in another.
- Different prices can be charged for the same goods: e.g. prices are cheaper in cities compared to rural areas; bulk purchases are cheaper than small ones.[5]
- Average figures assume that resources are shared evenly within the household, but studies show that women and girls receive less of everything than boys and men.
- Poverty levels can be overstated if non-monetary benefits are left out.
- Inflation distorts things: poverty lines are not re-measured every year even if prices have changed by double-digits.

---

[5] In many poor countries, items such as flour, rice, and soap powder may be bought by the hand or cupful, rather than by the packet. Similarly, the per unit price of electricity, water and telecommunications can vary immensely. A telephone call made using a pre-pay card usually costs much more than a call made from a home land-line phone.

- People may overstate their poverty if there are financial or other benefits arising from being identified as poor, or they may understate long-distant and forgotten sufferings.
- A person surviving on $1.05 a day may be little better off than another living on $0.95, but the former may be categorised as 'non-poor'.
- A slight increase in the number of people living under the poverty line may slightly raise the percentage of people defined as "poor" while masking a dramatic worsening of conditions for the worst off.
- Translating from $ prices to national currencies introduces problems. Between 1999 and 2000, South Africa saw the number of people living on less than $1 day fall from 24% to just 12%, while Turkmenistan went from 5% to 21%. But both changes were largely due to revised estimates of the purchasing power of the national currencies – where purchasing power is the measure of the value of a currency in terms of the amount of goods and services it can buy.

Given these limitations, why are these indicators so widely used? Firstly, they are simple, easily interpreted, and readily incorporated into international, inter-regional or inter-temporal studies. They are intuitively appealing, and their eye-catching nature makes them a powerful tool for advocacy purposes – it is easier to imagine life on $1 a day than it is to conceptualise complex subjective indexes comprised of many different components.

Secondly, the information is relatively easy to obtain. Even the poorest countries regularly conduct household and income surveys, so the data exists. Finally, the use of monetary measures enables comparison with other monetary variables, such as income, GDP, or foreign aid flows. However, given their limitations, readers will not be surprised to know there is an ongoing search for new and better indicators.

Non-monetary indicators

The Human Poverty Index (HPI), developed in 1977 by the UNDP, captures poverty not just in terms of lack of income but in a much broader way, as being the denial of a person's capabilities and opportunities in life. It draws heavily on the conceptual framework of Amartya Sen, bringing together in a composite index a number of the various features of deprivation that characterise the lives of the poor. The index is made up of three components:

   i. *longevity* – the percentage of people who do not live to 40 years
   ii. *knowledge deprivation* – the percentage of people who are illiterate

Table 2.5 Different indicators reveal a different picture

Country	% living on $1 day	% living on $2 day	HPI index	GDP $/person
Venezuela	15	32	11	5,380
Columbia	8.2	22.6	10	6,370
Philippines	14.6	46.4	28	4,170
Peru	18.1	37.7	23	5,010
China	16.6	46.7	24	4,580
South Africa	7.1	23.8	52	10,070
India	34.7	79.9	48	2,670
Zimbabwe	36	64.2	91	2,400
Ethiopa	37.9	78.4	89	780
Mali	72.8	90.6	93	930

Source: UNDP, *Human Development Report 2004.*

iii. *deprivations in the standard of living*, measured as:
  (a) the percentage of people without access to health services,
  (b) the percentage without guaranteed access to safe water and
  (c) the percentage of malnourished children under the age of five.
There are other non-monetary indicators of development, for example the Human Development Index (HDI). The advantage of the HPI over indicators such as the HDI[6] is that it focusses squarely on the experience of poverty, and does not take into account monetary variables at all.

To illustrate the fact that one measure will rarely capture the full picture, Table 2.5 summarises some data on a range of different countries and indicators. This shows, for example, that South Africa has high GDP per person compared to a number of other developing countries (at $10,070).

However 'GDP per capita' is simply a measure of total GDP divided by the population – it does not mean that wealth is shared equally. In fact, despite its high GDP per capita, South Africa scored worse in terms of the HPI than China, Peru, Philippines, Columbia and Venezuela. On the other hand, with the exception of Columbia, South Africa had a smaller proportion of people living on less than $2 and $1 per day. This could reflect the fact that South Africa offers targeted income support to its very poorest (through for example its policy of paying a pension to all elderly people) but nonetheless, South Africa performs less well on broader targets such as literacy, longevity and access to water.

---

[6] The HDI balances broad measures of development – literacy rates and mortality rates, with a monetary measure – GDP per capita.

Annex 2.2 – Raw data

Table 2.6 Change in poverty, exports of goods and services, and investment

	1	2	3	4
	% change in proportion of population living on $1/day	Annual average GDP growth per capita	% change exports	Investment: % change GCF
Lao PDR	−2	3.5	19.8	15
Bangladesh	−3.4	3.3	7.2	4.6
Uganda	−16.1	3.1	3.6	5.3
Bhutan	−19.2	3	5.1	15.3
Cape Verde	−6.3	2.9	9.1	12.6
Mozambique	−3.6	2.5	3.4	11.1
Nepal	−14.3	2.4	12.7	2.8
Solomon Islands	−4.1	1.4	18.2	–
Benin	−6.1	1	2.6	4.2
Malawi	−20.4	0.9	4.3	−5.4
Ethiopia	−1.2	0.8	6.6	1.6
Lesotho	22.3	0.7	9.5	6.1
Burkina Faso	−6.5	0.4	1.5	7.5
Mali	8.7	0.1	8.6	−0.4
Senegal	0.8	0	8.7	6.2
Central African Republic	23.3	−0.8	1.4	0.9
Chad	2.5	−1.3	3.5	5.8
Vanuatu	3.5	−1.3	15.8	−0.7
Guinea-Bissau	25	−1.6	9.8	−22.6
Madagascar	4.5	−1.8	5.6	0.2
Comoros	11.8	−3.5	7.5	−5.9
Angola	1.5	−3.8	23.6	10.8
Mauritania	−6.2	1.6	−10.5	−6.8
Guinea	−7.4	0.8	−9.1	1.2
Gambia	−16.3	−0.9	−2.9	−0.2
Togo	−1.7	−2	−9.8	−2.7
Niger	5.1	−2	−1.9	−4.1
Rwanda	13.1	−2.9	−0.5	0.5
Burundi	11	−3.4	−1.7	−9.5
Haiti	14.9	−3.5	−4	−3.3
Sierra Leone	37.2	−5.7	−2.2	−5.8
Minimum	**−20.4**	**−5.7**	**−10.5**	**−22.6**
Maximum	**37.2**	**3.5**	**23.6**	**15.3**
Mean	**1.63**	**−0.20**	**4.7**	**1.6**

Using logs and estimating elasticities

Demand for air travel

Economic issues include:
- Inverse demand curves
- Elasticities
- Income and substitution effects
- Normal, inferior and Giffen goods

Econometric issues include:
- Model specification: using logs to estimate elasticities
- Running regressions using Excel
- Hypothesis testing: one-tailed *t* tests

Data issues include:
- Data constraints
- Proxy variables

3.1   The issue

If you were the manager of the London Underground or American Airlines would you raise ticket prices, or drop them? Which strategy would maximise your firm's profits? The 'law of demand' states that if prices are lowered then there will be rises in demand. But this doesn't necessarily mean that a firm should just lower prices if it wants to boost revenue. Other effects operate too and the net result will depend on how sensitive consumers are to changes in price. If for some reason consumers are determined to have only a certain amount of a particular good or service then lowering prices may make little difference to the amount demanded and so a firm's revenues might fall because they are selling similar quantities but at lower prices. For example, if you manage an airline and your consumers don't care much about price; if they are not motivated to travel more even when flights are cheaper, then total revenues would fall, perhaps so much that costs could not be covered (and you would probably be looking for a new career). The question of pricing is therefore critical – whether one is a private firm trying to maximise profits, or a government agency trying to provide public transport.

But some producers have more control over prices than others. For producers of tomatoes, wheat or other goods and services for which there are many sellers and buyers: products are fairly homogeneous, and markets more closely approximate perfect competition. In these markets, each producer must set prices no higher than anyone else's, or they will lose their customers. However when firms have a degree of monopoly power the question of what price to charge, and to whom, is critical. For the transport industries, there may be limited competition – for example the London Underground competes only against other forms of transport; there is no other underground train service in London and so if buses are not good substitutes for tube trains, then London Underground will have a lot of control over the price. But they will still need to judge pricing decisions carefully. If prices are too low, they will fail to cover costs and may go bust, particularly if the government is unwilling to bail them out!

In this chapter, we examine these issues using the example of transport pricing in the airlines industry; we introduce the theoretical concepts of an 'inverse' demand curve, income/substitution effects and elasticities; and we show how econometric analysis can be used empirically to model the price elasticity of demand for air travel.

3.2   The theory

For our analysis of air travel, we expect consumers to be price-responsive; we expect the demand for air travel to rise as prices fall, either because more people buy flights when prices are lower, or because the same people fly further and more often when prices are lower.

In understanding more deeply why quantity demanded of any good usually rises as prices fall, we need to make distinctions between effects that are subtle. When a price changes, there are two effects: the substitution effect and the income effect.

The **substitution effect** captures the way that a consumer alters his or her purchasing decisions on the basis of the change in relative price (i.e. one good's price in comparison with other goods). For example, as airline travel becomes relatively cheaper compared to other goods and services, we expect consumers to substitute their purchases towards more airline travel, and away from other goods and services.

Price changes will also have knock-on **income effects**. Lowering the price of one good or service will lead to a rise in effective income or purchasing power. For example, if we have an income of £100 per week and we want to buy a plane ticket costing £20, we'll have £80 left to buy other things; but if there's a 50% cut in plane fares and we only have to spend £10 on our plane fare, then we will have £90 left to buy other things. Assuming that the prices of other things remain unchanged, we'll be able to afford more of everything. We would be able to have the same 'basket' of the other goods that we had before but with some extra income to spend because air travel is cheaper. If relative prices had not changed, the only way this would have been possible would have been via a rise in income. So even though our take-home pay of £100 hasn't changed, the purchasing power of our income has changed via this income effect.

But the impact of the income effect is more complicated than that of the substitution effect. We don't necessarily increase our demand for everything as our incomes rise; there are some things we prefer to stop consuming as our purchasing power increases; for example perhaps we would be able to afford to give up eating bread, or potatoes or tripe. This is the difference between a normal good and an inferior good. For **normal goods** quantity demanded rises as income rises. By comparison, for **inferior goods**, quantity demanded falls as income rises – if people tend to eat less bread when income rises because they can afford cake, then bread is an inferior good.

In assessing the net impact of price changes we need to think carefully about the balance of the income effect and substitution effect, keeping in mind whether we are considering normal goods or inferior goods. For normal goods, the income and substitution effects will reinforce each other because they will move in the same direction. A fall in the price of something will make it relatively cheaper and so we will demand more of it. Unsurprisingly, there will be a negative substitution effect: prices decrease, demand rises. The falling price will also release income increasing our ability to consume and our demand for a normal good will increase with this overall increase in purchasing power. So there will be a negative income effect too: prices fall, effective purchasing power of income rises and demand rises too. Overall, there will be an unequivocal increase in the quantity demanded.

But for inferior goods, the net impact of the substitution effect and income effect is more complex. The substitution effect will work in exactly the same way as for a normal good, i.e. a fall in the relative price of a good will encourage increasing demand for that good. Again, there will be a negative substitution effect. But the freeing up of income allowed by the fall in price will *discourage* consumption of inferior goods: the income effect on its own will encourage falling demand and there will be a *positive* relationship: the income effect will generate a tendency for decreased demand. This creates a trade-off because the income effect operates in the opposite direction to the substitution effect; and the precise outcome will depend on the relative magnitude of these separate effects. If the income effect is large enough then it may entirely cancel out the substitution effect.

How likely is it that the income effect will overwhelm the substitution effect? Most goods are **ordinary goods**: with ordinary goods, demand increases as prices fall. As explained above, all normal goods are ordinary goods because there is no trade-off between the income and substitution effects for normal goods. But there are two sorts of inferior goods: ordinary goods and **Giffen goods**. For ordinary inferior goods the perverse income effect explained in the last paragraph is not sufficient to overwhelm the substitution effect.

Giffen goods are an extreme type of inferior goods for which the income effect is enough to overwhelm the substitution effect and so a fall in prices is associated with a fall in demand. To explain why this happens: the price fall makes the Giffen good relatively cheaper so demand rises via the substitution effect. But this effect is not as strong as the income effect; via the income effect the price fall releases purchasing power and effective income allowing the consumer to buy a lot less of the inferior good. Overall, the perverse income effect has overwhelmed the substitution effect. So for Giffen goods: a fall in price leads to decreases in the quantity demanded first, because the income and subsitution effects are operating in opposite directions and second, because the income effect is larger than the substitution effect. Examples of Giffen goods are rare but one often-cited example is potatoes during the Irish famine: as the price of potatoes rose, purchasing power fell and demand for potatoes rose because consumers could no longer afford more expensive staples.

In Box 3.1 the different types of goods are illustrated to emphasise the difference between normal goods, inferior ordinary goods and Giffen goods.

It is not always easy to predict the net effect of the substitution effect and income effect in advance. Applying these concepts to our chapter example, the airline industry: the intensity of the effects will vary from case to case,

---

Box 3.1 Types of goods: Normal versus inferior, ordinary versus Giffen

Price changes: The law of demand states that, other things being equal, a fall in the price will lead to an increase in the amount demanded.

Income changes: With a **normal good** an increase in income raises the quantity demanded. With an **inferior good** an increase in income reduces the quantity demanded.

Changes in price generate **substitution effects** and **income effects**. For normal goods the substitution effect is the effect of a lower relative price in increasing quantity demanded. For normal goods, falls in prices generate an income effect which reinforces the substitution effect from a price change: lower prices mean an increase in purchasing power and so, for normal goods, demand rises. All normal goods are **ordinary goods**: falls in price lead to rises in demand.

But inferior goods have opposing income and substitution effects, and which one dominates cannot be assumed in advance. If the substitution effect is stronger than the income effect, it will be an ordinary inferior good. If the income effect is stronger than the substitution effect, then it will be a **Giffen good**.

The following table illustrates the various possibilities, where P = price and Q = quantity demanded:

	Substitution effect (SE)	Income effect (IE)	IE vs SE	Net effect
Normal goods	$\downarrow P \rightarrow \uparrow Q$	$\downarrow P \rightarrow \uparrow Q$	IE reinforces SE	$\downarrow P \rightarrow \uparrow Q$
→ All normal goods are ordinary				
Inferior goods:				
Ordinary inferior	$\downarrow P \rightarrow \uparrow\uparrow Q$	$\downarrow P \rightarrow \downarrow Q$	IE<SE	$\downarrow P \rightarrow \uparrow Q$
Giffen (inferior) goods	$\downarrow P \rightarrow \uparrow Q$	$\downarrow P \rightarrow \downarrow\downarrow Q$	IE>SE	$\downarrow P \rightarrow \downarrow Q$

depending on the reason people are travelling, and whether distances travelled are short or long. But here we will keep things simple by assuming that air travel is a normal good: people will want to consume more of it when their income rises. Price falls will release purchasing power and, because we are assuming that air travel is a normal good, this positive income will reinforce the substitution effect. Unequivocally, price falls will lead to increases in demand. So overall we expect that air travel will have a conventional looking downward sloping demand curve.

A downward sloping demand curve is called the **inverse demand curve**. Why? Mathematically, it is conventional to put the dependent variable on the vertical axis and the explanatory variable on the horizontal axis. Yet economists usually depict the relationship between price (P) and quantity demanded (Q) using (for ordinary goods) a downward sloping demand curve – with P on the vertical axis and Q on the horizontal axis, even though demand is the dependent variable. However, P *is* the dependent variable for supply relationships (i.e. all things being equal a rising price encourages increased production) so to make the demand function consistent with this, it must be mathematically inverted to give an 'inverse' demand curve with the dependent variable (Q) on the horizontal axis.

Another issue to consider is the shape of our demand function. Mathematically, the shape of a demand curve will be determined by the **elasticity** of a consumer's response to price changes. Elasticity is a very general concept. There are all sorts of elasticities in economics: the elasticity of output with respect to inputs of labour; the elasticity of imports and exports to currency fluctuations. And there are elasticities in other subjects (in fact the term elasticity has its origins in physics, which defines elasticity as the ability of a solid to recover its shape when an external force is removed). Here we will concentrate on price elasticities and in particular on two types of price elasticity: the **own-price elasticity of demand**, as explained in Box 3.2, and the **cross-price elasticity of demand**.

The cross-price elasticity of demand is the change in quantity demanded for one good in response to a change in the price of another. If two goods or services, for example planes and trains, are close substitutes, then a fall in the price of trains will lead to a fall in demand for planes. In this case the formula for the cross price elasticity of demand will be:

$$\eta_{\text{Planes, Trains}} = \frac{\Delta Q_{\text{Planes}}}{\Delta P_{\text{Trains}}} \cdot \frac{P_{\text{Trains}}}{Q_{\text{Planes}}} \qquad (3.1)$$

Price elasticities of demand will depend on the absolute and relative magnitudes of the income and substitution effects. Similarly, elasticities will also vary depending on whether a good is a necessity or a luxury. Demand for necessities (such as drinking water) is likely to be highly inelastic; demand for luxury goods tends to be relatively elastic. Certain types of travel (for example supersonic or zero gravity flights) are likely to be luxury goods.

Elasticities also have implications for the revenue generated (or not) by a change in prices. Revenue is price paid multiplied by quantity sold. If the own-price elasticity is greater than 1, i.e. if demand is elastic, then a fall in price will lead to a greater proportionate rise in quantity demanded and so revenue will increase. Total revenues accrued to a firm facing this kind of demand will rise if they push down prices (assuming no changes to the firm's costs). On the

Box 3.2 Own-price elasticities of demand

The *own-price elasticity of demand* measures the relative sensitivity of demand to changes in price. It is measured as the percentage change in quantity demanded resulting from a given percentage change in price. For example, if a 1% increase in price leads to a 1.5% fall in quantity demanded, then the own-price elasticity is 1.5. This is an *elastic* response, i.e. the proportional change in quantity demanded is larger in absolute terms than the proportional change in price. If, on the other hand, the 1% rise in price had led to only a 0.5% reduction in quantity demanded, then this would be an *inelastic* response: the consumers' proportionate response in terms of quantity demanded is relatively small (in absolute terms) in comparison with the proportionate change in price.

Mathematically, this means that the own price elasticity is defined as the ratio of percentage change in quantity demanded to percentage change in price:

$$\eta = \frac{\Delta Q/Q}{\Delta P/P} = \frac{\Delta Q}{\Delta P} \cdot \frac{P}{Q} \tag{3.2}$$

where P and Q represent the price and quantity demanded respectively and ΔQ and ΔP represent the change in quantity and price demanded.

The various scenarios for own price elasticities are shown below:

$\eta = -\infty$	$\eta = -1$	$\eta = 0$	$\eta = +1$	$\eta = +\infty$

Terminology	Numerical measure	Definition
Perfectly or completely inelastic	$|\eta| = 0$	Quantity demanded does not change as price changes.
Inelastic	$0 < |\eta| < 1$	Quantity demanded changes by a smaller percentage than the price.
Unit elasticity	$|\eta| = 1$	Quantity demanded changes by exactly the same percentage as the price.
Elastic	$1 < |\eta| < \infty$	Quantity demanded changes by a larger percentage than the price.
Perfectly or completely elastic	$|\eta| \to \infty$	Consumers are prepared to buy all they can get at one price, but none at all at a different price.

Practical examples of these measures of elasticity are shown in Box 3.4.

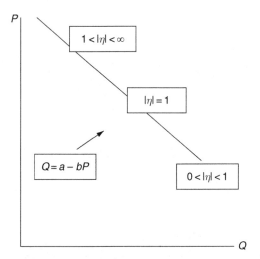

Figure 3.1   Elasticity varies along a linear demand curve

other hand, if the consumer response is inelastic, the rise in consumption will be relatively small in comparison with the falling price. And so total revenue will fall as prices fall.

What is the relationship between elasticities and inverse demand functions? As explained above, the formula for the own-price elasticity of demand is given by Equation (3.3):

$$\eta = \frac{\Delta Q}{\Delta P} \cdot \frac{P}{Q} \tag{3.3}$$

What happens to this elasticity along a linear demand function, such as the one depicted in Figure 3.1?

From Equation (3.2) you can see that the elasticity (η) will vary along a linear demand function. The slope of a line is constant i.e. $\Delta Q / \Delta P$ does not change along the line. But the ratio of price to quantity (P/Q) will vary along the line: at the top left of this line, the ratio P/Q will be relatively high and so η will be relatively large in absolute terms (i.e. elastic); in the bottom right-hand corner P/Q will be relatively small and so η will be too (i.e. the price elasticity of demand will be inelastic).

In economic analysis we often want to concentrate on *constant elasticity of demand* functions. These take the following *non-linear* form:

$$Q = AP^\eta \tag{3.4}$$

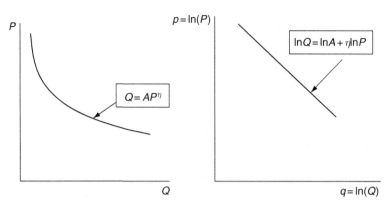

Figure 3.2   Constant elasticity of demand curve: linear vs. logged scales

where η is the elasticity of demand. This type of demand function is depicted in Figure 3.2 – in the first panel using a linear scale. The elasticity is constant for this sort of function because, moving towards the bottom right, the slope of the curve will flatten and $\Delta P/\Delta Q$ will fall (i.e. $\Delta Q/\Delta P$ will rise) and, at the same time, P/Q will fall. Thus the changes in the slope are being balanced by changes in the price-quantity ratio and so the elasticity remains constant.

Constant elasticity demand curves of the form (3.4) will exhibit a non-linear, logarithmic relationship. We can capture this by taking the natural log of both sides of the equality from Equation (3.4):

$$\ln(Q) = \ln A + \eta \ln(P) \tag{3.5}$$

So the plot of p $(= \ln P)$ against q $(= \ln Q)$ will be linear. This logged transformation of (3.2) is depicted in the second panel of Figure 3.2. (Also see Box 3.3 for a fuller explanation of the elasticities and the logarithmic functional form.)

Box 3.3 Logs and elasticities, model specification

As explained in Chapter 1, Ordinary Least Squares (OLS) is a linear estimation technique and therefore will only work properly if we can assume **linearity in the parameters**. This does not necessarily mean that non-linearity in the *variables* is a problem because we may be able to transform our model into a form that is linear in the parameters. We can do this for our example of air travel, as follows.

Equation (3.4) shows a constant elasticity of demand function:

$$Q = AP^\eta \tag{3.4}$$

Equation (3.4) is a non-linear function; it is not linear in the variables because, in its untransformed form, it is not an **additive function**; the various components are not being added together. Rather it is a **multiplicative function** in which the variables are being multiplied by each other. So what can we do? We can take natural logs, as we did to get Equation (3.5), and this specification *is* linear in the parameters:

$$\ln(Q) = \ln A + \eta \ln(P) \qquad \rightarrow q_t = a + \eta p_t \qquad (3.6)$$

where $q = \ln(Q)$, $p = \ln(P)$ and $a = \ln(A)$

This sort of function can be estimated effectively using OLS because it is an additive function and so satisfies the Gauss–Markov assumption of linearity in the parameters.

We can also show that the slope parameter on $\ln(P)$, i.e. η is the own-price elasticity of demand using a little bit of differential calculus. Following from Equation (3.1):

$$\eta = \frac{dQ}{dP} \cdot \frac{P}{Q}$$

$$\frac{dQ}{dP} = \eta A P^{\eta - 1} = \eta \frac{Q}{P} \quad \text{because } A P^{\eta - 1} = \frac{Q}{P}$$

so $\dfrac{dQ}{dP} \cdot \dfrac{P}{Q} = \eta$ $\qquad (3.7)$

Functional forms: lin-lin, log-log, log-lin or lin-log?

This illustrates the difference between lin-lin, log-log, log-lin and lin-log models. The model that we are using in Equation (3.6) is a **log-log model** or **double-log model** – we've logged both the dependent and explanatory variables. We explained that the slope parameter on $\ln(P)$, i.e. η is the own-price elasticity of demand.

A **lin-lin model** is one in which the dependent and explanatory variables are not logged, i.e. are left in their linear form.

Other forms of log relationships include **semi-log models**. There are two basic types of semi-log models: in **log-lin models** only the dependent variable is logged and the slope coefficient measures the relative change in Y for a given absolute change in X. This is often used when the explanatory variable is a time trend. For example, in the model $\ln(Y) = a + \beta t$, t is a **deterministic time trend** changing by one unit as each year passes, and the coefficient β simply measures the rate of growth over a year. This sort of log-lin model is sometimes called the **constant growth model**.

Another form is the **lin-log model**, where only the explanatory variable is logged. In this case the slope coefficient measures the absolute change in Y for a relative change in X.

Log-log, log-lin and lin-log forms are used frequently in applied economics because we are often interested in elasticities and proportional responses rather than absolute responses. For example as we've shown in this chapter, with a log-log model we are capturing an elasticity – the % change in one variable relative to the % change in another variable. With logged models, we can abstract from the units of measurement used and so we can interpret results more easily. Using logs can also help to moderate some econometric problems, e.g. **heteroscedasticity**, explored in Chapter 6.

In our empirical section, we will illustrate how these exponential/logarithmic relationships can be used in practice when estimating the price elasticity of demand for air travel. This will illustrate some very important points about how correctly to specify an empirical model, particularly when, as in much of economics, you're interested in unit-free elasticities of response rather than absolute responses.

But before moving onto our own empirical analysis, we should conclude this section by examining existing evidence. In any research project it is useful to have a look at the methods and findings of other researchers and in Box 3.4 we summarise some empirical evidence relevant to estimating own-price elasticities of demand for air travel.

Box 3.4 Existing evidence shows heterogeneity in patterns of demand for air travel

Demand for any good or service depends on a variety of factors, including tastes, income, price and quality, the price of other goods, especially substitutes, and any number of other factors. We must assume that these other influences remain constant when estimating demand elasticity – which is more easily said than done in practice. One example is given by a recent Canadian government survey of 21 domestic and international air travel demand studies (Canadian Department of Finance 2003), see Table 3.1. This study separated the findings into six distinct market segments each of which were influenced by very different sets of non-price factors. For example, business travellers are less flexible about dates or routes than are leisure travellers; and long-haul business travellers do not have substitute options, such as going by car or train.

As expected, this 'meta' study found that long-haul business travellers were much less responsive to price changes than all other types of consumers. This is evident not only in the average elasticity but also in the range of estimates. For long-haul international business travellers these range from $+0.19$ (perhaps long-haul air travel is an inferior good for some business travellers if richer companies can afford video-conferencing facilities?) to -0.48, with a median of -0.26. In contrast, the estimates for international leisure travellers ranged from -0.56 to -1.7, with a median of -1.04, and short-haul domestic leisure travellers, who could just as easily go by bus, car or train, were the most responsive to price changes. The lesson from this is that an airline wishing to boost its total revenues should seek means of raising prices for business travellers (particularly long-haul), and lowering them for holiday-makers (particularly short-haul).

These on average negative estimates of the own-price elasticity of demand confirm that air travel is a normal (and therefore ordinary) good. Ranking these sample estimates against

Table 3.1 Elastic demand from leisure travellers, inelastic from business

Market segment		Median own-price elasticity
Short-haul leisure	(SHL)	−1.52
Long-haul domestic business	(LHDB)	−1.15
Long-haul domestic leisure	(LHDL)	−1.10
Long-haul international leisure	(LHIL)	−1.04
Short-haul business	(SHB)	−0.70
Long-haul international business	(LHIB)	−0.26

Source: Derived from Department of Finance, Canada 2003.

the continuum of definitions of elasticity shown below and including the sign, we see that business travel (both short haul and international) is inelastic, meaning that its elasticity was less than zero but greater than −1 ($-1 < \eta < 0$), i.e. the responsiveness of quantity demanded was less than the responsiveness of price. Demand in all the other market segments was elastic with respect to price, with estimates that were less than −1 but greater than (negative) infinity ($-\infty < \eta < -1$). We can show these estimates on the continuum of own-price elasticity of demand as follows:

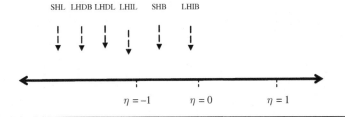

3.3   The data

In this chapter we want to investigate how consumers change their demand for air travel as the price of air travel changes and in this section we explain how we selected the data and some of the data constraints that we faced.

Broad trends

For our analysis we have used International Civil Aviation Organisation (ICAO) data on number of passengers worldwide travelling on scheduled

Table 3.2 Data on aviation demand and revenue

	International Civil Aviation Raw Data		Data transformed into natural logs	
	Number of passengers (millions)	Revenue per passenger-km US cents	Number of passengers	Revenue per passenger-km
1991	1135	9.60	7.03	2.26
1992	1146	9.20	7.04	2.22
1993	1142	9.20	7.04	2.22
1994	1233	9.20	7.12	2.22
1995	1304	9.40	7.17	2.24
1996	1391	9.10	7.24	2.21
1997	1457	8.80	7.28	2.17
1998	1471	8.60	7.29	2.15
1999	1562	8.30	7.35	2.12
2000	1672	8.30	7.42	2.12
2001	1640	7.90	7.40	2.07
2002	1639	7.80	7.40	2.05
2003	1691	8.00	7.43	2.08
2004	1887	8.20	7.54	2.10
Change	0.66	−0.15		

national and international flights as a measure of demand and revenue per passenger km as a proxy for price, as shown in Table 3.2. (We will say more about proxies in the following section on data constraints.)

Demand, as measured by passenger numbers, increased over the years from 1991 to 2004. The total number of passengers in 2004 was estimated to be 1,887 million, up from 1,135 million in 1991, a 66% increase. There was a fall in passenger numbers at the end of 2001, reflecting increased caution following the terrorist attacks of 11 September 2001 but even this fall proved to be short-lived. With the increasing dominance of the budget airlines, it is expected that future trends will reflect ever more growth, in spite of potentially severe impacts on the environment (an issue to be examined in Chapter 7).

For the price proxy, overall there was a 15% drop in revenue per passenger km over the years 1991 to 2004. There was a slight increase (with fuel price rises) in 2004 but overall our measure of demand (passenger numbers) and our proxy for price (revenue per passenger km) have moved in opposite directions, suggesting that there is an inverse relationship consistent with an inverse demand curve.

Dealing with data constraints

In conducting empirical analyses, data limitations are often an important constraint and it is important to acknowledge and justify these constraints from the outset.

One major constraint emerges from a **sampling bias**: we are interested in demand for air travel from all consumers everywhere but our data is only capturing travel on scheduled flights; it excludes chartered flights, flights on private jets etc. The exclusion of particular categories of flights may distort our results. Also, even without potential sampling bias, the data just for passengers on scheduled flights may not fully capture demand. Did two passengers travel 50 miles each, or was it one passenger travelling 100 miles? Were they business or holiday travellers? Did they travel to capital cities or to small local airports? Did they travel first or economy class? And so on. We have lumped everyone together into a crude measure of 'passenger kilometres' but this does not allow us to distinguish between short trips and long ones.

For the analysis in this chapter, we have an additional set of constraints because one of our aims is simply to illustrate OLS for simple regression analysis, i.e. using one explanatory variable. This focus on just one explanatory variable can be justified by assuming *ceteris paribus* (all things being equal) but if we did want to analyse a wider range of influences on demand for air travel, we might have problems collecting data on the many other influential variables, e.g. income trends, airline loyalty schemes, prices of substitutes and complements to air travel, costs of carbon offsetting etc. etc. A more detailed study would require us to gather price and quantity demanded data for a single carrier, over a single route, for a single class, and perhaps even with the same booking conditions.

What about the data on prices? Passengers can pay different prices to travel exactly the same number of miles, depending on the airline with which they are flying, what class ticket they bought, whether they booked on the Internet or through a travel agent, and whether they booked weeks or just hours in advance. In fact, it is difficult to collect any sort of data specifically on prices. It is a common problem in statistical analysis that the phenomenon an econometrician would like to analyse is not easily measurable. One solution is to use a *proxy variable*. A good proxy will be strongly correlated with the missing variable but uncorrelated with the error term of our regression. What's a good proxy for price in this example? As noted above, we have used ICAO on revenue per passenger per kilometre as a proxy; we would expect revenue per passenger km to be strongly correlated with prices. Again to keep things simple, we will also assume that revenue per passenger km is uncorrelated with the error term.[1] Using this proxy will also allow us to abstract from the complexities of routes and distances. On the other hand, price could have stayed the same, while passenger numbers could have increased for some other reason unrelated to price (e.g. rising incomes) and these two factors together would be manifested as falling revenue per passenger km. So overall, is it feasible to use revenue per passenger km as a proxy for prices? For our purposes we can justify the use of this variable on the basis that industry studies confirm that it is a good proxy but nonetheless we should acknowledge that **measurement errors** associated with using an imperfect proxy may affect our results.

Another problem for our data set is the small sample size – we have just 14 annual observations from 1991 to 2004. It would be better, for example, if we had evidence from the 1960s and 1970s to extend the data set but we do not have easy access to a longer set of time-series data and the accuracy of our empirical results will be compromised by the limited information in our small sample. We are using annual data because we are trying to capture long-term patterns and estimates of long-run elasticities. These are of more interest to policymakers and company accountants because data gathered over 12 full months reflects the time that consumers have to change their behavioural patterns, towards or away from air travel compared to choices that might be more rigid in the shorter term. But the small sample size will probably affect the accuracy of our estimations.[2]

One solution, if we were particularly interested in short-term elasticities, would be to search for data gathered more frequently. Another solution would be to create larger data sets, e.g. **panel data** sets that combine cross-sectional and time series data. Panel estimation requires more complex techniques specifically designed simultaneously to capture spatial and temporal effects.[3]

---

[1] This allows us to assume **exogeneity**. The violations of this assumption (i.e. the endogeneity problem) is beyond the scope of this chapter. See Chapter 8 for a discussion of related isssues.

[2] The problem of a small sample size is the problem of **micronumerosity**. This problem leads to inaccurate estimation and will be manifested in wider confidence intervals and t tests that are statistically less significant so a key consequence of micronumerosity is the increased probability of Type II error, i.e. the t test will be less powerful. But as our statistical results will show, our t tests are statistically significant so micronumerosity cannot be leading us into Type II errors for the example illustrated in this chapter.

[3] Panel estimation techniques are explained in Chapter 11.

3.4   Empirical methods and results

In setting up our empirical model of the data-generating process (DGP) for demand for air travel we have to think carefully about the specification of our model. We assume that air travel is a normal good and therefore we expect that the income effect and substitution effect will reinforce each other; there should be an unequivocally negative relationship between the price and quantity. In capturing these assumptions we need to select the correct **functional form** of our regression model. The issue of correct model specification is extremely important because, with a misspecified model, our OLS estimates will not be BLUE.[4]

For our example of demand for air travel we must consider whether to use a linear functional form (i.e. using unlogged variables) or a logarithmic functional form (i.e. using the natural logs of our variables). We are assuming that the own-price elasticity of demand is constant, implying that airline passengers are equally responsive to changes in the price of very low-priced tickets (say, for short flights), as they are to changes in the price of high-priced tickets (say for round-the-world tickets.). As explained in Section 3.2, this is not consistent with a function that is linear in the variables. A **log-log model** will fit best with our underlying theory because it will embed a constant elasticity (see Box 3.3).

Assuming a log-log specification, gives us the following model of the (DGP):

$$q_t = \alpha + \eta p_t + \varepsilon_t \tag{3.8}$$

where $q = \ln(Q)$ and $p = \ln(P)$ and η is the own price elasticity of demand for air travel. (We have transformed our raw data into natural logs in the final two columns of Table 3.2.) So we will be estimating the following sample regression function (SRF):

$$q_t = \hat{\alpha} + \hat{\eta} p_t + \hat{\varepsilon}_t \tag{3.9}$$

If we run a regression of q on p then our slope parameter estimate $\hat{\eta}$ will be an estimate of the elasticity of the air-travel demand with respect to our price proxy; it will show us the percentage change in Q for a percentage change in P. What magnitude would we expect $\hat{\eta}$ to take? For most of us, air travel

---

[4] A fuller discussion of some of issues surrounding model misspecification, including diagnostic testing, consequences and solutions, are outlined in Chapter 8.

is a luxury. So we would expect its own-price elasticity to be relatively high, i.e. $-\infty < \eta < -1$, i.e. the response of quantity demanded to changing price should be relatively elastic so the parameter on price will be more negative than -1.

In a preliminary assessment of our model we plot demand for air travel against our proxy for price over the period 1991 to 2004 (see Figure 3.3). This illustrates that passenger numbers have been rising whilst revenues have been falling, providing initial support for our hypothesis of an inverse relationship between demand and price.

Are we correct in assuming that this is consistent with a downward-sloping demand curve such as the one depicted in Figure 3.2? Figure 3.4 shows a scatter plot of air travel demand (logged) against the proxy (logged)

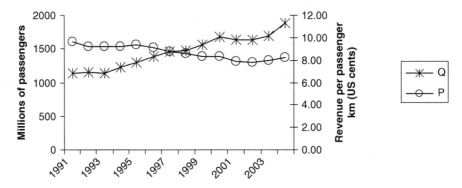

Figure 3.3   Rising global air travel, 1991–2004: rising demand and falling price

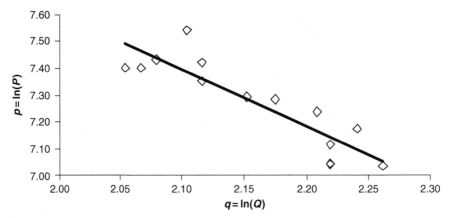

Figure 3.4   Scatter plot of air travel demand (in passenger miles) suggesting constant elasticity of demand for air travel

Table 3.3 Example of an Excel output table

Summary output log-log Model

Regression Statistics

R Squared	0.79
Adjusted R Squared	0.77
Standard Error	0.08
Observations	14

ANOVA

	df	SS	MS	F	Significance F
Regression	1	0.28	0.28	45.71	0.00
Residual	12	0.07	0.01		
Total	13	0.36			

	Coefficients	Standard Error	t Stat	P-value	Lower 95%	Upper 95%
Intercept	11.85	0.68	17.48	0.00	10.37	13.33
P	−2.12	0.31	−6.76	0.00	−2.80	−1.44

capturing the constant elasticity of demand relationship implied by our SRF (Equation (3.9)).

This is consistent with a logarithmic specification of the demand function for air travel and also suggests that there is a constant price elasticity of demand for air travel.

We can explore this pattern more rigorously by running an OLS regression using Excel's analysis tool: '*Regression*'. When we use Excel's regression tool, we get the Excel output table (Table 3.3) when we estimate the SRF from Equation (3.9).

We have included the whole table so you can see an example of an Excel output table. But there is a lot of extra information in the table that we will leave for subsequent chapters.

To summarise the essential information for this chapter, estimating our log-log model using Excel gives the following result:

$$Y = \quad 11.85 \quad\quad -2.12X \quad + \hat{\varepsilon}_t$$
$$(0.68) \quad\quad (0.31)$$
$$t = 17.48 \quad t = -6.76$$
$$R^2 = 0.79$$

(3.10)

The numbers in brackets are the standard errors for the parameter estimates.

We have a negative slope as expected, and the estimate of the own-price elasticity of demand indicates that the quantity of travel demanded increases by 2.12%, for a 1% fall in prices. As explained in Box 3.4, the estimate of $\eta = -2.12$ is described as an *elastic* response: in percentage terms, the demand for air travel has risen by a greater proportion than the percentage fall in the price of air travel.

To establish whether or not the inverse relationship between demand for air travel and our price proxy is statistically significant, we will test the hypothesis using a *one-tailed t test*. As explained in Chapter 1, we use a one-tailed test when we have some prior information about the sign of our parameters. In this case, we would expect our parameter to be less than zero; it is extremely unlikely that it would be more than zero because this would imply that air travel is a Giffen good, which is not a plausible hypothesis. So we set up the null and alternative hypotheses as follows:

H_0: $\eta = 0$

H_1: $\eta < 0$

For a one-tailed test, our decision rule is modified because we are concentrating on one tail of the t distribution. As explained in Chapter 1, as long as the one-tailed test is justified on the basis of prior information, a one-tailed test will have more *power* than a two-tailed test: the probability of *Type II error* (of incorrectly retaining H_0) will be lower because the rejection region associated with the 5% significance level will all be in one tail.

From statistical tables, a one-tailed test with a 5% significance level and degrees of freedom of $df = n - k - 1 = 14 - 1 - 1 = 12$ gives –1.782. So our decision rule will be: if $\hat{t} < -1.782$ then reject H_0. So, given our t value of –6.76, we can reject H_0 and conclude that our estimate of the own-price elasticity of demand for air travel is significantly less than zero at a 5% significance level.

We have tested a null that the elasticity is negative but we may also be interested in testing hypotheses about the absolute magnitude of the elasticity, e.g. that the absolute value of the elasticity is unitary, i.e. equal to 1 (see Chapter Exercise 3.7.1).

Our estimate is larger than the estimates reported in previous research (as summarised in Box 3.4). This may reflect data constraints, sampling bias, our small sample size and/or omissions from our model. As explained in the section on data constraints, we have made a number of assumptions so that we can illustrate some introductory statistical techniques. In a more rigorous multiple regression analysis (MRA) we would use the techniques explained in Part II of this book. More specifically, we would include additional explanatory variables to overcome any biases that are emerging because important explanatory variables have been left out. What sort of extra variables would we add in capturing demand for air travel? One possibility is an income variable. The observations on quantity and the price proxy used in this chapter do not allow us to distinguish between movements along the demand curve versus shifts of the demand curve. With a positive income elasticity for air travel (assuming that it is a normal good), and increasing per capita real income (as seen in most developed countries over the period) a regression omitting an income variable may have led to a distortion of the absolute price elasticity of demand.

What other variables could be used? The exclusion of prices of substitutes (e.g. prices of car travel) may also have biased the estimate of elasticity of demand for air travel. This omission might have particularly important consequences for the comparative analysis of short-haul travel versus long-haul travel so we could collect some data about the relative contribution of short-haul flights, compared to long-haul ones. We could also try to distinguish between leisure and business travellers given that previous studies have suggested that demand for leisure travel is more elastic than demand for business travel. Also, we have simplified by concentrating on the demand side and abstracting from the cost side. Some cost-side factors that may be relevant include fuel and security costs, changes in the airline industry (e.g. reflecting the entry of the budget airlines), changes to aviation taxation policies etc. etc. If we were to conduct a really robust econometric analysis taking full account of the supply side as well as the demand side, then we could use simultaneous equation estimation techniques. These techniques are beyond the scope of this book but some related issues are touched upon in Chapter 8.

These caveats allowing, we can conclude by saying that our evidence suggests that the demand for air travel is elastic. It is also broadly consistent with the much more detailed and sophisticated studies summarised in Box 3.4 (for leisure travel at least). This finding is good news for the airlines because an elastic response implies that a fall in price will lead to a larger rise in revenue: the distances travelled by air-travellers have risen by a greater proportion than the fall in the price of travel.

3.5   Implications and conclusions

The concepts analysed in this chapter have relevance to a range of policy issues. The microeconomic concepts will inform the marketing strategies of individual airline operators, explaining the many 'two for the price of one' or 'half-price weekend' deals that we frequently see advertised. Similar pricing deals operate in other industries – e.g. mobile phone companies. Discount deals such as these are not intended to be gifts or to comfort homesick expatriates – they are a sophisticated effort to map the demand schedule, and to discover the prices that will maximise corporate revenues. The evidence presented here suggests that, from the demand side at least, a strategy of lowering ticket prices would appear to be a profitable strategy. But for a fuller exploration of this issue we could look at the supply side too because pricing policies will depend also on the cost of running an airline.

More broadly, concepts of price elasticity are also important for macroeconomic policy. Elasticity analysis is used in the formulation of fiscal policy, e.g. in designing taxation strategies. Governments may want to tax some goods and services to raise revenue and/or to dampen consumer demand. Increasing taxation on goods for which consumers have inelastic demand may have positive fiscal and social benefits: for example, if the demand for tobacco/alcohol is inelastic then policy-makers can generate substantial tax revenues by introducing tobacco taxes and duties on alcohol, and some of this revenue can be earmarked for public health expenditure. Overall, the precise impact of such policies will depend on the own-price elasticity of demand for alcohol and cigarettes.

3.6   Further reading

Textbooks

Grant, S. and Bamford, C. (2006) *Transport Economics* (4th edition), Oxford: Heinemann Educational Publishers.

Varian, H. (2006) *Intermediate Microeconomics* (7th edition), London: W. W. Norton & Co. Chapters 5–6 and 15.

Journal articles

Brons, M., Pels, E., Nijkamp P. and Rietveld P. (2002) 'Price elasticities of demand for passenger air travel: a meta-analysis', *Journal of Air Transport Management*, vol. 8, no. 3, 165–75.

Ito, H. and Lee D. (2005) 'Assessing the impact of the September 11 terrorist attacks on the U.S. airline demand', *Journal of Economics and Business*, vol. 57, issue 1, 75–95.

Verleger, P. K. (1972) 'Models of the demand for air transportation', *Bell Journal of Economics and Management Science*, vol. 3, no. 2, 437–457.

Policy reports

Gillen, D. W., Morrison W. G. and Stewart, C. (2003) *Air Travel Demand Elasticities: Concepts, Issues and Measurement*, Department of Finance, Canada. See www.fin.gc.ca/consultresp/ Airtravel/airtravStdy_1e.html

3.7   Chapter exercises

1. In this chapter we have established that the estimate of the price elasticity of demand for air travel is significantly less than zero at a 5% significance level. But we might want to know whether or not there is an elastic response (rather than no response at all). Using the data provided in this chapter, test whether or not the demand for air travel is elastic by:
   (a) Reformulating the hypotheses and decision rules to test that the elasticity is less than or equal to unity in absolute value terms.
   (b) Calculate the t test accordingly.
   (c) Interpret your findings.
2. Using the data provided in Table 3.2:
   (a) Estimate (e.g. using Excel's 'Regression' tool) the relationship between passenger miles and the price proxy assuming a linear specification, i.e. a lin-lin specification. (Hint: run the regression on unlogged variables.)
   (b) What are the parameter estimates from this regression capturing?
   (c) Discuss your results focussing on the parameter estimates.
   (d) What differences do you notice between the results from your lin-lin estimation and the log-log specification estimated in this chapter? (Hint: have a look at your t tests and R^2.) Explain the differences.
   (e) Which specification is preferable? Why?

Hypothesis testing
Health expenditure and quality of life

Economic issues include:
- Public goods and externalities
- Asymmetric information and adverse selection

Econometric issues include:
- Hypothesis testing: using p values
- The F test of explanatory power

Data issues include:
- Household survey data
- Qualitative indexes

4.1   The issue

How much should the State spend on health? One might doubt this is a question for economists – perhaps medical professionals should decide on patients' needs and treatment costs or politicians should be asked about the desires of the electorate and its taxpayers. But economists can offer helpful tools with which to debate questions of this nature. No country has a blank chequebook, and public budgeting is a tense business of allocating scarce resources amongst competing needs. Economists can contribute helpfully to the debate on how resources might be best used by showing the relative costs and benefits of different strategies. This can help to reconcile, or at least to prioritise, diverse and sometimes conflicting objectives. Moreover, the question of how much governments should spend on health care is usually nested within the wider debate to which economists have long been central – namely, to what extent should the State be involved in the economy at all. In most countries this topic can be relied upon to produce heated argument from all ends of the political spectrum, in tones that are often highly ideological, and polemical. Our aim in this chapter is to shed some light on the heat by showing how empirical analysis can help raise the level of debate.

4.2   The theory

Most industrialised countries have seen government spending rise over the last century, as have many developing countries. Even in the USA, with its strong private sector ethos, government real expenditure increased from 2.5% of GDP in 1870 to over 20% by the end of the twentieth century; and in most countries the levels are much higher. Typically much of the spending goes to defence (often as much as half the total), followed by health, education, and infrastructure; and the figure would double if subsidies and transfer payments (such as unemployment benefits, pension payments and so on) were also included. Its rationale is usually the **public good** argument, that the State provides services that benefit everyone because services will not be properly provided by the market alone. State intervention is also justified by the need to compensate for negative *externalities* and to subsidise positive ones that the market would fail to address; or to ensure social equity. This was most dramatically marked in many leading economies during 2008, as governments nationalised banks and bailed out ailing industries in an attempt to contain the effects of the global credit crunch.

In the health sector, examples of these arguments include the public good aspect of vaccination against infectious diseases (where the vaccinations provide a non-rival and non-excludable benefit to the unvaccinated, by reducing the likelihood of their being exposed to disease). More recently, it is also argued that free and universal access to health care is a fundamental human right.

These ideas have a relatively long historical pedigree: Bismarck introduced public health insurance into Europe in 1883, and the idea spread so that by 1975 between 70 and 100 per cent of Europe's total labour force was covered. The USA developed a different tradition, with public insurance being directed only to the poor and the elderly, with the rest of the population insured privately. But both continents saw government spending on health increase, in both absolute terms and as a share of GDP. Expenditure slowed in the 1980s alongside a variety of attempts to reform the public sector and to control costs and amid fears that **government failure** was worse than the **market failures** it aimed to rectify. Critics doubted that the welfare state had added much to social or economic welfare, and thought that public spending could be cut without sacrificing important policy objectives. These challenges are reflected in the flurry of health-sector reforms that most countries have experienced since the 1970s, including deregulation, the introduction of **quasi-markets**, (public sector institutions designed to incorporate market features to promote economic efficiency) or even full privatisation.

The debate is still on with no country confident it has found the best means to provide the right quality and quantity of health services to its people. Moreover, costs are likely to keep rising as more sophisticated treatments are developed and our steadily increasing life expectancy and ageing population fuels demand. Public money generally predominates in the financing of health care and this strains government budgets for health services. Public health and prevention programmes, which are especially cost effective, account for on average only a small percentage of health-care spending (usually less than five per cent).

More controversially, turning to markets and market-based 'user pays' health services do not necessarily help solve the problem. Private sector insurers not only exclude those who cannot pay; they also exclude people who can pay but who have predictable or costly problems. Unless countries are willing to see these people abandoned by the health system completely, the State must step in. Congenital illnesses and pregnancy for example are often not covered by private insurers. Market-oriented health care is also criticised for inducing wasteful expenditures, including **supply-induced-demand** (fee-paid doctors may encourage patients to consume excessive amounts of care). There is also myopia: people may not purchase health insurance because they underestimate their future health costs.

One of the critical sources of market failure affecting the health sector is **asymmetric information**, creating many problems and inequities. Asymmetric information is a particular type of imperfect information in which one signatory to a contract has more information than another. Asymmetric information problems are very common in economics, as we will see in later chapters. One type of asymmetric information problem is **moral hazard**. This is a problem of 'hidden action': after contracts have been signed the beneficiaries of a contract may have an incentive to cheat on the contract. In a health-care setting this would be associated with patients trying to get the most of out their health insurance premium by over-consuming health-care services – they may continue to smoke without telling their health insurer for example.

Another asymmetric information problem is **adverse selection**. This is a pre-contractual problem of 'hidden attributes': before a contract is signed, signatories to a contract may be able to conceal relevant characteristics about themselves because those characteristics are not readily observable, e.g. to a health insurer. Akerlof (1970) illustrates the consequences of adverse selection problems using his **lemons principle**: in used car markets, average car prices will be pulled down by the quality of the 'lemons' until the market disappears completely.

The lemons principle can be applied to health insurance markets: adverse selection problems will mean that health insurance companies cannot distinguish between the healthy and the unhealthy. The more unhealthy people, who realise that they may need health care services in the future, will have a greater incentive to sign up to health insurance contracts; the most-healthy people will not and, because health insurers cannot easily tell the difference, they will set their premiums to match average healthiness. This premium will deter the relatively healthy from taking out health insurance contracts so they will leave the health insurance market. So average healthiness will fall and premiums will rise. This will deter the next-most-healthy group of potential customers; they too will leave the health insurance market, average health will fall again, premiums will rise again and so the process continues. Premiums will rise and there will never be enough relatively healthy members to keep the premium low unless mechanisms are put in place to reduce the asymmetric information (e.g. health screening by insurance companies, healthy people signalling that they're healthy via their lifestyle choices etc.).

In the extreme, this process will continue indefinitely until the market for health insurance disappears. On the other hand, forcing symmetric information might be considered unethical. So some countries have implemented a solution whereby health insurers are not allowed to exclude anyone, and can differentiate premiums only on the basis of age or gender, not by individual patient characteristics; in such systems all individuals are required to take insurance.

Overall the problems outlined above suggest that market solutions may not provide the best way either to finance or provide health care. But public health care is not perfect either. In developed countries, it is often criticised for being of poor quality and for relying excessively on rationing by queuing, where those with urgent problems are treated immediately. Those with minor problems have to wait a long time – sometimes so long that the minor problems become major problems. It is not always clear that tax-payers get value for money, or that the funds are used efficiently, let alone equitably. Under-investment in public health over a long period of time can create problems of poor infrastructure or lack of skilled professionals making it extremely difficult to boost quality and services, even if funds are eventually forthcoming.

The arguments are less heated in developing countries, where medical services are provided at a lower level of technology, lower costs and much lowered expectations about the quality of public health care. Much of the public expenditure in these countries is aimed at public health problems that the industrialised world resolved in the nineteenth century – with the very important exception of HIV/AIDS.

Does it matter whether the provision of health services is publicly or privately funded? The arguments above imply that higher public contributions to the total health budget encourage better health outcomes because, even in a country with high levels of expenditure overall, there are some sorts of services that private insurers will never cover, e.g. preventative health programmes and health education; these expenditures are typically the domain of the public sector. In this chapter we will focus on the impact of public health provision and statistically assess the relationships between healthiness and health expenditure across a cross-section of developed and developing countries.

4.3   The data

Collecting data on health and health expenditures is not straightforward because the value of healthiness is not easily measured in monetary terms. One approach is to use survey data. An example, from Tanzania, of the benefits of using appropriate survey data to examine and to guide health expenditure is described in Box 4.1.

The key to the success of the Tanzanian exercise was the careful collection of relevant data, and these data were then used strategically to guide the efficient spending of a limited health budget. This sort of data collection exercise can present special challenges in developing countries. Panel data household surveys (interviewing the same family on regular intervals) in Nairobi slums, for example, are affected by the fact that houses can disappear overnight. On the other hand, the benefits that can be achieved when we have better information about needs and priorities clearly make the effort worthwhile.

But a major problem for surveys is that they are prone to **sampling bias**, especially if a researcher is not careful to select a sample that is representative of the relevant population. Identifying **representative households** involves

---

Box 4.1 Health surveys in Tanzania: information as the best medicine

The benefits of data collection and analysis have been made strikingly clear in two poor, rural regions of Tanzania, where infant mortality fell by almost half in just six years following an innovative study into the causes of death. The results have been so dramatic that the data collection methodology is now being rolled out across the whole country.

One in ten children were dying before they reached their first birthday. So the Tanzania Ministry of Health began working with the Canadian aid agency, the International Development Research Centre (IDRC), to look for ways to improve the impact of their health expenditure. Together they searched for information about the causes of death, so that priority could be given to treatments that saved more lives at lower cost, and less priority given to treatments that saved few lives, at higher cost. This seems obvious now, but very few developing countries would readily have the information to ascertain this. Not least, most people die in their homes so very little information reaches the health planning authorities.

The project focussed on health outcomes in two rural districts over the period 1997 to 2003, to the south and east of the largest city, Dar es Salaam. Researchers on bicycles carried out door-to-door surveys, asking representative households whether any family member had died or been ill lately, and with what symptoms.

Figure 4.1 shows that there was no clear relationship between health expenditure priorities and the prevalence of disease. For example, malaria accounted for 30% of the years of lives lost in one region, but only 5% of the budget. A number of 'childhood problems' such as pneumonia, diarrhoea, malnutrition and measles claimed 28% of the life years lost, but got only 13% of the health budget. At the other extreme, 22% of the budget was directed

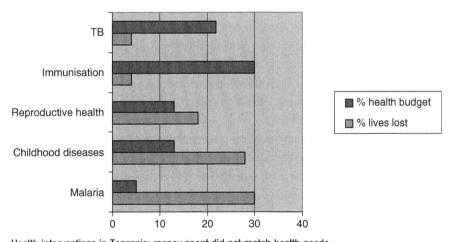

Figure 4.1   Health interventions in Tanzania: money spent did not match health needs

towards tuberculosis, which accounted for only 4% of deaths in the sample. The interpretation was not that the tuberculosis vaccination programme should be stopped: falls in the tuberculosis death rate no doubt reflected the success of the vaccination programmes. But in terms of future spending strategies, the falling tuberculosis death-rate was consistent with plans to lower expenditures on vaccination programmes.

The new information meant that medical efforts could be concentrated more effectively, and health status indicators improved as a consequence: the early results of better matching between health needs and health spending were staggering, with infant mortality dropping by 28% in just one year. Over six years of the mapping exercises, infant mortality dropped by 43% in one region, and 46% in the other.

The tragedy of the lives lost before this programme is that some of the most effective early treatments are not costly: for example, oral rehydration salts for children with diarrhoea cost only a few cents. Other more pricey treatments have been shown to be so effective that even poor households try to pay the cost. Insecticide impregnated mosquito nets, for example, seem expensive at $3 each but not in terms of the life years saved. Moreover, as families are able to stay healthy longer, they can also become less poor. Families that used to suffer malaria fevers every few months could stay well for a whole year, and even accumulate extra food and cash over that period.

Sources: Tanzania Essential Health Interventions Project, IDRC, Canada.

---

seeking information from particular households, rather than a random 'door-knock', in an effort to obtain a picture that is representative of the entire population. Calling on households at random could generate non-random results if, for example, the only people home to answer the survey were the unemployed, the aged, or the infirm.

For our quantitative assessment of the links between healthiness and health expenditure, we are examining healthiness at a broader scale. We examine the assertion that if one country spends more on health care than another, then its people should enjoy a healthier life and live longer and its babies should have a sturdier start in life.

Whilst it is relatively easy to make cross-country comparisons of health budgets using government health expenditure, survey data of the type used in Tanzania are not usually available for cross-country comparisons of healthiness. So how do we measure improvements in average health across countries? In this chapter we explore the relationships between healthiness and health expenditure using a sample of 24 high and low income countries.

Table 4.1 Infant mortality, life expectancy, and public expenditure on health

	1	2	3	4	5	6	7
	Life expectancy (average in years)	Infant mortality (deaths per 1000 live births)			Public health expenditure (% of GDP)		
	1999	1960	1999	Change (%)	1960	1998	Change (%)
Australia	78.78	20.20	4.90	−75.7%	2.40	5.90	145.8%
Austria	77.93	37.50	4.40	−88.3%	3.10	5.80	87.1%
Belgium	78.03	31.20	5.38	−82.8%	2.10	7.90	276.2%
Canada	79.03	27.30	5.30	−80.6%	2.30	6.40	178.3%
France	78.51	27.40	4.80	−82.5%	2.50	7.30	192.0%
Germany	76.99	35.00	4.83	−86.2%	3.20	7.90	146.9%
Ireland	76.12	29.30	5.50	−81.2%	3.00	4.70	56.7%
Italy	78.29	43.90	5.43	−87.6%	3.00	5.60	86.7%
Japan	80.63	30.40	3.60	−88.2%	1.80	5.90	227.8%
Netherlands	77.65	17.90	5.10	−71.5%	1.30	6.00	361.5%
New Zealand	77.39	22.60	5.23	−76.9%	3.50	6.20	77.1%
Norway	78.48	18.90	4.02	−78.7%	2.60	7.40	184.6%
Spain	77.91	43.70	5.30	−87.9%	0.90	5.40	500.0%
Sweden	79.26	16.60	3.60	−78.3%	3.40	6.70	97.1%
Switzerland	79.56	21.10	4.56	−78.4%	2.00	7.60	280.0%
UK	77.25	22.50	5.70	−74.7%	3.30	5.60	69.7%
USA	76.91	26.00	6.90	−73.5%	1.30	5.80	346.2%
Denmark	75.87	21.50	4.65	−78.4%	3.20	6.80	112.5%
Finland	77.26	21.40	4.08	−81.0%	2.30	5.20	126.1%
South Africa	48.47	88.60	61.52	−30.6%	...	3.30	...
Singapore	77.55	34.80	3.20	−90.8%	...	1.20	...
Malaysia	72.34	70.60	7.90	−88.8%	...	1.40	...
Indonesia	65.72	137.80	41.92	−69.6%	...	0.70	...
Bangladesh	60.74	154.80	61.20	−60.5%	...	1.70	...
Mean	75.28	41.71	11.21	−78.0%	...	5.40	...

Sources: World Bank *World Development Indicators*, OECD *Social Expenditure Database: 1980/1998*.

These data are summarised in Table 4.1 and were gathered from the following sources:

World Bank *World Development Indicators*: www.worldbank.org

OECD *Social Expenditure Database: 1980/1998*: www.oecd.org

Other potential sources of data include the World Health Organisation (WHO), United Nations Development Programme (UNDP) and the national accounts of individual countries.

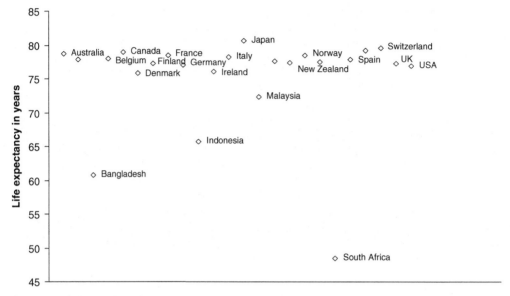

Figure 4.2   Life expectancy for a cross-section of countries, 1999

Indicators of health

The measure of healthiness that we use here is **life expectancy**, a frequently used indicator of national health standards. There are other ways to measure healthiness: another possibility is the **infant mortality rate** – the number of infant deaths per 1,000 live births.

The life expectancy data (column 1 of Table 4.1) shows a wide range of outcomes across the sample with a relatively short average lifespan (of just over 48 years) in South Africa but a relatively long average lifespan (of almost 81 years) in Japan.

These data are plotted in Figure 4.2 to give a visual impression of the spread of life expectancy outcomes. This plot shows that there is a clear division between the performance of the rich, developed countries – all of which have approximately similar average life expectancies of between 76 years and 81 years and the poorer less-developed countries, which experienced average life expectancies ranging between 48 and 72 years.

Infant mortality rates are another measure of the healthiness of a nation and data on infant mortality in 1999 relative to infant mortality in 1960 are shown in Table 4.1 (columns 2 to 4). In general, infant mortality has improved over the past 40 or so years, even in countries that still have a relatively high number of infant deaths. Bangladesh recorded 61 infant deaths per 1,000 live births in 1999, compared to 155 in 1960. Developed countries such as the USA and UK registered even greater improvements, despite their better baseline (relative improvements are harder when performance is already good!).

There may be other aspects of healthiness captured neither by life expectancy measures nor by infant mortality measures. For this reason, qualitative and composite indicators may also be helpful (see Box 4.2 for an outline of quality of life indicators).

Measuring health expenditure

To capture health expenditure in this analysis we use OECD data on *public expenditure on health as a percentage of GDP* (see columns 5 and 6, Table 4.1). Expenditure is measured relative to GDP to control for the economic size of the countries in our sample. It would be distorting to compare the absolute expenditures of large countries such as the USA with the absolute expenditures of smaller countries with otherwise similar health-related factors (e.g. similar levels of development, education or life-styles etc.) Just to focus on absolute figures would capture neither the relative commitments of governments to health expenditure nor the relative demands on health services given the economic or demographic size of a country. For example, the *UNDP Human Development Report* reveals that 2002 health expenditure in the USA amounted to $1,545 billion but the UK spent $128 billion in the same year. This doesn't mean that the UK government had less of a commitment to health than the US government; it reflects that fact that the UK is a smaller economy. So we can 'weight' each country's expenditure by expressing expenditure as a proportion of GDP.

Also, when comparing health expenditure between countries (or even within one country over time), we cannot say that $1 worth of health care bought the same quality of services in all situations. There is no readily available equivalent to indices of **purchasing power parity** (PPP) i.e. measures of the value of a currency in terms of the value of goods and services it can buy. PPP measures can provide a very useful means to compare the real purchasing power of different currencies but economists have struggled to develop reliable PPP indicators for health services.

By comparing the performance in 1960 (column 5, Table 4.1) and 1998 (column 6, Table 4.1) we can calculate the % change in expenditure (column 7, Table 4.1). These data reveal a sustained increase in governments' commitment to public health expenditure: health expenditure increased from a mean

---

Box 4.2 Measuring healthiness: The Quality of Life Index
and the Human Development Index

How should we decide on priorities for health spending? As described above, once a policy maker decides that a health budget should be set at some fixed amount, then priorities for spending have to be determined. One way to decide is on the basis of the benefits of various treatments. But defining and measuring these is extremely difficult, particularly because it involves making inter-personal comparisons or aggregating effects over a large number of individuals. It is not obvious how to compare the benefit of the same operation given to two different patients – for example, the benefit of a heart transplant to an otherwise healthy person, compared with the benefit to another patient with additional confounding health problems; or the benefit to a young person compared to an old one. And it is even more difficult to compare the benefits of different operations between different people – even if all the operations cost the same price. Measuring benefits in terms of their effect on labour productivity is one approach, but it is a very narrow definition of 'benefit'; moreover it is biased against elderly or low paid individuals.

Another method involves the use of **Quality of Life Index (QLIs)**, which ranks different health states, so one can compare the benefits to different patients of different sorts of treatments. Ranking patients' health status according to this scale produces a relatively objective measure of the benefits of various treatment options (McGuire *et al.* 1987). For example, physicians studying quality of life for people suffering from the inherited disease phenylketonuria (PKU) ranked 15 different health states, ranging between 'death' (=0.00) and 'no symptoms' (=1.00), and including: (a) confined to house, walking freely and able to care for oneself but not doing any major activities (=0.435), and (b) in hospital, walking freely but requiring assistance with self-care (=0.165).

The **Human Development Index (HDI)** is an example of a composite index that measures a country's performance across three areas of human development; life expectancy, literacy and standard of living (as measured by GDP per capita). This index allows us to rank countries that may have very similar levels of income but different outcomes in terms of infant survival rates and/or educational attainment. The United States, for example, ranked 6th on the 2002 HDI (scoring 0.939) while the United Kingdom ranked 13th (at 0.928). By comparison, Germany ranked 17th (0.925), South Africa ranked 107th (0.695), Bangladesh was 145th (0.478), and Sierra Leone was ranked lowest – in 173rd place (0.275).

The approach used in constructing the HDI can also be extended to measure poverty, capturing impacts that go far beyond simplistic income measures. For example, the Human Poverty Index (HPI), which was introduced in Chapter 2, includes the proportion of the population in each country with access to safe water supplies. The Gender-Related Development Index (GDI) adjusts for gender inequalities, to compare the positions of men and women between different countries. Sweden, which ranked 2nd in terms of the 2002 HDI, fell to 5th position in its GDI; the USA rose to 4th place in the GDI, and the UK rose to 12th place.

Source: http://hdr.undp.org/statistics

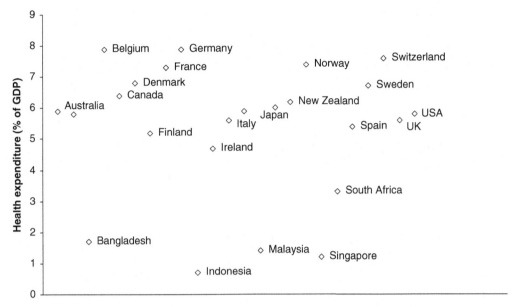

Figure 4.3   Health spending for a cross-section of countries, 1998

across this sample of only 2.5% of GDP in the 1960s to over 5.4% by 1998. The USA and Spain in particular recorded substantial increases of 346% and 500% respectively.

We plot 1998 health expenditure data in Figure 4.3 revealing again a broad division between the poorer, developing countries with health expenditures between 0.7% to 3.3% of GDP and the richer developed countries with health expenditures upwards of 4.7% of GDP.

Note that this broad pattern of health expenditure mirrors the pattern of life expectancies shown in Figure 4.2: the countries with longer life expectancies are the countries with higher health expenditures and this supports our hypothesis about a link between public health spending and healthiness. But it is important also to emphasise: firstly that a correlation between variables does not necessarily imply a causal mechanism and, secondly that there may be limitations on our data, as discussed below.

Data limitations

Before proceeding with a statistical analysis of these data, we should explore the limitations of our dataset. Firstly, a comparison of the life expectancy and infant mortality data illustrates that life expectancy may be an imperfect measure of a nation's healthiness. There are significant divergences between some countries' performance in terms of life expectancy versus infant mortality: for example, Canada had one of the highest life expectancies but alongside a relatively high infant mortality rate. Conversely, Singapore had a relatively low life expectancy but the best outcome across the sample in terms of low levels of infant mortality. In these cases, which measure more accurately captures healthiness? Probably neither or both!

Further biases are revealed in the life expectancy data. Figure 4.2 reveals that South Africa is a significant outlier (with a very low life expectancy) and the remaining developing countries in our sample (namely Malaysia, Indonesia and Bangladesh) have also experienced low life expectancies. Also, in terms of our analysis of the impact of health expenditure the clear divide between rich and poor countries captured in Figure 4.2 is likely to be a reflection of a complex range of factors some of which will be unrelated to our explanatory variable – public health expenditure.

In assessing our data we must keep in mind the constraints on cross-sectional comparisons. In analysing phenomena in poorer countries for example, missing data can be a common problem. Richer countries are more likely to have good data collection and they are probably also committed to relatively high levels of health expenditure. This sample is strongly skewed in favour of rich countries. This may create **sampling bias** so we need to keep in mind that the findings established in this chapter may not be robust in the countries which are poor.

Overall, it is important to recognise that our data may not perfectly measure the phenomena in which we are interested and so the results from our statistical analyses may not be completely reliable. We could perhaps perfectly measure our variables if we had populations of identical people, living identical lifestyles, with some spending a little on health care and others spending a great deal, to buy variable quantities of identical quality services. Such a data series would of course be impossible to find. Imperfect data series and impure associations are a fact of life in economics but hopefully we can find good proxies for the effects that we want to understand.

In this chapter we are illustrating some straightforward regression techniques and so we will assume away these complexities for the moment (though we will explore these problems in detail in later chapters).

4.4   Empirical methods and results

In this chapter, we are analysing the relationship between healthiness and health expenditure. As we are still focussing on simple regression analysis, we have to confine ourselves to one explanatory variable. It is important to remember that this may make our model vulnerable to **omitted variable bias** – a particular type of **model misspecification bias** occurring when OLS estimates of parameters are biased by the influences of excluded explanatory variables.[1] We assume that there is a linear relationship between the dependent variable and the explanatory variable and so the empirical model we are testing is:

$$Y_i = \alpha + \beta X_i + \varepsilon_i \tag{4.1}$$

where Y is healthiness measured as average life expectancy in 1999, X is public health expenditure as a proportion of GDP in 1998 and ε_i is a random error term. Note that we have used a **lag** on the explanatory variable. This is because we would not expect instantaneous effects of health expenditure on healthiness. Using the data from Table 4.1, we estimate an econometric model for a cross-sectional sample of 24 countries using the following SRF:

$$Y_i = \hat{\alpha} + \hat{\beta} X_i + \hat{\varepsilon}_i \tag{4.2}$$

Before running this regression we can draw some broad inferences about the plausibility of our model by inspecting the scatter plot in Figure 4.4. This shows a broadly positive association between life expectancy and health expenditure. But it is important to remember that not all observations in a sample will fit the broad pattern: here for example, Indonesia had the lowest spending but not the lowest life-expectancy; South Africa spent a relatively large amount on public health, but life expectancy was extremely low, at 48.5 years.

For our other measure of healthiness – infant mortality – low expenditure on public health was also associated with higher infant mortality rates: countries with higher spending tended also to have reduced infant mortality. But we cannot make clear cross-country comparisons. For example, although

---

[1] This and other problems of model misspecification will be addressed thoroughly in Part II – Multiple regression analysis.

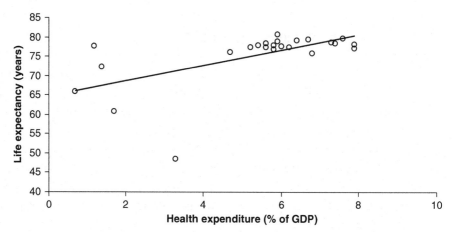

Figure 4.4   Longer life expectancy associated with larger health expenditures

the USA had the second highest increase in spending over the 40 years, it still had the fifth highest infant mortality rate. We won't analyse the link between infant mortality and health expenditure in any more detail here because we have left that for one of the chapter exercises . . .

Table 4.2 shows the Excel output table from running a regression of life expectancy on public health expenditure using our sample of 24 countries:

Table 4.2 Excel output table
Summary output

Regression Statistics	
R Squared	0.35
Adjusted R Squared	0.32
Standard Error	5.98
Observations	24

ANOVA

	df	SS	MS	F	Significance F
Regression	1	414.31	414.31	11.60	0.00
Residual	22	785.90	35.72		
Total	23	1200.21			

	Coefficients	Standard Error	t Stat	P-value	Lower 95%	Upper 95%
Intercept	64.69	3.34	19.37	0.00	57.77	71.62
Health Expenditure	1.98	0.58	3.41	0.00	0.77	3.18

These results can be summarised as follows:

$$\hat{Y}_i = \quad 64.69 + \quad 1.98X_i$$

$$\quad\quad\quad (3.34) \quad\quad (0.58)$$

$$\quad\quad\quad t = 19.37 \quad t = 3.41$$

$$\quad\quad\quad p = 0.00 \quad\quad p = 0.00$$

Standard errors are in brackets and we've also reported the **p-values**. We will explain these in more detail below.

The estimate of $\hat{\beta}$ suggests that a 1 point increase in the share of GDP devoted to public health is associated with an extension of life expectancy of just under 2 years. But is this finding statistically significant? We assess at a 5% significance level using a two-tailed t test with the following hypotheses and decision rules:

$$H_0 : \alpha = 0 \quad\quad\quad H_1 : \beta \neq 0$$

$$H_1 : \alpha \neq 0 \quad\quad\quad H_0 : \beta = 0$$

We have 22 degrees of freedom ($n = 24$ and we lose one degree of freedom in estimating our intercept and another degree of freedom estimating the slope parameter on health expenditure). So for a 5% significance level and a two-tailed test, $t_{crit} = 2.07$ and our decision rule will be: if $|\hat{t}| < t_{crit}$ then do not reject H_0 but if $|\hat{t}| > t_{crit}$ then reject H_0. For $\hat{\alpha}$: t=19.37 > 2.07; for $\hat{\beta}$: t=3.41 > 2.07 and so in both cases we reject H_0.

Focussing on $\hat{\beta}$, we can conclude that there is a positive association between life expectancy and health expenditure that is statistically significant at the 5% level. This confirms the patterns from our more casual inspection of the data in Section 4.3. For this sample of countries, countries that are spending more on public health have a healthier population.

There is another, quicker way to formulate decision rules – by using the **probability values (p values)** mentioned above. Notice that these are reported in the Excel Output Table to the right of the t statistics. As explained in Chapter 1, decision rules can be constructed around p values because they give us an **exact significance level**, capturing the boundary significance level at which we will start rejecting our null. They allow us to reformulate our decision rule in a very straightforward way. For example if we are using a 5% significance level our decision rule becomes: if $p > 0.05$, do not reject H_0; if $p < 0.05$ reject H_0.

For the results in this chapter, the p value on our t test of the null that the parameter on health expenditure is zero, i.e. $H_0 : \beta = 0$, gives p = 0.00 which is less than 0.05 and so we can reject H_0. Similarly we can reject the null that the intercept parameter is equal to zero (i.e. $H_0 : \alpha = 0$) because the p value for this parameter estimate is also 0.00.

The p values can be used for any sort of hypothesis test, including t tests, F tests and others. They are now widely reported in most statistical and econometrics packages. Using p values saves the time and trouble involved in looking up statistical tables but it is important to remember that they are formulated around a specific null hypothesis and this is usually the simplest possible null, e.g. that a parameter is equal to zero.

As is explained in detail in Chapters 1 and 2, R^2 is the coefficient of determination and measures the 'goodness of fit' of our estimated regression line. Here $R^2 = 0.35$ which indicates that 35% of the variability in life expectancy is captured by variability in health expenditure. But how can we judge this outcome? Is 35% too high, too low, or just right? We cannot say without a proper statistical test and to assess this question, we can use an F test of explanatory power, as outlined in Box 4.3. The result calculated there indicates that our R^2 is relatively high and our statistical model does capture a statistically significant proportion of the variability in life expectancy for our sample of countries. But it is important to remember (particularly as we are using simple regression analysis) that there will be many other factors influencing life expectancy apart from public health expenditure. Further analyses could focus on identifying the other determinants of life expectancy not only in a cross-sectional context but also in a time-series context.

Box 4.3 The F test of explanatory power

As explained in earlier chapters, when we want to test a single hypothesis, then one possibility is to use the Student's t test. But when we want to draw inferences about the overall explanatory power of a model, e.g. as captured by R^2, we can use the F test of explanatory power. As explained in Chapter 1, R^2 measures the proportion of the variability in the dependent variable that can be captured by the variability in the explanatory variables. So if we want to draw inferences about whether or not our R^2 is significantly different from zero, then we can test whether or not the slope parameter(s) are jointly equal to 0 using the **F test of explanatory power**.[2]

The formula for the F test of explanatory power is:

$$F_{k,\,n-k-1} = \frac{R^2/k}{(1 - R^2)/(n - k - 1)}$$

where k is the number of explanatory variables and n is the number of observations in our sample. For the model in this chapter, we have just one slope parameter ($k = 1$) but in its

---

[2] F tests and the F distribution are explained in detail in Chapter 1.

general formulation the F test of explanatory power tests the following null and alternative hypotheses for the slope parameters in a model with k explanatory variables:

$$H_0 : \beta_1 = \beta_2 = \ldots = \beta_k = 0$$

H_1: at least one of the parameters is not equal to zero

Decision rule: If $F > F_{crit}$, then reject H_0.

This F test of explanatory power is known as a **joint hypothesis test** because it is testing the overall explanatory power contributed by all the explanatory variables in the model. This and other F tests are particularly important to estimating models with more than one explanatory variable i.e. for multiple regression analysis (MRA) and so this and other F tests will be discussed more extensively in Part II of this book.

For simple regression analysis (SRA) the terminology above may seem confusing because of course we just have one explanatory variable and so just one slope parameter is included in our H_0. For the simple regression model in this chapter, R^2 is measuring the proportion of the variability in Y that can be captured by the one explanatory variable X. If we want to test whether or not our model overall captures a significant proportion of the variability in life expectancy, i.e. if we want to test whether or not the R^2 of 0.35 is significantly different from zero, then we can use the F test of explanatory power in the following way:

$$H_0 : \beta = 0$$

$$H_1 : \beta \neq 0$$

Decision rule: If $F > F_{crit}$, then reject H_0.

$$F_{k,n-k-1}\ F_{1,\,22} = \frac{R^2/k}{(1 - R^2)/n - k - 1}$$

$$= \frac{0.35/1}{(1 - 0.35)/(24 - 1 - 1)} = \frac{0.35}{0.03} = 11.67$$

You may have noticed that this F test result is also reported in the Excel output table as 11.60 (the very slight difference between these figures reflects rounding differences). Using our decision rule and a 5% significance level (i.e. with a 95% confidence interval), F_{crit} (1,22) = 4.30. So $F > F_{crit}$. Therefore we can reject H_0 and conclude that the model overall does capture a significant proportion of the variability in Y. This result verifies the result from our t test. In fact, in the SRA case the F test is just the square of the t test and (again allowing for rounding differences) $t = 3.41 \rightarrow t^2 = 11.63$ which is approximately equal to the F of 11.67 calculated above.

4.5   Implications and conclusions

The regressions in this chapter indicate that relatively high expenditures on public health are associated with longer life expectancies. Does this mean that governments should spend more? The simple answer may be 'yes' if we agree that a change in health expenditure can be compared on the same terms as a change in health outcomes. However before we can translate our findings into robust policy implications, more detailed work must be done.

Our empirical results may not be as clear-cut as implied above because several problems are likely to muddy our data and confound our results. Not least, our regression is a crude tool that compares broadly defined, total public health expenditure on the one hand, with a precise and narrowly defined healthiness indicator on the other. We may have over-estimated the importance of public health expenditure – public funds are spent on many health services completely unrelated to the mortality chances of new-born babies, such as adult cancer treatment, heart disease and hip replacements (all of which absorb large proportions of public health expenditure in many countries). We do not have information about the amounts devoted to infant or maternal care over the period studied. Finding more about these patterns of spending could also have important implications for the results.

Other problems may lie in the specification of our model. For this chapter we have been using simple regression analysis to estimate the impact of just one explanatory variable and this may generate biases in our estimation procedure. We will introduce **multiple regression analysis (MRA)** in the next chapter but, in the meantime, we should be cautious in the interpretation of results from a model with just one explanatory variable.

Last but not least, an extremely important question to consider is the issue of **correlation versus causation**: it is difficult, if not impossible, to separate correlation from causation. This is a key problem for most econometric analyses. In the context of healthiness, it could be that the causality operates in the opposite direction (people who live longer will demand more healthcare); or another variable may be affecting both health expenditure and life expectancy (e.g. effective governments are seen in countries at higher levels of development). Income may also have an impact, particularly in LDCs where higher incomes are associated with better health because of better sanitation, less starvation and so on.

Other factors such as diet, income, social status, genetic inheritance, education, and lifestyle choices (such as to smoke or not) may be as important as the quality and quantity of health care available. For infant mortality, the nutrition of both mother and infant will have critical impacts, as will water quality, sanitation and hygiene. In nineteenth-century Europe, for example, improvements in the quality of water supplies and sewage disposal, as well as the sterilisation, bottling and safe transport of milk, sharply reduced infant mortality; and the same is likely to be the case in the world's LDCs. The World Health Organisation (2008) has reported that there are important social determinants of health and these are captured by a **social gradient**: healthiness rises not only with income but also with relative social standing. So improving healthiness depends not only upon growing income but also upon a more equitable income distribution both within and across nations. Public policy will also have an effect: regulations requiring seatbelts to be worn in cars, or helmets to be worn when cycling, have a large impact on mortality and life expectancy even though such policies are not financed via public health expenditure. So even if we do find highly significant correlations between variables, we cannot assume that this reflects a causal link between the variables.

4.6   Further reading

Textbooks and lectures

Atkinson, A. B. and Stiglitz, J. (1980) *Lectures on Public Economics*, New York: McGraw-Hill.
Auerbach, A. J. and Feldstein, M. (eds.) (2002) *Handbook of Public Economics*, Amsterdam: Elsevier.
McGuire, A., Henderson, J. and Mooney, G. (1987) *The Economics of Health Care*, London: Routledge.
Stiglitz, J. (2000) *Economics of the Public Sector*, 3rd edition, London: W.W. Norton & Co., Chapter 12.

Journal articles

Akerlof, G. (1970) 'The market for lemons: quality, uncertainty, and the market mechanism', *Quarterly Journal of Economics*, vol. 84, no. 3, 488–500.
Arrow, K. (1963) 'The welfare economics of medical care', *American Economic Review*, vol. 53, no. 5.
Cutler, D. (2002) 'Equality, efficiency and market fundamentals – the dynamics of international medical care reform', *Journal of Economic Literature*, vol. 40, no. 3, 881–906.

Policy Reports

OECD (1985) *Social Expenditure 1960–1990: Problems of Growth and Control*, Paris: Organisation for Economic Cooperation and Development.
UNDP (annual) *Human Development Report*, Geneva: United Nations Development Programme.

World Bank (annual), *World Development Report*, Washington: World Bank Group.

World Health Organisation (WHO) (annual) *World Health Report*, Geneva: World Health Organisation.

World Health Organisation (WHO) (2008), *Closing the Gap in a Generation: Health Equity through Action on the Social Determinants of Health*, WHO Commission on Social Determinants of Health, Geneva: World Health Organisation.

4.7   Chapter exercises

1. In this chapter we have examined the relationship between health expenditure and life expectancy. Using the data from Table 4.1, analyse the relationship between infant mortality and health expenditure as follows:

   (a) Generate a scatter plot of infant mortality against health expenditure.

   (b) Estimate a line of best fit using the Excel Regression tool.

   (c) Discuss the findings from the hypothesis tests including

      i. *t* tests of single hypotheses

      ii. the *F* test of explanatory power.

   (d) For these hypothesis tests construct decision rules using

      i. *p* values

      ii. critical values from statistical tables.

   (e) Interpret your findings – is there an association between health expenditure and infant mortality? Is the association significant?

   (f) What are the limitations of your analysis?

2. In this chapter we've been using simple regression analysis on one explanatory variable. Other variables will have an impact on life expectancy.

   (a) Using some of the data sources outlined in this chapter, e.g. the World Bank's website, www.worldbank.org, collect some data on variables that you think may be important determinants of a nation's healthiness.

   (b) Set out an empirical model including more than one explanatory variable.

   (c) Using the Excel Regression tool, estimate your empirical model of healthiness using multiple regression analysis (MRA). (HINT: this is just a matter of incorporating extra columns within the "Input X Range" of the Excel 'Data Analysis – Regression' tool.)

   (d) What do you think might be some of the statistical and theoretical implications of using MRA rather than SRA?

Part II

Multiple regression and diagnostic testing

In Chapters 2–4, we introduced the basic OLS techniques associated with simple regression analysis (SRA). But, as explained in Chapter 1, OLS is the Best Linear Unbiased Estimator (BLUE) – i.e. the most reliable and accurate estimator of parameters – only when the Gauss–Markov (GM) assumptions are satisfied. In many cases, GM assumptions will be violated and OLS will be inadequately simple; for example the omission of important variables will generate biases in SRA. And there may be other econometric problems further compromising the BLUEness of OLS.

In Part II we introduce multiple regression analysis (MRA), i.e. regressions on models with more than one explanatory variable. We also outline some commonly used econometric tests and procedures, for example the diagnostic tests used to discover violations of the GM assumptions. We will also introduce some procedures for correcting violations of GM assumptions.

Multiple regression analysis
Housing demand in the UK

Economic issues include:
- Durable consumption goods
- Credit constraints and gearing

Econometric issues include:
- OLS using EViews
- Multiple regression analysis (MRA)
- F tests of restrictions

Data issues include:
- Hedonic pricing
- Capturing seasonality using dummy variables
- Dummy variable trap

5.1   The issue

Developments in housing markets have wide-ranging implications for the macro-economy. Increases in house prices will boost household wealth, thereby boosting consumption and fostering increases in aggregate demand. Increases in house prices may also affect consumer confidence and expectations, increasing general optimism within the economy. On the other hand, rigidities in housing markets have crucial implications for labour mobility, employment and unemployment. For example, housing market volatility will limit the ability of people to move in search of better jobs: Oswald (1997) observed that countries with fastest growth in home ownership in the 1980s and 1990s had the fastest growth in unemployment and attributed this to the labour immobility of owner occupiers in depressed housing markets, particularly those home owners who face **negative equity** (a situation which occurs when mortgage borrowings on a property exceed the value of the mortgaged property).

The **affordability** of housing will also affect householders' decisions to invest in housing: as house prices rise and incomes fall, people will choose other alternatives (e.g. renting, living with family) and cannot afford to enter the housing market either because their incomes are too low and/or because they cannot get easy access to mortgage credit. For many people in the UK and other OECD countries, declining affordability has meant that younger, poorer people have to wait a long time before becoming homeowners; in the meantime, the older/richer people who were able to afford housing a decade ago will have benefited from the spectacular rises in house prices that occurred from the late 1990s until 2007; they will have accrued an increased share of the stock of household wealth. In this way, volatile housing markets will have contributed to wealth inequalities.

House prices are affected by a wide range of other variables including the stock of housing, population growth and changing demographic patterns, government regulation and fiscal incentives/disincentives for owner occupation (e.g. stamp duty in the UK). House prices can also be volatile because of supply constraints; with inelastic supply, the price effects of shifts in demand are amplified. For new housing in particular, the supply of housing stock is inelastic in both the short term and the long term; firstly, because of the lags involved with housing construction and secondly, because the supply of land available for new housing is constrained, particularly in the UK. This shortage of housing land is one reason that governments may encourage the use of urban 'brownfield' sites for new housing developments.

More specifically, the UK housing market has experienced a lot of instability in the past few decades – particularly during the 1980s, with a sharp resurgence in volatility in 2007/8. This volatility may have its roots in the moves towards the deregulation of the UK's financial markets that started in the 1980s. Prior to 1981, the building societies were the key mortgage lenders, and they used the savings deposits of one set of customers to finance the mortgages of another set of customers. But from 1981 onwards, other lenders entered the mortgage market, including high street banks and other financial institutions. Other sources of credit were tapped, not only depositor savings but also short-term money markets. The increased volumes of mortgage lending enabled larger numbers of households to become homeowners; home-ownership was not as dependent on existing wealth/past savings as it had been in the past. In the 1980s and from the late 1990s onwards, increased liquidity in mortgage markets initially fuelled housing market bubbles, but then housing busts were precipitated in the early 1990s and again in 2007/8 as lending institutions became worried about the sustainability of high volumes of mortgage lending. During the 2007/8 credit crunch in particular, these fears were exacerbated by concerns about UK banks' excessive exposure to risky and unbalanced **sub-prime mortgage lending** (the relatively risky lending to borrowers who are more likely to default on their loans because of their straitened financial circumstances). Poor credit market conditions precipitated increasing pessimism amongst mortgage lenders, risk premiums on mortgage lending were increased and/or more stringent lending criteria were adopted thus constraining the availability of mortgage credit and magnifying house price falls.

Volatility is also affected by the sensitivity of UK mortgage markets to interest rate changes. A lot of European countries use fixed rate mortgages and so interest costs on mortgage borrowing change infrequently; in contrast, the high proportion of variable rate mortgages in the UK means that interest costs can change relatively rapidly and this makes UK mortgage holders more sensitive to changes in interest rates overall. UK housing markets were particularly affected by rises in interest rates in the late 1980s, when interest rates were raised in order to curb inflationary pressures throughout the macroeconomy; these rises fed through into higher mortgage rates, stalling housing demand and contributing to large falls in house prices from the early 1990s onwards. Interest rate costs have less relevance for the 2008 housing credit crunch because the Bank of England's base rate was relatively low and then fell dramatically, though lending pessimism did contribute to relatively large risk premiums on mortgage lending.

The aim of this chapter is to assess the various determinants of fluctuations in UK housing demand, focussing in particular on credit constraints – including the cost and availability of mortgage financing. But to begin with, we will examine some of the theory explaining **owner occupation**, i.e. why people choose to buy their own houses to live in, rather than renting.

5.2   The theory

Why do people buy houses? There is the obvious answer: because it's somewhere to live. But why not just rent? People buy houses if they expect their house to gain value over time and/or if living in their own house is cheaper than renting. One of the factors affecting this decision is the **affordability** of houses. Affordability can be captured by the ratio of average incomes to average house prices but income is not the only financial constraint on home-ownership; credit constraints are also important, as explained below.

Owner-occupiers face a complex set of decisions when they buy and sell their houses. On the consumption side, houses are durable goods and so exhibit **lumpiness**: lumpy goods are not easily divisible into small, easily traded quantities. So buying a house involves a once-off purchase of a large 'bundle' of services associated not only with shelter but also with a complex mix of necessities and luxuries. Houses are also goods that people expect to consume throughout their lives delivering utility over a long time-horizon.

The ownership of housing assets is also a key source of household wealth and, similarly mortgage borrowings are a key source of household debt. In accumulating housing wealth, owner-occupiers will try to maximise the capital gains of owning housing assets by timing their housing purchases carefully to take advantage of rises and falls in house prices, hopefully maximising speculative gains. But households face credit constraints: most households do not have sufficient current income and accumulated savings to cover the high cost of housing assets that will deliver utility and returns over a long time-horizon. So financial markets will play an important role in filling the shortfall because households can use borrowings to **leverage** the purchase of assets that they could not otherwise afford. So for most owner-occupiers, buying a house will accompany a significant set of decisions, i.e. the financial decisions associated with getting a mortgage.

The extent to which a household is dependent on mortgage borrowings can be measured by the **gearing ratio**: this captures the proportion of the housing purchase that is funded via mortgage borrowings rather than a household's income and savings: if you want to buy something that costs £100 but you only have £20, then you may be able to borrow £80; in this case your gearing ratio will be four – your borrowings will be four times as much as your own contribution. Gearing means that the purchase of an asset is not constrained by a person's current income or wealth.

The extent to which households use their own savings as opposed to gearing their purchases will affect their own stake or 'equity' in their housing assets, but it will also have wider implications in terms of housing market volatility. For example, if a house buyer is buying a house for £100,000 and if a building society or bank is prepared to give them a 100% mortgage (i.e. lend them the full £100,000) then the house buyer will have used none of his/her own savings and is therefore holding zero equity in the house. In this case, any house price appreciation will come at zero cost (assuming no transactions costs); if the house appreciates and is sold for £120,000, then the home-owner will not have had to use any of their own cash to make the gain; they'll have £20,000 of pure profit. But gearing purchases is a risky strategy because what happens if house prices fall? Capital gains from house price appreciation will be eroded by house price falls; if a home owner has borrowed £100,000 to buy a house that a year later is worth £80,000 then they're facing £20,000 of pure loss (excepting any gains made because they haven't had to pay rent). This situation of **negative equity** occurs when borrowings exceed the value of an asset.

Highly geared housing purchases may also have implications if the cost of borrowing rises because, as interest rates rise, an increasing proportion of households will be unable to afford their mortgages and if they default on their payments then their houses may be **repossessed**. These events will have implications for other borrowers too because mortgage lenders will respond to the instability created by negative equity and rising levels of default and repossession by increasing risk premiums on mortgage lending, contributing to further volatility and instability.

Minsky (1964) analysed the role played by financial constraints in propelling boom–bust cycles and put forward the **financial fragility hypothesis**, arguing that optimism during expansionary phases contributes to financial bubbles by encouraging excessive lending; however, this excessive lending will also plant the seeds of eventual crisis because, as lending increases to unsustainable levels, defaults will increase concomitantly, triggering pessimism amongst lenders. Risk premiums will also rise and credit constraints will intensify thus precipitating credit crunches and financial crisis. These ideas have much relevance for today's housing market volatility.

Muellbauer and Murphy (1997) also analyse the role of financial factors in arguing that, during the UK housing boom of the 1980s, high gearing ratios were more important than the low interest rates. The financial deregulation of mortgage markets had affected gearing ratios by allowing easier access to mortgage financing. With more competition in mortgage lending markets, accompanying increases in the volume of mortgage finance encouraged mortgage lenders to take greater risks in order to attract customers. 100% mortgages based on large multiples of borrowers' incomes were not uncommon. So households' equity in their houses decreased and gearing ratios increased. Whilst house prices were rising, homeowners who had high gearing rates on their housing purchases benefited from house price appreciation but for some homeowners those benefits were short-lived; by the 1990s, a large number of unlucky home owners were saddled with negative equity. And rapid house price falls in the UK following the 2007/8 credit crunch contributed to a resurgence of negative equity from 2008 onwards.

5.3   Data

In this chapter we are going to examine the impact of financial factors such as lending and interest rates on housing demand. Using house price growth as our dependent variable, we will regress this on mortgage rates and the growth in mortgage lending. We will also assess the impact of seasonal factors using **dummy variables**, as will be explained below.

But where does housing market data come from? Housing market data for a range of countries are published by the OECD (www.oecd.org). For the UK, some housing market data are available via the Office of National Statistics (ONS) website (www.statistics.gov.uk). The building societies are also useful sources of house price data and in our analysis we use house price data from the Nationwide building society to calculate house price growth (see www.nationwide.co.uk). For the financial variables used in this chapter, we have collected data on volumes of mortgage lending from the Council of Mortgage Lenders (CML) (www.cml.org.uk/cml/statistics). Data on mortgage rates comes from the Office of National Statistics (ONS) (www.statistics.gov.uk).

There are a number of limitations for these data. For the UK overall, it is important to remember that housing markets in England and Wales operate in a different way from housing markets in Scotland and so a lot of British housing market data is really data just for England and Wales.

Measuring house prices is further complicated by the fact that not all houses are of the same quality. Houses are not homogenous: they are **heterogenous goods**, i.e. they are essentially different objects of mixed quality. Even houses in the same area may be different things; for example if Mr Bloggs buys a house in the same street as Mr Jones, he may be prepared to pay a lot more for his house if it has a loft conversion or a modern bathroom or kitchen. But he will also have to pay more if Mr Jones bought his house during a depressed period whilst Mr Bloggs bought his house during a boom. House price indices abstract from heterogeneity. This creates measurement errors in housing data. It will also be difficult to separate the impact of general house price inflation from specific increases in the quality of housing services reflecting renovations etc. The building societies in particular have recognised this problem and in recent years have started to adopt **hedonic pricing** methods (Wood, 2005). Hedonic pricing and some of the measurement issues that emerge from the heterogeneity of housing goods are explained in Box 5.1.

Box 5.1 House price indices and hedonic pricing

Sources of house price data

Wood (2005) has identified at least seven main house price indices for the UK:

The Land Registry collects statistics on:

1. average prices from records on all completed house sales.

Mortgage lenders also collect data on house prices from the mortgage applications of their customers. The Office of the Deputy Prime Minister collates these house price data from its Survey of Mortgage Lenders (SML) to construct two indices including:

2. a simple average index; and
3. a mix-adjusted index – which is a weighted average of house prices from a representative selection of house sales.

Building societies collect house price data too, for example:

4. the Halifax index; and
5. the Nationwide index.

Building societies data are collected from mortgage lending records but building society survey data was more representative 25 years ago than it is today because, as explained above, building societies are no longer the only major mortgage lenders. Today, many other types of financial institution are involved with mortgage lending and if there are significant differences in the profiles of the average bank mortgage-holder versus the average building society mortgage-holder, then the building society data will suffer from sampling bias.

House price indices are also generated by real estate agents including the:

6. Hometrack index; and
7. Rightmove index.

Hedonic pricing

The collection of these house price data is complicated by the fact that houses are heterogeneous. So how do economists separate the influences of quality difference from house prices inflation? One way is to use **hedonic pricing** methodologies to compile house price data controlling for quality improvements. Hedonic pricing builds upon the idea that different characteristics of a good or service impact differently on the pleasure of consumption. For housing it involves econometric analysis to assess the value of certain property characteristics (e.g. a large garden, a modern kitchen). Prices are then adjusted to remove the idiosyncratic influence of these sources of heterogeneity to give an unbiased estimate of the 'raw' price. In the *Financial Times* (30 June 2004), hedonic prices are described which show that whilst the price of shelter rose from the late 1990s, the price of desirable attributes did not. This suggests that general house prices inflation had a greater impact on house prices than quality improvements.

Summary of some web links for housing market data:

Council of Mortgage Lenders (CML)	www.cml.org.uk
Land Registry	www.landreg.gov.uk
Office of the Deputy Prime Minister (ODPM)	www.odpm.gov.uk
Office of National Statistics (ONS)	www.statistics.gov.uk
Nationwide	www.nationwide.co.uk/hpi/

What do the data show about housing demand in the UK? Figure 5.1 plots Nationwide data on UK house prices alongside data on mortgage lending from the CML over the period 1975Q1 to 2008Q1.

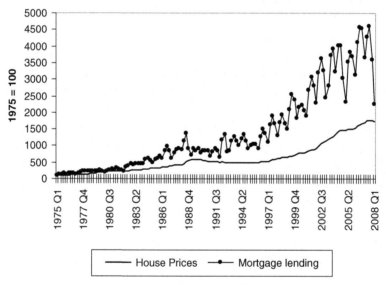

Source: Nationwide Building Society, CML.

Figure 5.1   UK house prices and mortgage lending, 1975Q1 to 2008Q1

Figure 5.1 shows that there has been a sustained upward trend in house prices from the 1970s through to early 2008; this is matched by exponential rises in mortgage lending suggesting that house prices are positively associated with mortgage lending. At the end of the period, there were strong signs that these trends were reversing from 2008 onwards.

Using these data patterns as a basis for our empirical model, we will assess the relationship between house prices, mortgage lending growth and mortgage rates using the following data:

Variable	Source	Website
House prices	Average Price for 'All Houses' (from mortgage application records)	www.nationwide.co.uk/hpi/ downloads/UK_house_price_ since_1952.xls
Mortgage lending	ONS data on composite Banks and Building Societies mortgage rate. From *Economic Trends Annual Supplement* (AJVT)	www.statistics.gov.uk
Mortgage rates	All loans for house purchases by mortgage lenders	www.cml.org.uk/cml/statistics

The house price and mortgage lending variables have been deflated using the consumer price index from the ONS (*Economic Trends Annual Supplement*'s Table 3.2, variable D7BT). We will also use dummy variables to capture seasonal influences, as explained below.

5.4   Empirical methods and results

In this empirical section we analyse some of the factors influencing UK housing demand, as measured by house prices. In the theoretical section we explained that housing demand is determined by a number of potential explanatory variables. The rise in house prices depicted in Figure 5.1 has outstripped rises in household disposable incomes and has coincided with the declining affordability of housing. So rises in affordability do not fully explain the pronounced boom–bust cycles in UK house prices since the 1980s.

In exploring these boom–bust cycles, as is common in econometric analysis, we will have to abstract from the complexity of relevant factors to concentrate on what we judge to be the most important factors. Building upon some of the theoretical ideas outlined above, we will examine the role of credit constraints and mortgage lending. Financial deregulation from the 1980s onwards boosted gearing ratios and led to increased mortgage lending on riskier terms; the increased risk may have translated in a greater probability of default. More recently, deregulated financial markets and the growth of complex financial products again encouraged lenders to engage in risky over-lending, encouraging house prices to accelerate at unprecedented rates throughout the late 1990s through to the 2000s only to collapse in the early 1990s and from 2008 onwards. These factors may help to explain destabilising boom–bust cycles in house prices.

Specifically to assess the impact of financial factors, we collected 45 quarterly observations for the UK between 1995Q1 and 2006Q1 using the data sources outlined above and we use these data to estimate the following empirical model:

$$h_t = \alpha + \beta_1 l_t + \beta_2 r_t + \beta_3 Q1_t + \beta_4 Q2_t + \beta_5 Q3_t + \varepsilon_t \tag{5.1}$$

where h is house prices (logged); l is mortgage lending (logged); r is the mortgage rate; Q1, Q2 and Q3 are dummy variables (capturing shifts in means for the Winter, Spring and Summer quarters respectively), and ε is a random error term.

Our SRF will be:

$$h_t = \hat{\alpha} + \hat{\beta}_1 l_t + \hat{\beta}_2 r_t + \hat{\beta}_3 Q1_t + \hat{\beta}_4 Q2_t + \hat{\beta}_5 Q3_t + \hat{\varepsilon}_t \tag{5.2}$$

In addition to the financial factors discussed above, we have also introduced seasonality into our model and this is captured using **seasonal dummy variables**, as explained in Box 5.2.

Box 5.2 Using seasonal dummies to capture seasonality

Dummy variables are **categorical variables** and are often used to capture non-measurable influences, for example the effect of seasonal factors on housing demand. Dummy variables are **binary** – they take the value 1 if something is true and the value 0 if something is false. For example, in the model below Q1 will capture differences in house prices in the winter quarter. We introduce a winter quarter dummy variable and ask the question for each observation in our data set: is this observation in the winter quarter? If the observation is in the winter quarter then we set Q1 = 1; if not, we set Q1 = 0. So for all observations taken from winter quarters Q1 = 1 and for spring, summer and autumn quarters Q1 = 0.

The following extract from our data file shows how the dummy variables are constructed in practice.

	Q1	Q2	Q3	Q4
1975 Q1	1	0	0	0
1975 Q2	0	1	0	0
1975 Q3	0	0	1	0
1975 Q4	0	0	0	1
1976 Q1	1	0	0	0
1976 Q2	0	1	0	0
1976 Q3	0	0	1	0
1976 Q4	0	0	0	1
1977 Q1	1	0	0	0
etc. etc.				

With dummy variables it is easy to fall into the **dummy variable trap**. Imagine that we had included all four seasonal dummies as well as an intercept into the SRF set out in Equation (5.2). The most obvious problem is one of interpretation. What would the parameters on Q1, Q2, Q3 and Q4 mean? These parameters are designed to capture all the constant factors affecting house prices in a given quarter. So what is the intercept capturing if we have four quarterly dummies in our model? More importantly, if we include all of the seasonal dummies then we will have a perfect correlation of +1 between the intercept and the sum of the dummies. To explain this: the intercept in a regression model is always a constant. The four quarterly dummy variables will always sum to 1 because the seasonal categories are mutually exclusive and exhaustive. (Ignoring the weather, officially it is always *either* winter *or* spring *or* summer *or* autumn; it is never more than one of these at once.) So the sum of the dummies will be a constant; because the intercept is also a constant, the correlation coefficient between them will be exactly equal to +1. This means that it will be impossible empirically to separate the influences of the intercept and dummies.

In statistical terms, the dummy variable trap emerges because of **perfect multi-collinearity** between the intercept and the sum of the four quarterly dummies. Multicollinearity is the general term for the existence of linear associations between explanatory variables. With **imperfect multicollinearity** the correlation coefficients between variables are high but less than 1 in absolute terms. With imperfect multi-collinearity estimation will be less accurate and this may affect our inferences. Perfect multicollinearity is the extreme version of multicollinearity and occurs when there are *perfect* linear associations between explanatory variables and/or groups of explanatory variables, i.e. when the correlation coefficients between them are exactly equal to ±1. With perfect multicollinearity (e.g. in the case of the dummy variable trap), OLS will not work at all because when there is a perfect linear association between groups of explanatory variables it is impossible to separate their influences: variances will be infinitely large and confidence intervals will be infinitely wide. And your econometrics software will give you an error message!

To escape this dummy variable trap for this analysis, we will have to drop one dummy variable and use its corresponding set of observations as our **reference category**. For our estimations we will use Q4 (autumn) as the reference category. The intercept then captures the impact of constant factors in autumn. The parameter estimates on the other dummies will represent *shifts* in the intercepts for other seasons. Another solution could be to drop the intercept and have four quarterly dummies, with the parameters on each representing the intercept for the relevant quarter, but this would complicate the interpretation of R^2 and for this reason it is better to keep one category as a reference category.

What does this imply for our model? We are estimating the following model:

$$h_t = a + \beta_1 l_t + \beta_2 r_t + \beta_3 Q1_t + \beta_4 Q2_t + \beta_5 Q3_t + \varepsilon_t \tag{5.1}$$

where h is house prices (logged), l is mortgage lending (logged), r is the mortgage rate, Q1, Q2 and Q3 are dummy variables (capturing shifts in means for the Winter, Spring and Summer quarters respectively), and ε is a random error term.

As explained above, we are using Q4 as our reference category and so the intercept from the model is capturing the constant factors in Q4. Different combinations of values on the dummy variables will affect the intercept of this model as follows: When it's autumn, i.e. when $Q1 = Q2 = Q3 = 0$

$$\rightarrow h_t = a + \beta_1 l_t + \beta_2 r_t + \varepsilon_t \tag{5.1a}$$

When it's winter, i.e. when $Q1 = 1$ and $Q2 = Q3 = 0$:

$$\rightarrow h_t = (a + \beta_3) + \beta_1 l_t + \beta_2 r_t + \varepsilon_t \tag{5.1b}$$

When it's spring, i.e. when $Q2 = 1$ and $Q1 = Q3 = 0$

$$\rightarrow h_t = (a + \beta_4) + \beta_1 l_t + \beta_2 r_t + \varepsilon_t \tag{5.1c}$$

When it's summer, i.e. when $Q3 = 1$ and $Q1 = Q2 = 0$

$$\rightarrow h_t = (a + \beta_5) + \beta_1 l_t + \beta_2 r_t + \varepsilon_t \tag{5.1d}$$

So we've estimated four different models in one go!

Notice that the intercept is being augmented in each case – the parameters on the dummy variables are shifting the intercept upwards. We aren't trying to capture shifts in slopes in this example and the mean of the product of the slope parameter estimates and the explanatory variables is constant across all seasons.[1] The average for a given season, e.g. winter is given by:

$$h_t = (\bar{a} + \bar{\beta}_3) + \beta_1 \bar{l}_t + \beta_2 \bar{r}_t + \varepsilon_t \tag{5.3a}$$

The mean of a constant is just that constant, and this will be the same for all four seasons. It follows that the mean of the parameter on an additive dummy is just that parameter. The mean of the error is zero and so for winter we can capture the difference between winter's mean and the overall means as follows:

$$h_t - a - \beta_1 \bar{l}_t - \beta_2 \bar{r}_t = \beta_3 \tag{5.3b}$$

In this way, the seasonal dummies are capturing the shifts in the means of house prices as the seasons change. To summarise: the additive dummy variables are capturing the **differences in group means** across the four seasons.

---

[1] If we wanted to capture changes in slopes then we would use a multiplicative dummy variable, and these are explained in Chapter 9.

The main innovation of this chapter is, for the first time in this book, we have more than one explanatory variable; in fact we have five explanatory variables ($k = 5$). This means that we will have to use **multiple regression analysis** (MRA) to analyse house prices. One of the main advantages of MRA is that it allows us to avoid **omitted variable bias** by specifying our empirical models to include as many variables as are indicated by the relevant theory. This is useful in the context of our model of house prices because we have identified a number of explanatory variables that might capture house price fluctuations.

MRA also involves an extension of the various tests and measures used for SRA and so the coefficient of determination, our measure of the goodness of fit, must be adapted to account for the presence of more than one explanatory variable, as explained in Box 5.3.

Box 5.3 Multiple regression analysis (MRA)

Multiple regression analysis (MRA) involves the extension of the OLS techniques outlined in previous chapters to empirical models that have more than one explanatory variable. This means that we can separate out the influences of different explanatory variables; the parameter on one explanatory variable will be capturing the impact of that variable holding the other explanatory variables constant. This allows us to capture the direct effect of each explanatory variable more effectively; we are **controlling** for the influences of the other explanatory variables included in the model. Whilst the mathematics of multiple regression are more complex than for simple regression, in practice the techniques are much the same and the computer packages are programmed do all the extra work. It's not a good idea to try to do multiple regressions "by hand" unless you have lots of spare time!

Measuring goodness of fit

In simple regression we were using just one explanatory variable. In multiple regression we may use many more. What implications does this have for the coefficient of determination – our measure of goodness of fit? As explained in Chapter 1, in simple regression analysis there is a straightforward association between the correlation coefficient – r and the coefficient of determination – R^2. For MRA, this relationship is more complex and $R^2 \neq r^2$: r will just capture the two-way correlation between Y and one explanatory variable; r will not control for the indirect influences of other explanatory variables. On the other hand, R^2 is capturing the collective association between Y and all the explanatory variables. So, whilst $R^2 \neq r^2$ it can still be calculated using the following formula:

$$R^2 = \frac{ESS}{TSS} = \frac{\sum(\hat{Y} - \bar{Y})^2}{\sum(Y_i - \bar{Y})^2}$$

(1.12 from Chapter 1)

Another complication that applies to MRA is that each time we add a new explanatory variable, our goodness of fit necessarily increases because we are adding in an additional source of 'explained' variance and so R^2 will inevitably increase. This means that, all things being equal, R^2 in models with lots of explanatory variables will be greater than the R^2 in models with few explanatory variables, even though the latter may have more real substance. At the extreme (degrees of freedom permitting) that might tempt us into **data mining** i.e. just adding in as many variables as possible without much consideration of their theoretical underpinnings. One way to correct for the 'size' of a model is to use $\bar{R}^2$ (the adjusted R^2). This is an adjustment using degrees of freedom as follows:

$$\bar{R}^2 = 1 - \left[(1 - R^2) \times \frac{n - 1}{n - k - 1}\right]$$

(5.4)

where k is the number of explanatory variables and n is the number of observations in the sample. This formula ensures that, in a model with many explanatory variables (and lots of slope parameters), the R^2 will be adjusted downwards accordingly; in this way $\bar{R}^2$ penalises the inclusion of 'trash' variables.

In the preceding chapters on simple regressions, we used either the relatively unwieldy method of running regressions using Excel or the *definitely unwieldy* method of running regressions by hand. But for multiple regression analysis it is quicker and easier to use tailor-made econometrics packages. With these packages, running a regression just involves typing a list of variable codes and clicking on a couple of buttons. The package automatically produces a table of estimation results together with a wide range of accompanying statistics that can be cut-and-pasted directly into your various documents. Another key advantage of such packages is the detail and sophistication of the econometric techniques embedded within them, including a wide range of diagnostic and corrective tools that are not available via spreadsheet packages.

In this chapter we introduce running regressions using the econometrics package EViews. With EViews, there are a number of data input options including typing the data in by hand, but the easiest method is probably to collect data in Excel and then cut and paste across into EViews. Running our estimation of Equation (5.3a) using EViews gives results as summarised in Table 5.1 – a summary of the EViews printout.

Table 5.1 Summary of EViews printout

Dependent Variable: Real house prices (logged)
Method: Least Squares
Sample: 1995Q1 2006Q1
Included observations: 45

Variable	Coefficient	Std. Error	t-Statistic	Prob.
Intercept	2.880	1.076	2.675	0.011
Mortgage lending (logged)	0.854	0.089	9.650	0.000
Mortgage rate	− 0.004	0.033	− 0.112	0.912
Q1	0.203	0.062	3.283	0.002
Q2	− 0.080	0.061	− 1.311	0.197
Q3	0.009	0.060	0.145	0.886
R-squared	0.86	F-statistic		47.74
Adjusted R-squared	0.84	Prob(F-statistic)		0.00
Sum Squared residuals	0.76			

You will notice that there is a lot of detail in this table. For the moment, we are just going to concentrate on the t tests, the adjusted R^2 (explained above) and some related statistics.[2] But the results from the estimation of the SRF can be summarised by the following equation:

$$\hat{h}_t = \underset{\substack{(1.076) \\ t = 2.675 \\ p = 0.011}}{2.880} \underset{\substack{(0.089) \\ t = 9.650 \\ 0.000}}{+0.854l} \underset{\substack{(0.033) \\ t = -0.112 \\ 0.912}}{-0.004r} \underset{\substack{(0.062) \\ t = 3.283 \\ 0.002}}{+0.203Q1} \underset{\substack{(0.061) \\ t = -1.311 \\ 0.197}}{-0.080Q2} \underset{\substack{(0.060) \\ t = 0.145 \\ 0.886}}{+0.009Q3}$$

$$(5.5)$$

Single hypothesis test

Here we will use a two-tailed t test to test the nulls that the parameter on the intercept is equal to zero, i.e.:

$H_0 : \alpha = 0$
$H_1 : \alpha \neq 0$

---

[2] You may also have noticed that the estimations are performed on logged variables because we wanted to estimate the elasticities (see Box 3.3). You can transform variables in EXCEL but it is also possible to transform your variables using the 'Quick – Generate Series' option from the EViews toolbar. See EViews 'Help' options for further instructions.

and for the slope parameters that each individual parameter on each explanatory variable is equal to zero, i.e.:

$$H_0 : \beta_1 = 0 \quad H_0 : \beta_2 = 0 \quad H_0 : \beta_3 = 0 \quad H_0 : \beta_4 = 0 \quad H_0 : \beta_5 = 0$$
$$H_1 : \beta_1 \neq 0 \quad H_1 : \beta_2 \neq 0 \quad H_1 : \beta_3 \neq 0 \quad H_1 : \beta_4 \neq 0 \quad H_1 : \beta_5 \neq 0$$

These hypotheses for the slope parameters can be summarised as:

$$H_0 : \beta_k = 0$$
$$H_1 : \beta_k \neq 0 \tag{5.6}$$

We have 39 degrees of freedom in our t test ($n - k - 1 = 45 - 5 - 1$) and from statistical tables we get the critical values for t at a 5% significance level of $t_{crit} \approx 2.02$. So our decision rule is:

if $|\hat{t}| > 2.02$, then reject H_0; if $|\hat{t}| < 2.02$ then do not reject H_0

A quicker alternative would be to use a decision rule based around the p values, as explained in Chapters 1 and 4. Our decision rule for a 5% significance level is:

if $p < 0.05$, then reject H_0; if $p > 0.05$ then do not reject H_0

This is equivalent to rejecting the null if $|\hat{t}| > t_{crit}(5\%)$.[3] Using these decision rules: for the intercept, mortgage lending and the winter dummy, we can reject H_0; for the parameters on the mortgage rate and the other seasonal dummies, we cannot reject H_0.

How do our statistical findings link with our theoretical analysis? For mortgage lending there is a positive and significant association: rising house prices are associated with rises in mortgage lending. This is consistent with the assertion that increases in mortgage lending will foster house price bubbles and conversely, that credit constraints will precipitate house price slumps. This may reflect the gearing and credit constraints explained in the theoretical section: higher volumes of lending allow owner-occupiers to gear-up their property purchases and this fuels rising house prices and house price bubbles. For mortgage rates, there is a negative association – as hypothesised but this is insignificantly different from zero at a 5% significance level (i.e. with a 95% confidence interval). This is consistent with our theoretical analysis to the extent that rising mortgage rates are associated with dampened demand for housing but the effect is not large.

As for the dummy variables, the parameter on Q1 is positive and significantly different from zero at a 5% significance level and this suggests that the

---

[3] We will use p value decision rules from now on because they are easier to use and p values are reported in most modern spreadsheet and econometrics packages including Excel and EViews.

mean house price in Q1 is significantly higher, at a 5% significance level, than the mean house price in the other quarters. For the other quarters, there are no significant differences in the group means.

Testing for a unitary elasticity

The t tests discussed above are testing the null hypothesis that mortgage financing has no effect on house prices. However, if we want to make more specific hypotheses about the magnitude of responses, we can adapt the hypotheses within our t tests. We have logged both the house price and mortgage lending variable so, as explained in Chapter 3, this means that our parameter on the mortgage lending variable is capturing the elasticity of house prices with respect to mortgage lending. It will capture the percentage increase in house prices associated with a percentage increase in mortgage lending. If we want to find out whether or not this is a **unitary elasticity** (an elasticity equal to one), i.e. whether or not a 1% rise in mortgage lending is associated with a proportional 1% rise in house prices, then we can test this using a one-tailed t test as follows:

$$H_0 : \beta_1 = 1$$
$$H_1 : \beta_1 < 1$$

$$\rightarrow \hat{t} = \frac{\hat{\beta} - 1}{se(\hat{\beta})} = \frac{0.854 - 1}{0.089} = -1.64 \tag{5.7}$$

For a one-tailed t test with a 5% significance level ($df = 39$), $t_{crit} \approx -1.68$. So we do not reject H_0 and conclude that whilst there is a significant association between house prices and mortgage lending the elasticity is insignificantly different from one. This suggests that there may be an elastic response of house prices to mortgage lending but the decision is marginal; note that with a different significance level, the inferences would be different, e.g. with a 10% significance level (i.e. a 90% confidence interval) $t_{crit} \approx -1.30$ and we would reject H_0. In this case, our inferences are sensitive to the significance level used. This underscores the fact that, in any interpretation of statistical results, the researcher must remember the trade-offs between Type I and Type II errors (as summarised in Chapter 1).

Goodness of fit

With MRA analysis our individual t tests, being single hypothesis tests, cannot give us information about the contribution of all our explanatory variables as a

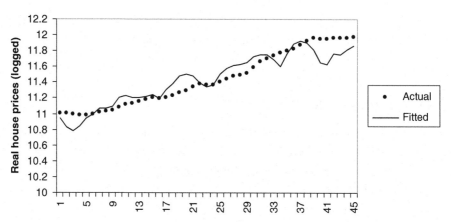

Figure 5.2   Actual vs. fitted values from estimation of Equation (5.3a)

group and so assessing goodness of fit becomes slightly more complicated. Also individual scatter plots of our dependent variable against each of our explanatory variables would be unwieldy and in any case would not control for the contribution of other explanatory variables. So in MRA it is more usual to get a visual impression about the 'fit' of our model by plotting actual (i.e. observed) values against our predicted or fitted values from the multiple regression model. Figure 5.2 shows the plot of actual versus fitted values for our SRF as summarised in Equation (5.3a).

This plot suggests a broad correspondence between observed and predicted house prices but there are a number of periods when our estimated model is consistently under-predicting or over-predicting house prices; we seem to have some systematic patterns in our residuals. This reflects a problem of **autocorrelation**. Exploring autocorrelation in depth is beyond the scope of this chapter.[4]

As for the goodness of fit, if we want an objective measure of goodness of fit in multiple regression analysis we use the $\bar{R}^2$ – **the adjusted R^2**. As explained in Box 5.3, $\bar{R}^2$ is weighted to take account of the number of explanatory variables in an empirical model, ensuring that a model with lots of explanatory variables does not necessarily give a better goodness of fit than a model with very few explanatory variables. Applying the formula for $\bar{R}^2$ from (5.3a) to our model gives:

---

[4] Autocorrelation is explained in detail in Chapter 7.

$$\bar{R}^2 = 1 - (1 - R^2) \times \frac{n-1}{n-k-1}$$

$$= 1 - \left[(1 - 0.86) \times \frac{45-1}{45-5-1} \right] = 0.84 \tag{5.8}$$

This is consistent with the $\bar{R}^2$ recorded underneath the ordinary R^2 in Table 5.1 – the EViews results table. It indicates that, after adjusting for the contribution of all the explanatory variables, about 84% of the variability in real house prices can be captured by the variability in the explanatory variables together.

Putting together the high adjusted R^2 and the fact that some of the slope parameters are significantly different from zero indicates that house prices and the various explanatory variables are varying together; there is *some* sort of statistical relationship between the variables.

But what if the researcher wants to find out if this overall relationship is significant? In this case, he/she will use the *F* test of overall explanatory power, as explained in Box 5.4. We can also test hypotheses about sub-groups of variables (in this case we will try the parameters on the dummy variables), using the **F test of restrictions**. This is also explained in Box 5.4.

Overall, our results do confirm that there is a significantly positive relationship between house prices and mortgage lending, though the impact of mortgage rates seems to be less important. There are however important caveats. The systematic pattern in the residuals, as noted above, may be a sign of potentially serious problems with the specification of our model.

There are some specific disadvantages of MRA that emerge because we are estimating more parameters than we would in a SRA. One problem, mentioned above, is imperfect multicollinearity. As explained above, imperfect multicollinearity occurs when the correlation coefficients are relatively high but less than 1 in absolute value terms. Imperfect multicollinearity is not a violation of a Gauss–Markov condition. Our OLS estimators will still be BLUE but the overall accuracy of estimation procedures will be compromised. OLS will give us definite results; but these results may not be very accurate because we will be estimating our parameters less precisely: the variances and standard errors of our parameter estimates will be higher, our confidence intervals will be wider and we will be more likely to retain a false H_0, i.e. we will be more prone to Type II errors.

A related problem is the problem of **(imperfect) micronumerosity**. Micronumerosity is the problem of having a relatively small number of degrees of freedom; for example if we have 10 observations and 6 explanatory

---

Box 5.4 Joint hypothesis tests

Building up from earlier discussions of F tests in Chapters 1 and 4, the **F test of explanatory power** can be conducted using the following null and alternative:

$$H_0 : \beta_1 = \beta_2 = \beta_3 = \beta_4 = \beta_5 = 0$$

H_1: At least one of the slope parameters is not equal to zero

   The F test of explanatory power (introduced in Chapters 1 and 4) tests the joint restrictions that all slope parameters are jointly equal to zero. The formula is used in this example as follows:

$$F(k, n - k - 1) = \frac{(R^2/k)}{(1 - R^2)/(n - k - 1)} = \frac{(0.860/5)}{(1 - 0.860)/(45 - 5 - 1)} = 47.91$$

$$(5.9)$$

where k is the number of explanatory variables and $n =$ number of observations. Broadly the same result is reported in Table 5.1 – EViews printout as the 'F-statistic', with its associated p value of 0.00 (discrepancies reflect rounding differences). Given that $p < 0.00$ we can reject H_0 at a 5% significance level and conclude that there is a significant association between house prices and all our explanatory variables, i.e. our model as a whole. The variability captured by our explanatory variables is a statistically significant proportion of total variability in our house price variable. We would come to the same conclusion if we looked up our critical value for the F statistic using statistical tables. From these tables (using a 5% significance level), $F_{crit}(5,39) \approx 2.45$. This is less than 47.91 so, again, we reject H_0.

The F test of restrictions

We can also use F tests to test sub-sets of restrictions, for example if we wanted to test the importance of groups of variables. The formula for the F test of restrictions is:

$$F(d, n - k_u - 1) = \frac{(RSS_r - RSS_u)/d}{RSS_u/(n - k_u - 1)} \tag{5.10}$$

where the subscripts r and u denote the restricted and unrestricted models respectively, k is the number of explanatory variables, n is the number of observations and d is the number of parameters restricted.

   To explain this formula intuitively: it is capturing changes in RSS – the residual sum of squares. When we 'restrict' a model, i.e. by imposing restrictions upon the estimates of parameters within our model, then our estimations are less likely to fit the real world neatly. Statistically, this translates into a fall in our goodness of fit and a rise in our residuals and thus an increase in the RSS. The F test of restrictions is designed to capture the relative size of this increase in RSS by comparing the RSS in the 'unrestricted' model with the RSS in the 'restricted' version; the restricted model will incorporate the null hypothesis about the parameter values.

Using the example in this chapter to illustrate, if we wanted to test that the seasonal influences were zero, i.e. that the constant factors were more or less the same for all quarters, we could use an F test of restrictions to compare the RSS_u (RSS from the unrestricted model with the seasonal dummies in) with the RSS_r (RSS from a restricted model with the dummies out). If the RSS increases by a significant amount when the dummies are ignored, then this suggests the dummies are important variables and should be left in. On the other hand if the increase in the RSS is insignificant when the dummies are ignored, then this suggests that the dummies do not add explanatory power and could be left out.

To illustrate, we will test a null that incorporates our restriction that the parameters on the dummies are jointly equal to zero i.e.:

$$H_0 : \beta_3 = \beta_4 = \beta_5 = 0$$

H_1: At least one of the parameters on the seasonal dummies is not equal to zero

When we impose the restriction that the parameters on the dummies are jointly equal to zero we will estimate a restricted model of the following form:

$$h_t = a + \beta_1 l_t + \beta_2 r_t + \varepsilon_t \tag{5.11}$$

Our unrestricted model, in which the parameters on the dummies can take whatever values fit the data best, is Equation (5.3a).

Estimating Equation (5.11) using EViews we get $RSS_r = 1.145$. We have already run Equation (5.3a) above and the RSS_u from this is recorded in Table 5.1 as 'Sum squared residuals' so $RSS_u = 0.762$. We have restricted three parameter values and so $d = 3$. Incorporating these numbers into our formula we calculate:

$$F(d, n - k_u - 1) = \frac{(RSS_r - RSS_u)/d}{(RSS_u)/(n - k_u - 1)} = \frac{(1.145 - 0.762)/3}{0.762/(45 - 5 - 1)} = 6.53 \tag{5.12}$$

In practice, EViews will do all the mathematical work for us. We can estimate the unrestricted model by using the EViews toolbar to click through 'View – Coefficient Tests – Redundant Variables', inputting Q1, Q2 and Q3 as our 'redundant variables'. Then EViews will show an output table with the estimated F together with its associated p value. The F will be more-or-less the same as the one calculated in Equation (5.12) (any small discrepancies will reflect rounding differences). So from EViews we get the p value from the F test in Equation (5.12), i.e. $p = 0.001$. So $p < 0.05$ and we can reject H_0. At a 5% significance level, the dummy variables as a group are contributing significant explanatory power to our model of house prices.

> This result implies that the residuals do increase markedly when the seasonal dummies are dropped: the increase in the RSS is relatively large when we impose the restriction that the parameters on the seasonal dummies are zero, and our *t* tests of individual significance suggest that this mainly reflects the influence of shifting house prices in Q1.

variables (6 slope parameters and 1 intercept parameter to estimate), then we will have only 3 degrees of freedom left (i.e. not many).[5] Imperfect micronumerosity has much the same consequences as imperfect multicollinearity: variances and standard errors are larger, confidence intervals are wider and our hypothesis testing is more prone to Type II errors.

Just as there is an extreme version of multicollinearity (perfect multicollinearity) so there is an extreme version of micronumerosity: **perfect micronumerosity**. This occurs when we have fewer observations than parameters to estimate and so we have no degrees of freedom. With perfect micronumerosity, as with perfect multicollinearity, there will be no solution using OLS estimation. Again our software will send us an error message to remind us to check our data set!

5.5   Implications and conclusions

It is important in any empirical analysis to state the limitations of the findings. This is just our first illustration of MRA and so we have kept it simple by focussing on just a sub-set of possible explanatory variables. We have also neglected the influence of lags and in the chapter exercises we make some suggestions about how to introduce lags into an empirical model. There may be other important variables, for example changes in disposable income, demographic factors, government policy etc. etc. Furthermore, findings for other countries and/or time periods might be different, reflecting institutional differences and structural changes.

An additional technical issue to keep in mind is that we haven't tested for violations of the Gauss–Markov assumptions outlined in Chapter 1. Until we have done these tests, we cannot be sure that our OLS estimations are giving reliable and accurate results. For this analysis, there *were* hints of a potential problem with our residuals when we plotted our actual versus fitted values

---

[5] Imperfect micronumerosity was a problem that we were facing with the necessarily elementary illustrations of simple regression analysis in Chapters 2–4.

(see Figure 5.2). How to detect and correct potential violations of Gauss–Markov assumptions is explained in more detail in the following chapters.

These caveats stated, overall the results from this chapter suggest that there was a significant positive association between mortgage lending and house prices in the UK over the period 1995 to 2006. We identified an elastic response with rises in mortgage rates matched by proportionate rises in house prices. The impact of seasonal changes also had an impact. On the other hand, the impact of fluctuations in mortgage rates was insignificant.

Overall, if these findings are robust, then there are some important policy implications. The fact that mortgage rates have an insignificant impact suggests that more emphasis could be placed on constraining lending excesses during boom periods in order to avoid credit crunches and housing crashes when those boom periods end. Financial deregulation during the 1980s means that mortgage lenders are now more 'self-regulating' than they were in the 1970s; but, as the 2007/8 sub-prime mortgage crisis has amply illustrated, private financial institutions do not always have the incentives or information to manage their lending policies prudently. Public institutions can play an important role in smoothing volatility.

In containing the UK credit crunch of 2007/8 for example, the Bank of England responded by providing facilities to swap risky mortgages for Treasury bonds, in this way injecting liquidity into the system. Regulatory authorities also have the potential to play a key role in the management of financial crises. The UK's Financial Services Authority (FSA) – a non-governmental institution given statutory powers to regulate the financial services industry including mortgage lenders via the *Financial Services and Markets Act 2000* – responded to the 2007 Northern Rock banking run by recognising that the UK's deposit protection policies were inadequate and had the potential to trigger banking runs. So the FSA focussed on devising a robust system of deposit insurance to sustain public confidence in the banking system. These examples illustrate that a combination of more prudent mortgage lending and a more effective monetary policy institutional framework are important in moderating boom–bust cycles in the future.

5.6   Further reading

Academic articles and working papers

Baddeley, M. C. (2005) 'Housing bubbles, herds and frenzies: Evidence from British Housing Markets', *CCEPP Policy Brief No. 02–05*, Cambridge Centre for Economic and Public Policy, Cambridge, UK. See www.landecon.cam.ac.uk/

Helbling, T. F. (2005) 'House price bubbles – a tale based on housing price booms and busts', *BIS Papers No. 21 – Real Estate Indicators and Financial Stability*, Bank for International Settlements, 30–41.

Minsky, H. P. (1964) 'Longer waves in financial relations: financial factors in the more severe depressions', *American Economic Review*, vol. 54, no. 3, 324–35.

Muellbauer, J. and Murphy, A. (1997) 'Booms and busts in the UK housing market', *Economic Journal*, vol. 107, no. 445, 1701–27.

Oswald, A. J. (1997) 'The missing piece of the unemployment puzzle', Inaugural Lecture, University of Warwick.

Wood, R. (2005) 'A comparison of UK residential house price indices', *BIS Papers No. 21 – Real Estate Indicators and Financial Stability*, Bank for International Settlements, 212–27.

Policy reports and newspaper articles

Andre, C., Catte, P., Girouard, N. and Price, R. (2004) 'Housing markets, wealth and the business cycle', *OECD Economics Department Working Papers*, No. 394, Paris: OECD Publishing.

The Economist (2005) 'The global housing boom: in come the waves', 16 June 2005.

Financial Times (2004) 'Every house price index tells its own story', 30 June 2004.

5.7   Chapter exercises

1. For the model in this chapter, we have implicitly assumed that mortgage lending and mortgage rates have immediate impacts on house prices. Using the data from the websites mentioned in the data section, assess this assumption as follows:

   (a) Adapting Equation (5.2), estimate a model of house prices that also includes lags (of up to 4 quarters) on mortgage rates and mortgage lending.

   (b) Using t tests and p values, statistically assess the individual significance of the parameter estimates.

   (c) Use an F test of restrictions, assess whether or not lags on the explanatory variables are jointly associated with fluctuations in house prices.

2. Housing demand is affected by the cost of housing. In this chapter, we have assessed one aspect of housing costs, i.e. borrowing costs as measured by mortgage rates, but personal incomes will also be important.

   (a) Using the ONS website (www.statistics.gov.uk) collect data on personal disposable income (PDI).

   (b) Incorporate current and lagged PDI (in logged form) into an extension of the house price model estimated in this chapter.

   (c) Assess the statistical significance of logged PDI using t tests and F tests.

   (d) Interpret your findings. What are the policy implications?

Heteroscedasticity

R&D, invention and innovation

Economic issues include:
- Invention versus innovation
- Role of technology

Econometric issues include:
- Homoscedasticity and heteroscedasticity
- Heteroscedasticity tests: the Goldfield–Quandt test, White's test
- Weighted Least Squares (WLS)

Data issues include:
- Measuring innovation and knowledge: an innovativeness index
- Working with outliers

6.1 The issue

Innovation is essential for economic growth and development, whether for countries that are technological leaders at the frontier of knowledge or for countries that are 'latecomers', catching up on technical advances made elsewhere. Globalisation has interacted with rapid technological change and trade has become increasingly open and competitive, transport costs have fallen, and capital and labour have become more and more mobile. International competitive pressures have become more pronounced and all countries, rich and poor, have had to innovate constantly.

Innovation can also involve finding new ways to do the same old things – for example in introducing new processes that can reduce the price and/or raise the quality of traditional products – such as wine. Overall, being innovative is important everywhere; it has important implications for developing countries as well as developed ones (UNCTAD, 2007); it is as important to individual firms as it is to nations as a whole. It is also important to individual people – we need to keep investing in and refreshing our personal human capital; in modern economies for example, there are many good reasons (social as well as professional) to be computer literate, i.e. to 'invest' in our human computing capital.

In this chapter we will analyse the relationships between inputs into the innovative process (measured as R&D expenditure) and outputs (measured as number of patents) across a sample of countries. We will illustrate that, in getting accurate statistical information about the relationship between these inputs and outputs, we have to account for the specific econometric problem of **heteroscedasticity**.

6.2   The theory

What is the difference between invention and innovation? Invention is about new ideas and technologies; innovation is about turning those new technologies into products and processes, i.e. it is about introducing new inventions into production. So invention is just the first stage in a long process. Figure 6.1 illustrates the pyramid of activities that mark progress from invention to innovation: invention is at the top of the pyramid (there can be no innovation without some inventions to precede it); the next segment of Figure 6.1 illustrates that inventions are then improved in a way that will boost productivity and competitiveness; then, as shown in the next segment, new technologies are adapted to fit in with existing productive processes; the final segment of the pyramid illustrates the final stage in which workers and managers are trained to use these new technologies in their everyday activities.

The nature of invention and innovation can vary immensely according to its function and according to the capabilities and capacities that are required to do it. Countries (and firms) that are more innovative will have a better economic performance than those that are not: they will be quicker to pick up the latest technologies; they will be faster to bring new products to the market; they will be more competitive; and they will gain market share. Linked with these benefits should be sustainable job creation and increased economic growth. But before any of this can start, a country or a firm must decide to devote resources to the innovative process and this is where research and development (R&D) comes in. R&D is not the only element in the innovative process, but it is an essential one. Also, R&D expenditure is the most widely available and best-developed statistical indicator of inputs into the process of innovation activities. According to international guidelines, R&D comprises creative work

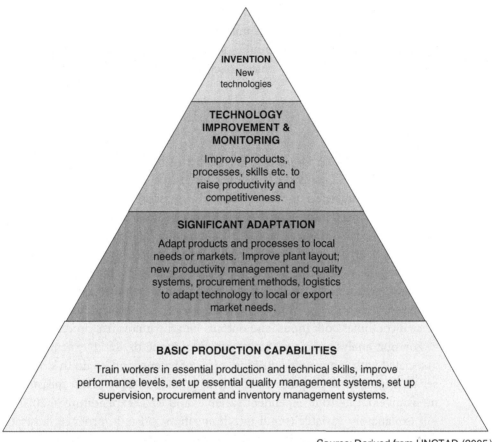

Source: Derived from UNCTAD (2005).

Figure 6.1   Invention vs. innovation: the pyramid of innovative activities

undertaken systematically to increase the stock of knowledge and used for devising new processes (OECD, 2002). It includes basic research – research that advances scientific knowledge but has no specific immediate commercial applications; applied research – which has specific commercial objectives with respect to products, processes or services; and finally development – which involves systematically applying research knowledge to the production of prototype goods and services, new materials, and new methods, etc.

The theory tested in this chapter is that investing more in R&D increases a country's innovativeness. Whilst we are not focussing specifically on the relationship between R&D, innovation and economic growth, our findings will have implications for the economic growth because R&D will contribute to innovation and innovation boosts economic growth. Here we will focus on this very first stage of the innovative process by asking: How can we boost a country's performance in terms of innovation? What is the relationship between inputs and outputs into the innovative process? Framing the questions in this way will give us some hooks onto which policy initiatives can eventually be attached.

6.3   The data

How can we measure innovation? A number of benchmarking exercises have been carried out, as many countries are concerned about their innovation capacities and performance. For example, Box 6.1 summarises proxies for both inputs and outputs used by Innovation Policy in Europe in its calculation of the Summary Innovation Index (SII) (see Figure 6.2), a measure of the relative innovativeness of a sample of countries over time. Other widely used measures include the Technological Activity Index (TAI) and the Human Capital Index (HCI).

The SII gives a useful picture of innovation for a selection of countries but it is not a widely available or widely tested measure of innovation across all nations. Also, it combines both inputs and outputs into the innovative process.

For our analysis we will assess whether input of R&D expenditure is associated with innovative output in terms of patents and, to do this, we will separate inputs and outputs, using patents granted in 2001 as our measure of innovative output (our dependent variable) and R&D expenditure in 2000 as our explanatory variable (input into innovation). Also, in order to illustrate the problem of heteroscedasticity (the econometric focus in this chapter) we will use two measures of R&D: total R&D expenditure and R&D intensity (i.e. R&D as a proportion of GDP).

The sources for these data are as follows:

Variable	Source	Website
Number of patents	US Patents Office	www.uspto.gov/
Real R&D expenditure	OECD (2004) *Science and Technology Industry Outlook*	www.oecd.org

As discussed in previous chapters, it is important to state from the outset any potential problems with our data. Firstly, data on these issues is not yet widely published and so we have a cross-sectional data set that includes only 29 observations: this will generate two potential problems: sampling bias (a problem introduced in Chapter 4) and imperfect micronumerosity (explained in Chapter 5). Unfortunately we cannot do much about these problems

---

> **Box 6.1** Mirror mirror on the wall, who is most innovative of all …
>
> The Summary Innovation Index (SII) is an index of innovative activity and has been calculated for a range of countries. This index has been constructed using the following indicators of innovation:
>
> 1. **Human resources**
>   (a) Science and engineering graduates (% of 20–29 years age cohort)
>   (b) Population with tertiary education
>   (c) Participation in life-long learning
>   (d) Employment in medium-tech and high-tech manufacturing
>   (e) Employment in high-tech services
> 2. **Knowledge creation**
>   (a) Public R&D expenditures
>   (b) Business expenditures on R&D as % GDP
>   (c) European Patent Office high-tech and general patent applications
>   (d) United States Patent Office high-tech and general patent applications
> 3. **Transmission and application of knowledge**
>   (a) Small and medium sized enterprises (SMEs) innovating in-house (% of all SMEs)
>   (b) SMEs involved in innovation co-operation
>   (c) Innovation expenditures (% of total turnover)
>   (d) SMEs using non-technological change
> 4. **Innovation finance, output and markets**
>   (a) Share of high-tech venture capital investment
>   (b) Share of early stage venture capital in GDP
>   (c) Sales of 'new to market' products
>   (d) Sales of 'new to the firm but not new to the market' products
>   (e) ICT expenditures (% of GDP)
>   (f) Share of manufacturing value-added in high-tech sectors
>
> As Figure 6.2 shows, according to the SII, Sweden and Finland remain the innovation leaders within the European Union, ranking below Japan and above the United States in terms of global innovation levels.

because the data just isn't there (yet). But we should be careful to interpret our findings cautiously and hope that future studies (based on improved data) will confirm our findings.

There are some more specific data problems too. For innovative output, patent data is not a perfect measure, not least because many innovations are not patented. In addition, knowledge can be created and transferred tacitly, in which case there will be no tangible measure of it. Also, some countries are

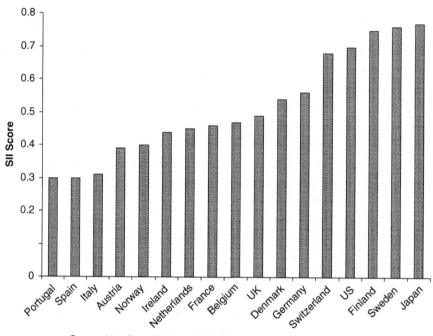

Source: http://trendchart.cordis.lu/scoreboards/scoreboard2004/indicators.cfma

Figure 6.2   Summary Innovation Index, 2004

new to the patent process and so will not put the same emphasis on patenting their innovations as countries that are not necessarily more innovative in real terms. Patenting is a costly exercise, and some countries may do less of it than others because of the administrative or legal costs involved. Finally, we can measure only the number of patents taken, not their value, either in terms of potential revenue streams, or in terms of their contribution to knowledge and innovation. Much valuable R&D that is conducted in the public sector, in universities and R&D institutions, is not patented; sometimes because it does not have a ready business application, although it may contribute to many subsequent valuable applications. In some countries, individuals working in university labs or faculties are not allowed to patent their work. Nonetheless, patents are one of the most frequently used measures of innovation mainly because the data are readily available.

For R&D expenditure – it is the most frequently used measure of inputs into the innovation process but many developing countries may not collect or publish R&D data and, even if they do, the information may be outdated. Not all countries use the same definitions of R&D; and in some countries, firms have tax incentives to report activities as R&D when perhaps, under other circumstances, they would not be defined as such. For the purposes of industrial innovation and activities that are likely to result in patents, an important measure is likely to be Business Enterprise R&D (BERD), but data on this component of R&D is scarce so we use total R&D as a proxy.

6.4   Empirical results and interpretation

As explained above, we will be investigating the link between inputs into the innovative process (R&D expenditure) and innovative output (measured as number of patents) using 2000 and 2001 data. We might expect to find that higher levels of R&D expenditure in 2000 will result in larger numbers of patents in 2001. To assess this assertion we investigate the following model:

$$Y_{i,t} = \alpha + \beta X_{i,t-1} + \varepsilon_{i,t} \tag{6.1}$$

where Y = number of patents granted for country i in year t, and X = general expenditure on R&D for country i in year $t-1$, and ε_i is the random error term.
  The SRF will be:

$$Y_{i,t} = \hat{\alpha} + \hat{\beta} X_{i,t-1} + \hat{\varepsilon}_{i,t} \tag{6.2}$$

The explanatory variable X is lagged because investing inputs of R&D expenditure will not immediately generate patents; the lag is included in the recognition that the process will take time.
  Our basic hypotheses will be that there is a significant association between R&D and patents granted in the following year:

$H_0 : \beta = 0$

$H_1 : \beta \neq 0$

Table 6.1 shows the results from estimating the SRF using a cross-section of 29 countries with 2001 data on patents and 2000 data on R&D. From Table 6.1, these results can be summarised as follows:

$$
\begin{aligned}
\hat{Y}_i = \quad &-826.23 \qquad\quad 0.31X \\
&(358.24) \qquad\quad (0.01) \\
&t = -2.31 \qquad\quad t = 42.42 \\
&p = 0.03 \qquad\quad\, p = 0.00 \\[4pt]
&R^2 = 0.99
\end{aligned}
\tag{6.3}
$$

(Standard errors in brackets)

Table 6.1 EViews output table: OLS regression

Dependent Variable: Number of patents
Method: Least Squares
Sample: 1 29

Variable	Coefficient	Std. Error	t-Statistic	Prob.
Intercept	−826.23	358.24	−2.31	0.03
General expenditure on R&D	0.31	0.01	42.42	0.00
R-Squared	0.99	Mean dependent variable		4800.00
Sum squared residuals	86712468.00	F-statistic		1799.31
		Prob(F-statistic)		0.00

These results suggest a positive and significant (at 5%) association between patents granted and R&D expenditure: with a p value of 0.00 on our t test, we can reject our null that the parameter on R&D is insignificantly different from zero at a 5% significance level.

This is confirmed by our R^2 of 0.99 which suggests that 99% of the variability in patents granted is captured by variability in R&D expenditure. The F test of explanatory power (the F-statistic in the output table) also suggests a positive and highly significant relationship. So on first inspection our results look good (suspiciously good in fact!) but are they reliable?

The problem of heteroscedasticity

When we run a regression we need to think about whether or not the Gauss–Markov assumptions (outlined in Chapter 1) have been satisfied. In a full analysis of an empirical model, it is important to assess a range of potential violations of the Gauss–Markov assumptions but one of the aims of this book is to explain tests and techniques one at a time, with one problem as the focus of each chapter. For this chapter we will investigate **heteroscedasticity**.

Heteroscedasticity is an extremely common problem in applied econometrics. It is particularly characteristic of cross-sectional data, but can also occur in time-series data. Heteroscedasticity literally refers to 'differently dispersed' errors, and as such it violates one of the Gauss–Markov assumptions introduced in Chapter 1. Specifically, it violates the assumption of **homoscedasticity** i.e. that errors are 'similarly dispersed'. As explained in Chapter 1, OLS estimates are only BLUE if the error term is **homoscedastic** i.e. if $var(\varepsilon_i) = \sigma^2$ where σ^2 is a constant. This constancy of variance means that if we were to take repeated samples of data, the error variance for each observation would be the same as the error variance for all the other observations. This is difficult to conceptualise in economics because we usually have only one sample of data and it may be difficult to see how we can infer anything at all about the error variance for each observation if we have just one set of observations. One way to conceptualise homoscedasticity is to think about the conditional value of the error variance, i.e. ε_i 'conditioned' on a particular value of X. With homoscedasticity, we would not expect the error variance to vary systematically with our explanatory variables, i.e. the conditional variance should be constant across all realisations of X, i.e. $\text{var}(\varepsilon_i \mid X_i) = \sigma^2$. If we violate this assumption of homoscedasticity then we will have a heteroscedastic error term i.e. $\text{var}(\varepsilon_i \mid X_i) = \sigma_i^2$ – the conditional variance of the error term will vary across observations as our explanatory variable varies.[1]

In a sample context, homoscedasticity requires that the **residual variance** be constant across all observations in the sample, i.e. it should not vary as X varies. As explained in Chapter 1, variance is a measure of spread and is calculated by squaring deviations from means. The expected value of a residual is zero so the residual variance can be calculated just by squaring the residuals, adding them together and dividing by the degrees of freedom, as explained in Chapter 1. In a sample context, the actual value of the residual can be positive, or negative, relatively close to 0 and relatively far from 0, but the point is that it should be random; the residual and residual variance should not be systematically associated with the explanatory variable X. We do not want the spread of residuals to increase as X increases.

This can be explained intuitively using an example. If we are analysing consumption and expenditure patterns across households, then it is likely that we will find a greater dispersion of the kinds of choices made by wealthy households compared to poor households. When incomes are low, there can be little room for discretion on how to allocate one's money: we pay the rent, buy food and other essentials. Most other poor households do exactly the same. By comparison, rich households can exercise more choice over how to allocate their money: choosing between spending on holidays, original art, second homes, or various forms of savings and investments. The variability of choices made by rich households will be much larger than poorer households.

---

[1] This is also related to the problem of endogeneity – the problem that occurs when there is a systematic association between the error and one of the explanatory variables. This problem is beyond the scope of this chapter but endogeneity is briefly explained in Chapter 1 and explored in more detail in Chapter 8.

This will show up in a regression as a larger residual for observations on rich households than for observations on poor households.

Consequences of heteroscedasticity

With heteroscedasticity, our OLS parameter estimates will remain unbiased and consistent (as long as no other Gauss–Markov assumptions are violated) but they will not be minimum variance and other estimation methods will be needed to give us efficient parameter estimates – with smaller variances and narrower confidence intervals. In addition, the usual OLS formulae for variances and standard errors will be biased in the presence of heteroscedasticity and if we want to ensure that our hypothesis tests are correctly calculated, then we will have to use formulae for variances and standard errors that are adjusted to allow for heteroscedastic errors.

Most estimation packages (including EViews) will report **heteroscedasticity-robust standard errors** for the parameter estimates and so, with large samples of data, OLS may give accurate estimates and inferences as long as hypothesis tests are constructed using these robust standard errors (and as long as the heteroscedasticity isn't just a symptom of a more serious problem such as model misspecification). It is important to remember that the default option for calculation of the variances in EViews assumes homoscedasticity but it is easy to get results that include the robust standard errors by ticking the option for 'Heteroskedasticity Consistent Coefficient Covariance' in the EViews 'Equation Estimation' window.

What are the potential implications of heteroscedasticity for our analysis of innovation? Large economies will inevitably have larger absolute magnitudes of R&D expenditure. So as R&D expenditure is incorporated in absolute terms into our regression of (6.2), we may be picking-up systematic differences in R&D expenditure rather than a robust association between R&D and patents. Our residual variance may be varying systematically reflecting this. It is also possible that large or rich countries will have different patenting behaviours than small or poor countries. For example, it could be that rich countries have developed the infrastructure to specialise in R&D; economies of scale and scope may enable them to produce more patents per unit of R&D expenditure than poorer countries (even when R&D is measured in relative terms e.g. as a proportion of GDP). R&D may be more diversified in richer countries because their industrial structure has been adapted to R&D activities, particularly if large companies are trying to sustain monopoly advantages. Barriers to entry may prevent poor countries from using R&D expenditure to produce patentable inventions and innovations. In this case, our regression results may be distorted by the exceptional patent production of the richest countries, and our residual variance may be varying systematically reflecting these influences.

Diagnosing heteroscedasticity

Before we can use our OLS results to justify increased public or private R&D expenditure, we need to check whether or not our errors are heteroscedastic. How do we do this? As explained above, if our error variance is conditional upon the value of our explanatory variables, then we will have an heteroscedastic error term. So in a sample context, methods for detecting heteroscedasticity often focus on identifying systematic associations between the residual variance and the explanatory variables, including visual inspection and **diagnostic tests** – i.e. tests to diagnose specific violations of Gauss–Markov assumptions.

Visual inspection

The first and easiest thing to do is to inspect our data to look for systematic patterns in our residuals and residual variance. Figure 6.3 shows patents by country, ranked according to R&D expenditure; there is a clear non-linear relationship suggesting an exponential relationship between patents and R&D expenditure. In particular, Figure 6.3 shows extremely large patent outputs for the top R&D spenders i.e. for Sweden and the former G7 countries (USA,

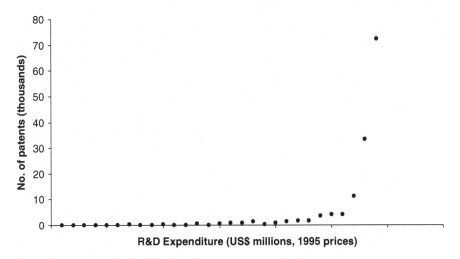

Figure 6.3   Patents by country, ranked by R&D expenditure

Japan, Germany, France, the UK, Canada and Italy).[2] These observations may distort our residual variance, particularly if we run a regression without controlling for units of measurement. In addition, these last eight observations are not particularly representative of the whole sample and yet could be influential observations given our small sample size of 29 observations. In particular, we would be concerned about the last two observations (which are for Japan and the USA) because they are quite clearly **outliers** – i.e. extreme observations. Given this asymmetry in our data set, we would not be surprised to see our residual variance rising for observations on countries with particularly large R&D expenditures.

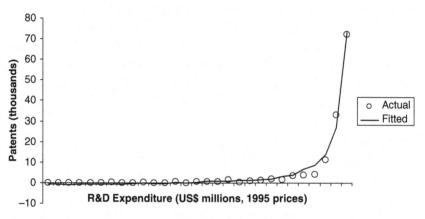

Figure 6.4   Actual and fitted values from estimation of Equation (6.2)

We can also look at the plots of actual versus fitted values because the spread of observed values around the fitted line will give us a visual impression of the residual variance and so will capture the accuracy of our estimation. Figure 6.4 shows the plot of actual and fitted values from the estimation of Equation (6.2). On first inspection, there does seem to be a good fit but it is difficult to see what's happening for the more average countries in the sample; in fact, for some countries in our sample, our initial model is generating negative fitted values for patents, which is a ridiculous result. So what's happening in this plot? One of the problems with our initial model is that, because we have not (yet!) weighted or transformed our variables, we are not getting a clear impression of the patterns for countries with relatively low levels of R&D expenditure: the absolute magnitude of the residuals for these observations is small when plotted on a scale that captures the very large number of patents produced by the countries with very large number of

[2] Unfortunately, data is not available for Russia so we cannot include all the G8 economies.

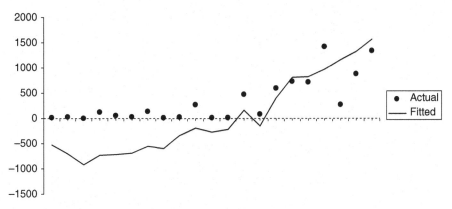

Figure 6.5   Actual vs. fitted values from Equation (6.2) for observations 1–20

patents (and high levels of R&D expenditure). So it is difficult to infer what might be happening with the residual variance for the smaller economies.

To give a clearer impression, in Figure 6.5 we have plotted the actual and fitted values just for the more representative countries (excluding the eight countries with the very highest patents output) to illustrate how the unadjusted inclusion of these eight extreme observations is distorting the predicted values for patents for countries with more average R&D expenditure (i.e. most of the countries in our sample).

This figure suggests that the accuracy of the patent estimates as captured by the fitted line is limited for the smaller countries but for most of the big R&D spenders the accuracy of the estimation improves: there is a clear systematic pattern and from this we could infer that the residual variance is not constant. Our visual inspection of this data suggests that we cannot assume that our errors are homoscedastic.

Diagnostic tests

Above we have shown a fairly clear pattern of heteroscedasticity in our plots of actual and fitted values. But patterns of heteroscedasticity are not always so easy to detect via visual inspection and so it is always a good idea to conduct some diagnostic tests. EViews (and most other econometrics packages) will report tests specifically designed to detect heteroscedasticity. There are many tests for heteroscedasticity and they revolve around identifying a systematic association between the residual variance and the explanatory variable(s). Here we will focus on just two tests: the Goldfeld–Quandt test and White's test.

The **Goldfeld–Quandt (GQ) test** can be used when one, rather than several, of the explanatory variables is suspected as the heteroscedasticity culprit. In multiple regression analysis, conducting the GQ test would involve constructing a new test for each explanatory variable but here our task will be relatively straightforward because we have only one explanatory variable – R&D expenditure. The intuition underlying the GQ test is that if the residual variance is changing as the explanatory variable changes, then we would expect to see a residual sum of squares (RSS) from the 'top' end of the sample (i.e. with the high values on X) that is significantly different from the RSS at the bottom end. So the GQ test involves calculating the ratio of the RSSs.

The GQ test tests the following null and alternative hypotheses:

H_0: $\mathrm{var}(\varepsilon_i \mid X_i) = \sigma^2$ i.e. a homoscedastic error

H_1: $\mathrm{var}(\varepsilon_i \mid X_i) = \sigma_i^2$ i.e. a heteroscedastic error

The construction of the GQ test involves the following stages:

Step One: Rank the raw data according to ascending values of X.

Step Two: Cut out a number of the central observations, breaking the data set into two distinct sets: one with low values of X and one with high values. One of the problems with the GQ test is that there is no clear rule about how many observations to delete and this means that there will always be an element of subjectivity to the GQ test. The general advice is to delete around 10–20% of observations – e.g. delete 4 observations for a sample size of 30 and delete 10 observations for a sample size of 60.

Step Three: Run the regression for the first set of observations, to obtain RSS_1.

Step Four: Run the regression for the second set of observations, to obtain RSS_2.

Step Five: Calculate the F ratio of RSSs as follows:

$$F(n_1 - k - 1, n_2 - k - 1) = \frac{RSS_1/(n_1 - k - 1)}{RSS_2/(n_2 - k - 1)} \tag{6.4}$$

In deciding how to split our sample, we have followed Thomas (1997) in deleting 4 central observations from our sample size of approximately 30 observations (Thomas 1997, p. 287). We will also incorporate an asymmetric split because our plot of actual versus fitted values indicates that the pattern changes for our eight top R&D spenders and we want to see how the residual variance differs for these top eight observations. So we will calculate RSS_1 from a regression on the first 17 observations, delete the next 4 observations and then calculate RSS_2 from a regression on the last 8 observations.

Running the regressions on observations 1 to 17 gives $RSS_1 = 65666650$; running another regression on observations 22 to 29 gives $RSS_2 = 9129452$ so we calculate the F test as follows:

$$F(n_1 - k - 1, n_2 - k - 1) = \frac{RSS_1/(n_1 - k - 1)}{RSS_2/(n_2 - k - 1)}$$

$$\rightarrow F(15, 6) = \frac{65666650/15}{9129452/6} = 2.88$$

(6.5)

From statistical tables, $F_{\text{crit, 5%}}(15,6) \approx 2.79$ and so we reject the null and, on the evidence of the GQ test, conclude that there is significant evidence of heteroscedasticity at a 5% significance level.

We have rejected the null of homoscedasticity but with only a narrow margin. This may reflect the fact that the GQ test is not a powerful test (it has a relatively high probability of Type II error, i.e. of falsely retaining the null of homoscedasticity). This lack of power may emerge because, by deleting central observations, we are losing degrees of freedom and therefore potentially valuable information. There are other problems with the GQ test: the intuition underlying the deletion of the central observations is that it will accentuate the differences in the RSSs but there are no clear rules about how many central observations to delete and this introduces an element of subjectivity into the GQ test. Also, the GQ is sensitive to differences in the way the sample is split (this problem is illustrated in the chapter exercises). Also, in a multiple regression context, the test would have to be run a number of times using each explanatory variable. Finally, it is important to remember always to put the larger residual variance in the numerator otherwise the test will have no power at all! (If we calculate the GQ test the wrong way round then F will always be less than 1; always less than the relevant critical value and so the null of homoscedasticity would be retained even for very large and systematic changes in the residual variance.)

Luckily, there are newer and more powerful heteroscedasticity tests, for example **White's test**. The intuition underlying White's test is much the same as the basic intuition underlying the GQ test: it focusses on identifying systematic patterns between the residual variance, the explanatory variable(s) and the square of the explanatory variable(s). It is relatively straightforward to perform and one variant can be constructed as follows:

1. Save $\hat{\varepsilon}_i$ i.e. the residuals from the initial SRF (Equation (6.2)).
2. Square the explanatory variable.
3. Run an **auxiliary regression** (i.e. a regression using output from the estimation of the SRF) by regressing the squared residuals on the level and square of the explanatory variable:

$$\hat{\varepsilon}_i^2 = \phi + \gamma_1 X_i + \gamma_2 X_i^2 \qquad (6.6)$$

where $\hat{\varepsilon}_i^2$ is the squared residual for each observation i, ϕ is the intercept for the auxiliary regression and γ_1 and γ_2 are the parameters on the explanatory variable and its square.

4. Conduct an F test of explanatory power to give White's test statistic.
5. If $F > F_{\text{crit}}$ then reject the null of homoscedasticity, i.e. reject H_0: $\text{var}(\varepsilon_i \mid X_i) = \sigma^2$.

The intuition underlying this procedure is that if there is a systematic association between the residual variance and X, then the R^2 from this auxiliary regression will be relatively high.

White's test has a number of advantages over the GQ test, most of which centre around the fact that less subjectivity is involved in the testing procedure: there is no room for error in selecting an explanatory variable to capture the heteroscedasticity because all explanatory variables are included (degrees of freedom permitting); and there are no decisions to be made about how many central observations to exclude. All information is used which makes it, *ceteris paribus*, a more powerful test than the GQ test.

It has the added practical advantage that it is calculated automatically by EViews. For our example, see Table 6.2 for the EViews output table which

Table 6.2 EViews output table: White's heteroscedasticity test

White's Heteroscedasticity Test:

F-statistic	43.48	Probability	0.00
Obs*R-squared	22.33	Probability	0.00

Test Equation:
Dependent Variable: RESID^2 (= squared residuals)
Method: Least Squares
Sample: 1 29

Variable	Coefficient	Std.Error	t-Statistic	Prob.
Intercept	−1986402.00	967760.60	−2.05	0.05
R&D expenditure	583.79	62.90	9.28	0.00
R&D expenditure squared	0.00	0.00	−8.68	0.00

records White's F test and its associated p value: because $p < 0.05$ we can reject H_0 at a 5% significance level (and at much lower significance levels too). Thus White's test result suggests that there is strongly significant evidence of heteroscedasticity for our initial estimation, a result that is consistent with the GQ test and our visual inspection of actual versus fitted values.

Remedial measures

Visual inspections of the data and both the GQ and White's tests have indicated a problem with heteroscedastic errors for our estimation of (6.2). So our initial OLS results will not be giving us the most accurate impression of the relationship between patents and R&D expenditure. Heteroscedasticity means that our OLS estimators are no longer efficient, which undermines the usual hypothesis-testing procedures. What can we do about it? Luckily there is a range of possible solutions though a process of trial and error is often needed in identifying the best solution. Some potential solutions are outlined in Box 6.2.

Box 6.2 Correcting heteroscedasticity

Heteroscedasticity can emerge for a number of reasons and, in the context of a sample, identifying a solution often involves a process of trial and error. For regressions of linear models, one quick and simple approach is to transform the data into logs, because this compresses the scales in which variables are measured. For example if we had used levels data: the raw value of real USA expenditure on R&D in 2000 at US$243,271 million is more than a thousand times larger than the US$207 million spent by Iceland. When transformed to natural logs the differences between them are sharply compressed to 12.4 (United States) and 5.33 (Iceland). Estimating log-log models may also have theoretical plausibility if we want estimates of unit-free elasticities to capture the percentage changes in Y associated with a given percentage change in X. (Elasticities and log-log models were introduced in Chapter 3.)

If heteroscedasticity is a symptom of the influence of an outlier or small groups of outliers then, given the central limit theorem (discussed in Chapter 1), the problem may become unimportant in large samples. Note from above that OLS is still consistent in large samples even though it is inefficient (but unbiased) in small samples. So we may be able to reduce the problem by increasing our sample size. We could also delete the outlier observations but this would involve a loss of degrees of freedom. It will also involve a willing abandonment of potentially important information: those apparent outliers may in fact give some important clues about our empirical model.

If justifiable in terms of the relevant economic theory, we can transform our model and 'normalise' the data to minimise the likelihood of heteroscedasticity; for example we could transform data by expressing data per capita or as a proportion of GDP. This sort of informal weighting process can also eliminate outliers without abandoning observations.

Alternatively, we can use more rigorous estimation procedures specifically designed to 'homogenise' our sample variance. If we had information about the error variance from the relevant population, then we could use **weighted least squares** (WLS) a type of **generalised least squares** (GLS) procedure.[3] In the rare case when we know exactly the underlying error variance, we can use this information in transforming our model. To illustrate this, we start with the following model:

$$Y_i = a + \beta X_i + u_i \tag{6.7}$$

Let's pretend that we know that the error variance (conditional on the value of X_i) takes the following form:

$$Var(u_i \mid X_i) = \sigma^2 X_i^2 \text{ where } \sigma^2 \text{ is constant} \tag{6.8}$$

Then we can divide both sides of (6.7) by X_i to give:

$$Y_i/X_i = (a/X_i) + \beta(X_i/X_i) + (u_i/X_i) = a\left(\frac{1}{X_i}\right) + \beta + \varepsilon_i \tag{6.9}$$

Notice that the error in (6.9) has been transformed into $\varepsilon_i = \dfrac{u_i}{X_i}$.

Next we must assume that our explanatory variable is **non-stochastic** for a given observation i (i.e. even though the explanatory variable must vary *within* a sample, the value of each *individual* observation on the explanatory variable will be a constant *across* samples). This means that the value of X will be fixed for each observation i. This is difficult to conceptualise with only one sample of data but it means that the X values be fixed *across* all samples; if this is true, then the value of X for each *individual* observation i, will be a constant and so we can take X_i outside the variance expression, squaring it as we go (following the mathematical rules of variance). So the variance of ε_i becomes:

$$\text{var}(\varepsilon_i) = \text{var}\left(\frac{u_i}{X_i}\right) = \frac{1}{X_i^2}\text{var}(u_i) \tag{6.10}$$

From Equation (6.8), we incorporate the expression for var(u_i) as follows:

$$\text{var}(\varepsilon_i) = \frac{\text{var}(u_i)}{X_i^2} = \frac{\sigma^2 \times X_i^2}{X_i^2} = \sigma^2 \tag{6.11}$$

and so ε_i is equal to the constant σ^2: it is homoscedastic.

---

[3] The WLS models that we show illustrate just one example of how the basic principle of least squares (i.e. of minimising the sum of squared residuals) can be generalised; another is shown in the following chapter – on autocorrelation.

Our WLS estimation will give accurate and reliable estimates (provided all the other Gauss–Markov assumptions are satisfied too) and WLS will be a BLUE estimation technique. This illustrates that sometimes (not always!) when Gauss–Markov assumptions are violated, the least squares principle can be adapted to give GLS estimators; these estimators will be consistent and efficient even when OLS is not.

So, in theory at least (and given our assumptions), we could get a model with a homoscedastic error simply by regressing Y/X on $1/X$, though care is needed in interpreting parameter estimates from WLS. Notice in the transformed model set out in Equation (6.9) that the constant from (6.7) is being estimated by the slope parameter on $1/X$ in Equation (6.9); and the slope parameter on X is being estimated by the intercept from this transformed model.

There are some problems with taking this approach to a sample context and we will explain these below. But first we will explain the intuition underlying this sort of weighting procedure assuming that we can easily use this solution in samples of data. In a sample, if the residual variance is increasing as X increases, then fitted values associated with high values of X will be less reliable than fitted values associated with low values of X (the residuals and residual variance will be larger; there will be a larger divergence between observed values and fitted values). In dividing through each observation by X we are giving a greater weight to observations associated with low values of X (i.e. the observations that are being estimated more accurately) and a lesser weight to observations associated with high values of X (which are being estimated less accurately). So we are weighting observations according to reliability and the overall accuracy of our estimation will improve accordingly.

The main problem with WLS is that when we are working in the realm of social, rather than physical, science it is extremely unlikely that we will have much information at all about the hypothetical error variance – we have at best a large and representative sample. For this reason the above procedure is sometimes known as **infeasible WLS**: it's not a feasible procedure when (as is usually the case) we don't know the exact form of the heteroscedasticity.

But understanding the basic intuition underlying this infeasible WLS procedure is important because the same intuition underlies other GLS procedures. But when we don't know the error variance we need to select appropriate weights carefully. For example, take the case where the residual variance increases as the explanatory variable X increases; this implies that the accuracy of the model is decreasing as we get larger and larger values of the explanatory variable and so dividing through by X would not work.

One way to identify appropriate weights is to *estimate* the unknown population variance using our sample data. To do this, we would take the residuals from the OLS estimation, and square them. Then we could estimate the conditional residual variance by regressing the squared residuals on some function of the explanatory variable. We would take the square root of this conditional residual variance for each observation and use it to weight each observation (i.e. we would divide each observation by the square root of the conditional residual variance). This procedure is known as **feasible WLS (FLS)**. FLS will not be unbiased in small samples and the residual variance will not be an unbiased estimator of the error variance but FLS will be consistent so may work effectively with large samples of data.

OLS is consistent too so why bother with FLS? Remember from our discussion of consequences that the OLS formulae for standard errors and variances will be biased in the presence of heteroscedasticity and FLS does not suffer from this disadvantage.

For our analysis of innovation we tried various combinations of the solutions outlined in Box 6.2. One option would be to exclude the outliers but in doing this we would be ignoring observations that might convey valuable information about R&D (we do not want to lose USA and Japan and the lessons that their story might tell us). We tried estimating a log-log model to pick up an exponential relationship between R&D and patents; this did reduce the problem of heteroscedasticity but we were still forced to reject the null of homoscedasticity at a 5% significance level. The log-log model did not effectively control for the extremely large observations on real R&D expenditure for the G7 countries and Sweden. We considered expressing all the variables as ratios of GDP. Whilst this would be appropriate for R&D expenditure, expressing patents as a ratio of GDP would be problematic because patents as a proportion of GDP has no clear economic meaning and so interpreting results would be difficult. So finally we combined the solutions and identified the following model:

$$y_{i,t} = \theta + \lambda x_{i,t-1} + \xi_{i,t} \tag{6.12}$$

where y is patents (logged), x is R&D intensity (real R&D expenditure as a proportion of GDP); θ is the intercept, λ is the slope parameter and ξ is the error term.

From this we estimate the following SRF:

$$\hat{y}_{i,t} = \hat{\theta} + \hat{\lambda}\hat{x}_{i,t-1} \tag{6.13}$$

The results from the estimation of this model (including the White's test result) are reported in Table 6.3.

These results suggest a positive and significant relationship between patents and R&D intensity: with a p value of 0.00 on our t test, we can reject our null that the parameter on R&D is insignificantly different from zero. Given that patents is now logged, the parameter estimate suggests that an increase in R&D of 1% of GDP is associated with a 1.93% increase in patents granted the following year. The overall association between these variables is confirmed by our R^2 of 0.43; 43% of the variability in patents (logged) is captured by

Table 6.3 EViews output table: model with homoscedastic errors

Dependent variable: Patents (logged)

Method: Least Squares
Sample: 1 29

Variable	Coefficient	Std. Error	t-Statistic	Prob.
Intercept	2.48	0.82	3.04	0.01
R&D intensity	1.93	0.43	4.52	0.00
R-squared	0.43	F-statistic		20.42
Sum squared residuals	109.41	Prob(F-statistic)		0.00

White Heteroscedasticity Test:

F-statistic	1.36	Probability		0.27
Obs*R-squared	2.75	Probability		0.25

Dependent Variable: RESID^2

Variable	Coefficient	Std. Error	t-Statistic	Prob.
Intercept	2.90	3.86	0.75	0.46
R&D intensity	−1.02	4.58	−0.22	0.83
R&D intensity squared	0.71	1.18	0.60	0.55

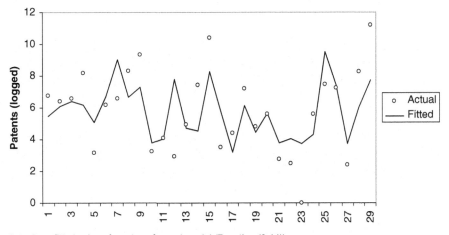

Figure 6.6   Actual vs. fitted values from transformed model (Equation (6.11))

variability in R&D intensity. The F test of explanatory power confirms that there is a highly significant relationship: we can reject the null hypothesis of no association between patents and R&D intensity at very low significance levels. A visual inspection of actual and predicted values (see Figure 6.6) suggests that the residuals and residual variance do not seem to be exhibiting systematic patterns.

Most importantly, our White's test result suggests that we can retain our null hypothesis of homoscedasticity at 5% and at 10% and in fact at significance levels up to 27%.

Why has this transformation worked so well? Dividing R&D by GDP to give a measure of R&D intensity reduced the association between the residual variance and explanatory variable; it has also reduced the distorting impact of the outliers. Logging the patents variable enabled us to capture the exponential relationship between patents and R&D expenditure as initially identified from an inspection of Figure 6.3. Overall, we have reliable evidence that there is a significantly positive association between R&D intensity in 2000 and patents in 2001 for the 29 countries in our sample.

6.5   Policy implications and conclusions

The empirical evidence of a positive association between inputs into the innovative process (as measured by R&D intensity) and innovative outputs (as measured by patents granted) suggests that boosting R&D intensity can have beneficial impacts in terms of innovative activity. But what policies can be put in place to boost R&D spending and thus encourage innovative activity?

In some countries and/or industries, particularly less-developed countries and industries, innovative activities are undertaken informally, without the trappings of formal R&D departments. As countries mature however, R&D begins to appear as a distinct activity. As firms tackle increasingly significant technological improvements, and as consumer demand for new products grows, firms will want to introduce new product and process innovations and so the role of formal R&D will become increasingly important. Firms may set up specialised units to monitor new developments, to adapt and improve on existing technologies, and/or to develop something completely new. R&D can also be conducted in low-tech and medium-tech sectors as much as in the high-tech sectors with which one usually associates R&D – in Italy for example, most business-related R&D takes place in the textiles and manufacturing sectors, i.e. in traditional sectors but ones in which Italy has created a strong comparative advantage.

There is evidence that R&D activity can generate **increasing returns**; as innovation opens up new industries, there may be special and widespread benefits particularly if innovation enables local people in LDCs to build-up their human capital in acquiring technological knowledge. In China and

India, massive amounts of R&D are being undertaken as a principal activity, reflecting China and India's comparative advantage in terms of endowments of large numbers of highly skilled scientists and engineers. In India, technological changes associated with computerisation have allowed her to become a global leader in software technology and innovations in telecommunications have allowed her to take advantage of the demand for call-centre outsourcing, with substantial benefits for the wider economy.

In the fast-moving, highly competitive and technologically advanced globalised world, maintaining innovative advantages will be essential for economic growth and progression and, in promoting innovation, governments can play a crucial role particularly for economies that do not have a well-established tradition of innovation within the private sector. Formal R&D is an essential part of the technological learning process but in countries without an established R&D tradition and/or where private firms are not willing or able to undertake R&D expenditure, governments can play a leading role.

6.6   Further reading

Textbooks

Fagerberg, J., Mowery, D. and Nelson R. (eds.) (2004) *The Oxford Handbook of Innovation*, Oxford: Oxford University Press.

Link, A. N. and Scherer, F. M. (eds.) (2006) *The Economics of R&D, Innovation, and Technological Change: Essays in Honor of Edwin Mansfield*, New York: Springer-Verlag.

Stock, J. H. and Watson, M. W. (2000) *Introduction to Econometrics*, Harlow: Pearson Education/Addison-Wesley, Chapter 4.

Thomas, R. L. (1997) *Modern Econometrics: An Introduction*, Harlow: Addison-Wesley, Chapter 10.

Wooldridge, J. M. (2003) *Introductory Econometrics: A Modern Approach* (2nd edition), Thomson South-Western, Chapter 8.

Academic articles and working papers

Klette J. and Kortum S. (2004) 'Innovating firms and aggregate innovation', *Journal of Political Economy*, vol. 112, no. 5, 986–1018.

Policy Reports

OECD (2002), *OECD Science, Technology and Industry Outlook 2002*, Paris: Organisation for Economic Cooperation and Development. Published annually.

UNCTAD (2005), 'World Investment Report 2005 – Transnational Corporations and the Internationalization of R&D'. New York and Geneva: United Nations Conference on Trade and Development. www.unctad.org/en/docs/wir2005overview_end.pdf

UNCTAD (2007), Knowledge, Technological Learning and Innovation for Development, Least Developed Countries Report, Geneva and New York: United Nations.

6.7   Chapter exercises

1. For the Goldfeld–Quandt (GQ) test estimated in this chapter, we have incorporated an asymmetric division of the sample. Using the data sources outlined in the data section:

   (a) Construct your own GQ test for heteroscedasticity by dividing the sample symmetrically, using RSS_1 from a regression on the first 12 observations and RSS_2 from a regression on the last 12 observations. Discuss your result.

   (b) What can you say about the power of this form of the GQ test?

   (c) Explain the divergence between your result and the result from the GQ test conducted in this chapter.

2. Using the data sources outlined in the data section:

   (a) Estimate a log-log model of the relationship between patents and R&D expenditure and discuss your results.

   (b) Construct two plots of your actual and predicted values – one for the whole sample and the other for the first 20 observations (i.e. excluding the G7 and Sweden). What do these plots suggest about the nature of the residual variance in your estimation?

   (c) Using EViews, conduct White's test for your log-log model. Explain why your results differ from the estimation of equation 6.13.

Autocorrelation

Tourism and the environment

Economic issues include:
- Tragedy of the commons and environmental externalities
- Game theory and the Prisoner's Dilemma
- Tourism life-cycles and sustainable development

Econometric issues include:
- Breusch–Godfrey LM and Durbin–Watson tests for autocorrelation
- Generalised Least Squares (GLS) and the Cochrane–Orcutt procedure

Data issues include:
- Measuring the environment

7.1   The issue

The tourism industry has great potential to boost incomes, growth and development in poorer countries. World Travel and Tourism Council (WTTC) estimates of the economic contribution made by tourism in 2005 include revenues of $6201.5 billion, employment of 221.6 million workers and an 8.3% share of GDP. For the Caribbean alone, a region heavily dependent on its tourism industry, 2005 estimates indicate that tourism has contributed 15% of GDP, 15% of jobs and $45.5 billion of revenue.

This growth in the tourism industry has not come without a cost. If tourism is not carefully planned then there will be negative consequences for the natural environment and for socio-economic and cultural institutions more generally. Even when judged in terms of prospects for the tourism industry alone, if the environmental resources on which tourism depends are exploited and destroyed by rapid growth in tourism demand then the contribution of tourism to sustainable development in the long term will be limited.

In managing a tourism industry that will be sustainable in the future, policy makers need to take account of the environmental consequences. So there are a lot of difficult issues confronting policy makers in those countries that are promoting sustainable development via their tourism industries.

7.2　The theory

In assessing the relationships between tourism, the environment and sustainable development, a number of theoretical issues are important. In this chapter we focus on analyses of the 'tragedy of the commons' and the relationships between tourism life cycles and sustainable development.

The tragedy of the commons

The **tragedy of the commons** is a problem that emerges from the over-use of natural resources held in common ownership. Hardin (1968) described this problem as emerging in the use of common grazing land before the English parliamentary enclosures movement of the eighteenth century. (See also *The Economist* (2008) for a modern analysis of the problem.) According to Hardin, when land was commonly owned, local villagers had an incentive to have more cows grazing on the land than was economically efficient. This was because each villager always had an incentive to put more cows on the land as long as they could afford it because if they didn't make use of the land with their own cows, then the other villagers would use the land instead. The parliamentary enclosures movement provided a solution to this problem by creating a system of private property rights; these encouraged each property owner to consider the efficient and sustainable use of their own land, consequently reducing the over-grazing problem.

This tragedy of the commons principle can be applied to the use of environmental resources in a modern context too. Modern tragedies of the commons exist when environmental resources are over-used by tourism industries. The essence of the problem can be explained using concepts from **game theory**. Game theory involves the analysis of strategic interactions between small groups of 'players'. In its simplest form, game theory focusses on interactions in 2-player games. The over-use of natural resources illustrates a commonly observed game: the **Prisoner's Dilemma (PD)**. In PD games the market mechanism does not operate efficiently to coordinate individuals' self-interested actions and Adam Smith's Invisible Hand goes into reverse: players pursuing their own self-interest will generate a sub-optimal social outcome.

The PD game can be used to illustrate the tragedy of the commons and here we apply the ideas to analyse environmental impacts of tourism. Imagine that there are two hotels in Goa: the Taj Mahal Hotel and the Amber Palace Hotel. An environmental resource on which they will both depend is a clean sea. If there is sewage in the sea then customers will stay away and each hotel will lose revenue. We begin by assuming that, for each hotel, tourism revenues will fall by 3.5 million rupees for the number of hotels without a sewage plant. So if one has a sewage plant and the other doesn't, each hotel's revenues will fall by 3.5m rupees. If neither have a sewage plant, then their revenues will fall by 7m rupees each. On the other hand, if a hotel wants to build a sewage plant then it will cost them RS5m. These figures can be incorporated into a **pay-off matrix** which shows the financial consequences of the hotels' strategies, see below noting that we have negative pay-offs in this matrix because we are examining the *costs*.

	Taj Mahal Sewage into sea	*Taj Mahal Buy sewage plant*
Amber Palace Sewage into sea	Amber Palace: –7m rupees Taj Mahal: –7m rupees	Amber Palace: –3.5m rupees Taj Mahal: –8.5m rupees
Amber Palace Buy sewage plant	Amber Palace: –8.5m rupees Taj Mahal: –3.5m rupees	Amber Palace: –5m rupees Taj Mahal: –5m rupees

If you imagine that you are managing the Taj Mahal Hotel, you will see that your costs will be minimised if you pump your sewage into the sea. This is the **dominant strategy**, i.e. the best strategy regardless of the actions of the other player. The game is symmetrical, i.e. the same strategy will work for the Amber Palace Hotel. So the net result is that both hotels will pump sewage into the sea incurring 7m rupees in lost revenue for each hotel, a total loss for the industry of 14m rupees. This is the **Nash equilibrium** of the game. The Nash equilibrium is a game's point of stability, i.e. the point at which there is no incentive for either player to change their strategy. But in terms of the **Pareto optimal** strategy: if both hotels had bought sewage plants, then their total losses would have been 10m rupees – the best overall outcome even when judged just in terms of the two hotels' costs. In terms of the broader environmental impacts, the social benefits would have been even greater. But each hotel had no guarantee that the other hotel would buy a sewage plant so there was no incentive for either of them individually to pursue the socially desirable strategy.

The essence of this tragedy of the commons idea is that the use of natural resources in common ownership creates **negative externalities**: exploiting natural resources may benefit private individuals but if no-one is taking responsibility for maintaining those resources (because those resources are in common ownership), then the use of natural resources will not take account of the total social costs.

The social costs of environmental change will impact in a number of ways: environmental change may limit the future viability of the tourism industry, particularly for countries dependent upon an abundance of natural resources. Environmental change will also have global impacts e.g. in terms of climate change.

Environmental impacts on tourism in LDCs

These negative externalities have implications for the length of **tourism life-cycles**. The tourism life cycle describes the stages of growth and decline in tourism production. The tourism life-cycle concept illustrates how the tourism industry goes through a cycle of growth and decline in response to different motivators of demand. In the early stage, facilities for tourists are limited but as tourism demand grows, **external economies** develop. External economies emerge when the economic activities undertaken by an individual person/business benefit all people/businesses within an industry or area. For our example of tourism development, external economies take hold and so the construction of some infrastructure encourages the creation of more infrastructure; new hotels have to construct roads, lighting, drainage etc. and the presence of these services encourages the building of more new hotels. The tourism industry will grow rapidly until it reaches a peak. Then, particularly given the fashions and fads in tourism demand, resorts will lose their novelty appeal. Overcrowding and congestion will discourage tourists from returning. Some tourists will in any case only want to re-visit a resort once. Once these negative factors take hold, the resort will head into decline (Baddeley, 2004).

The tourism life-cycle hypothesis illustrates that many of the negative environmental impacts emerging from the development of tourism resorts emerge only over a relatively long time horizon. In poorer countries, the focus is by necessity often on the short term. When there are mouths to feed today it doesn't make much sense to worry about the long-term profitability of tourism resorts let alone environmental sustainability more generally. If the tourism industry is to provide a long-term development solution, some of the problems outlined above must be resolved. Tourist areas should be encouraged to develop in a way that provides local incomes allowing local infrastructure to develop but in a way that is sustainable – both in terms of prolonging the life-cycle of tourism resources but also in a way that preserves the environment.

Global environmental impacts: climate change

Above we have outlined some of the issues affecting the development of tourism in particular areas. There are also significant global implications. Clear air and clean seas are natural resources in common ownership and so private incentives will not automatically ensure that these resources are maintained. This has created particular problems in the last few decades. Growing demand for international tourism has led to rapid rises in demand for air travel (an issue that was also addressed in Chapter 3). In particular, with more and more tourists flying to more exotic locations, the demand for air travel has increased with significant implications for climate change. The Stern Review (Stern 2006) gave an extensive assessment of the future environmental and economic consequences of human-made environmental change, advocating that governments invest now to ameliorate environmental damage in the future. The implications of aircraft emissions for the global environment have also been the focus for recent policy reports from groups such as the Intergovernmental Panel on Climate Change (IPCC) and the UN Framework Convention on Climate Change (UNFCCC). For example a recent IPCC report has highlighted the impact of international aviation on climate change; this report notes that international passenger traffic has grown by approximately 9% per year since 1960 – exceeding growth in GDP by a factor of 2.4. (Penner *et al.*, 1999, p. 23) Technological improvements and improved operational procedures have mitigated the impacts of this growing demand for aviation but nonetheless, reductions in emissions from these changes have not kept pace with the rises in aviation emissions from increased demand for air transport. Penner *et al.* also project that future rises in passenger traffic will exceed future growth in GDP.

In this chapter we explore some of the impacts of tourism on the environment by analysing the relationship between international tourist traffic and aircraft emissions using the data described in the following section.

7.3   The data

In this chapter, we use time-series data to investigate the relationship between aviation emissions and international flows of tourists. It is important to remember that aviation emissions, and emissions more generally, are just one factor affecting the environment. Some of the broader issues involved in measuring the environment and environmental resources are outlined in Box 7.1.

Box 7.1 Measuring the environment

Measuring the environment is difficult because there is no single measurable objective factor that defines the environment. Some traditional indicators have focussed on the categories of economic, social and biophysical environmental aspects but it is difficult objectively to rank and/ or select the individual criteria that define these categories. In terms of environment sustainability, e.g. of tourism developments, indicators such as the Index of Sustainable Economic Welfare (ISEW), the Environmental Pressure Index (EPI) and Genuine Progress Indicator (GPI) have been devised to give a general, broad picture of environment impact. However, there can be no completely objective criterion for assigning appropriate weights to the various components of these indicators. The Barometer of Sustainability (BS) gives equal weights to human well-being and eco-system 'well-being' but the judgement to weight equally involves some subjectivism; some might argue that human well-being should have a greater weight; others might think that *homo sapiens* is only one species and therefore assigning human and eco-system well-being equal weights involves an implicit over-estimation of human priorities. Approaches such as the Ecological Footprint (EF) methodology involve assuming that all space is equal in quality and importance. But again, is it appropriate to assume that all people should be entitled to the same environmental resources? Different people/organisations create different externalities, both positive and negative, in terms of their economic and social activities. Should a brothel have the same entitlement to land as a university? Also, all space is not equal in usefulness to people: many people would probably value an acre in Sydney more highly than 100 acres in the Simpson Desert.

For all indicators of environmental quality and impact, measurement will be particularly difficult for LDCs because collecting, harmonising and disaggregating data will be a difficult task. This all suggests that adopting a more disaggregated and partial approach to environmental assessment is a necessary compromise in a less than ideal world.

Our dependent variable is aircraft emissions and our explanatory variable is tourism flows and the data is collected from the following sources:

Variable	Source	Website
CO_2 emissions from international aviation bunkers	CO_2 Emissions from Fuel Combustion, International Energy Agency (IEA)	www.iea.org
International Tourism Arrivals	Tourism Market Trends – Statistical Annex, UN World Trade Organisation (UNWTO)	www.unwto.org

Figure 7.1 shows the time-plots of data on emissions and tourism arrivals between 1971 and 2003.

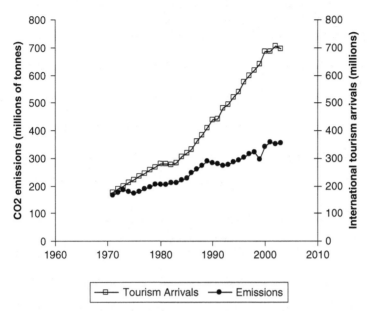

Figure 7.1   International aviation emissions and international tourist arrivals, 1971–2003

An initial inspection of these data suggests that aviation emissions increase with tourism arrivals and provide preliminary evidence in support of our hypothesis that there is a positive assocation between tourism demand and aircraft pollution. As always however, it is important to acknowledge the limitations of our data set. The emissions data is derived from records of fossil fuel used by the aviation industry. There are other measures of emissions. The UN Framework Convention on Climate Change (UNFCCC) requires countries to submit audits of CO_2 emissions but whilst the UNFCCC embeds a common reporting format for all countries, its geographical coverage is limited. Also, there are other types of aviation emissions and we have concentrated just on CO_2 emissions as they are relatively easy to measure. As for the tourism data, these will proxy for the growth in demand for international aviation from tourists. However, it is important to remember that tourists are not responsible for all aviation emissions and also, some tourists will use other forms of transport; the emissions from these alternative forms of transport will not be captured in aviation emissions data.

7.4   Empirical methods and results

Our overall hypothesis is that international tourism will generate negative environmental consequences. In particular, the increased aviation traffic

Table 7.1 EViews output table: OLS estimation

Dependent Variable: Aircraft emissions (logged)
Method: Least Squares
Sample: 1971 2003
Included observations: 33

Variable	Coefficient	Std. Error	t-Statistic	Prob.
Intercept	2.30	0.12	19.94	0.00
Tourist arrivals (logged)	0.54	0.02	27.90	0.00
R-squared	0.96	Mean dependent variable		5.50
Adjusted R-squared	0.96	F-statistic		778.16
Sum squared residuals	0.07	Prob(F-statistic)		0.00
Durbin-Watson statistic	0.74			

required to service rising demand for international tourism will generate CO_2 emissions with negative implications for climate change. To confirm this hypothesis we will estimate the following model (with lower case letters used to denote logged variables):

$$y_t = \alpha + \beta x_t + \varepsilon_t \tag{7.1}$$

where y is aviation emissions (logged) and x is tourism arrivals (logged).

Using this model we estimate the following SRF using time-series data from 1971 to 2003 ($n = 33$):

$$y_t = \hat{\alpha} + \hat{\beta} x_t + \hat{\varepsilon}_t \tag{7.2}$$

Table 7.2 shows the EViews output table from the estimation of (7.2).

The results from the estimation of (7.2) can be summarised as follows:

$$
\begin{array}{cccc}
\hat{y}_t & = & 2.30 & +0.54x_t \\
 & & (0.12) & (0.02) \\
 & & t = 19.94 & t = 27.90 \\
 & & p = 0.00 & p = 0.00 \\
R^2 = 0.96 & & &
\end{array}
$$

Durbin–Watson test $= 0.74$

Initially, these results look good and confirm our assertion that aviation emissions are associated with rises in international tourist traffic. Our t test on H_0: $\beta = 0$ versus H_1: $\beta \neq 0$, gives $p = 0.00$ and, at a 5% significance level, we can safely reject the null hypothesis of no association between y and x. The R^2 suggests that 96% of the variability in y is captured by variability in x – a high degree of 'explanatory' power and this is confirmed by the F test of explanatory power. The EViews printout also contains a statistic for a test not yet mentioned – the Durbin–Watson test which will be explained in detail below.

As emphasised in the preceding chapter, we cannot assume that these are reliable results until we have established that the Gauss–Markov assumptions underlying OLS estimation have been satisfied. In this chapter, we will focus on the problem of **autocorrelation** or **serial correlation** and we will explore this assumption in assessing our regression results.

What is autocorrelation?

To define autocorrelation mathematically and in terms of the Gauss–Markov theorem: it involves the violation of the Gauss–Markov assumption that $cov(\varepsilon_i, \varepsilon_j) = 0, i \neq j$. In words, autocorrelation is the violation of the assumption that the covariance between error terms is zero. For OLS to work effectively, the residuals from our regression should only capture random and excluded unimportant factors. Autocorrelation (in the residuals) is a problem that occurs when residuals from a sample regression are not random because they correlate with each other either over time or over space. If we have any sort of systematic pattern between our residuals, then some of the systematic influences that should be captured by the deterministic part of our model may be mistakenly picked up by the residual and OLS will be less accurate as a consequence. Whilst autocorrelation is commonly a time-series problem it can exist in cross-sectional datasets too. In a cross-sectional context, spatial autocorrelation may occur if neighbouring countries have similar conditions and institutional structures; also there may be spillover effects between countries that are close in terms of geography because those countries may also be similar in terms of socio-economic and cultural conditions.

It is important to note that the key symptom of autocorrelation is systematic patterns in the residuals and these can be a symptom of something other than pure autocorrelation, for example one or more of the following problems:
- heteroscedasticity (explained in Chapter 6)
- model misspecification (explained in Chapter 8)
- endogeneity (explained in Chapter 9)
- structural breaks (explained in Chapter 9)
- non-stationarity (explained in Chapter 10)

When systematic patterns in residuals are reflecting these more complex problems, the consequences may be more severe and the solutions more complicated. So it is important to spend some time identifying the exact cause of the autocorrelation in residuals before deciding what to do next.

Consequences of autocorrelation

When the 'no autocorrelation' assumption is violated, OLS will no longer be BLUE. OLS estimators will remain unbiased and consistent (as long as nothing more sinister is happening) but they will not be BLUE because they will not be the minimum variance unbiased estimator. (These consequences are similar to the consequences from heteroscedasticity, outlined in Chapter 6, because both are about systematic patterns in the random error term.) For OLS estimation in the presence of autocorrelation, the variances and standard errors will be larger and confidence intervals wider. This is because not all systematic information is being captured by the deterministic part of the regression model; instead, some of it is being mistakenly attributed to the residual.

Detecting autocorrelation

As explained above, autocorrelation is a problem that manifests itself via systematic patterns in the residuals from a regression. So the simplest method for identifying autocorrelation is a visual inspection of plots of residuals. In addition, various diagnostic tests exist which, in essence, quantify these systematic residual patterns. There are a number of different autocorrelation tests and here we will explain two common tests: the Durbin–Watson test and the Breusch–Godfrey LM test.

Visual inspection

Figure 7.2 is an EViews plot of the actual and fitted values from the OLS regression together with a plot of the residuals. (As explained in Chapter 1, the residual for each observation is the vertical distance between the observed value and the fitted value.) Visual inspection of these plots is often the first and quickest way to spot a potential problem.

What are we looking for? In Figure 7.2, you may notice that there are relatively long runs of initially negative but then positive gaps between actual and observed values; the residuals are not spread randomly across the sample, suggesting that there is some systematic positive correlation between residuals. These systematic waves of positive and then negative residuals suggest a problem of **positive autocorrelation**, which occurs when one residual is a positive function of its predecessor. (It is also possible to have **negative autocorrelation**; in this case one residual will be a negative function of its predecessor and the residuals would zig-zag up and down more frequently than randomly generated residuals. Whilst negative autocorrelation is a less

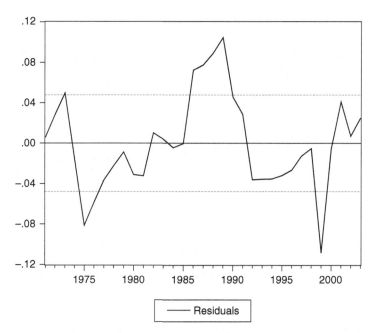

Figure 7.2   EViews plot of residuals from estimation of Equation (7.2)

common problem and has different underlying causes, nonetheless it will generate similar problems and consequences to positive autocorrelation.)

Diagnostic tests

Visual patterns can be difficult to detect and will inevitably involve some degree of subjectivity, particularly in borderline cases. So there are many autocorrelation tests designed to pick up correlations between residuals. The classic test for autocorrelation is the **Durbin–Watson (DW) test**, routinely reported by most econometrics packages. We explain this test here because it is so widely known and used but it is important to remember that the DW test suffers from a number of limitations, and these are discussed in more detail below.

The DW test is designed to pick up autocorrelation of the following form:

$$\varepsilon_t = \rho\varepsilon_{t-1} + \upsilon_t \tag{7.3}$$

where ε_t is the error term and υ_t is a **stochastic** error term. (A stochastic error is a randomly generated error process with a mean of zero and is sometimes referred to as a **white noise** error process.) The model in (7.4) focusses on the association between the error and one lag of itself, i.e. it is a first-order *autoregressive* process. In technical notation, it is an AR(1) process, i.e. a process in which a variable is a function of just one lag of itself (*auto* = self; *regressive* = related to the past). The DW test is designed to pick up AR(1) autocorrelation and so tests the following null and alternative hypotheses:

$$H_0: \text{cov}(\varepsilon_t, \varepsilon_{t-1}) = 0 \qquad (7.4)$$

$$H_1: \text{cov}(\varepsilon_t, \varepsilon_{t-1}) \neq 0$$

The Durbin–Watson statistic is constructed around the sum of squared differences between successive residuals expressed as a ratio of the residual variance and can be calculated using the following formula:

$$\hat{d} = \frac{\sum (\hat{\varepsilon}_t - \hat{\varepsilon}_{t-1})^2}{\sum \hat{\varepsilon}_t^2} \qquad (7.5)$$

If there is **negative autocorrelation** then the squared differences between successive residuals will be relatively large and *d* will be relatively large too, with an upper bound of 4. If there is **positive autocorrelation** then the squared differences between successive residuals will be relatively small and *d* will tend towards zero.

If there is **no autocorrelation**: the differences will be random and then *d* will fall between 0 and 4, i.e. somewhere around 2.

One of the limitations of the DW test lies in the complexity of its decision rules. In deciding whether or not the DW test result is revealing autocorrelation, the critical values for DW are found using *k* (the number of explanatory variables) and *n* (the number of observations). DW tables give two critical values each time, an upper value (d_U) and a lower value (d_L). The decision rules given these critical values are summarised in Table 7.2.

For our estimation, we have $\hat{d} = 0.74$ (see Table 7.1). From the DW tables (we have $k = 1$ and $n = 33$) using a 5% significance level, we get $d_U = 1.51$ and $d_L = 1.38$. Following the decision rules summarised in Table 7.2, since $\hat{d} < d_L$ we must reject H_0 and conclude that there is significant evidence of positive serial correlation in the residuals from our estimation of Equation (7.2).

Table 7.2 Decision rules for the Durbin–Watson (DW) test

If →	$0 < \hat{d} < d_L$	$d_L < \hat{d} < d_U$	$d_U < \hat{d} < 4 - d_U$	$4 - d_U < \hat{d} < 4 - d_L$	$4 - d_L < \hat{d} < 4$
Then →	Reject H_0	No decision possible	Do not reject H_0	No decision possible	Reject H_0
Inference →	Positive serial correlation	?	No significant serial correlation	?	Negative serial correlation

Problems with the DW test

There are a number of problems with the Durbin–Watson test. It is a clumsy test to use because, as noted above and in Table 7.2, there are two **zones of indecision** between the values $d_L < \hat{d} < d_U$ and $4 - d_U < \hat{d} < 4 - d_L$. In these zones no conclusions can be drawn at all. Also as mentioned above, the DW will only pick up AR(1) autocorrelation i.e. correlation between successive residuals; it won't automatically pick-up correlations with residuals that are more than one 'step' behind; for example in quarterly data we may expect that residuals in one period are correlated with residuals a year ago, i.e. four steps behind and the DW test will not capture this form of autocorrelation. Also, DW will not work when there's a lagged dependent variable in the model: in this case $\hat{d}$ will be biased towards 2 and so will not be a powerful test of our H_0. This is because the probability of Type II error (incorrectly retaining the false null of no autocorrelation) will be relatively high when $\hat{d}$ is close to 2 and so we will be more likely wrongly to conclude that there is no significant autocorrelation. This last problem can be addressed by adapting the procedure to derive **Durbin's h test**; Durbin's h test is a relatively powerful test for autocorrelation in the presence of a lagged dependent variable and it is easier to interpret because it follows a standard normal distribution. But, like the DW test, it will only pick up AR(1) autocorrelation.

Given the problems with DW, it is generally a good idea to conduct additional tests for autocorrelation. There are many alternatives to the DW test but a widely used test is the **Breusch–Godfrey Lagrange Multiplier test (BG test)**. This test can pick up higher-order autocorrelation and can be calculated by many econometrics packages, including EViews. It is also a more powerful test than the DW because it isn't biased towards a non-rejection of the null when a lagged dependent variable is included. This test is constructed by saving the residuals from the original regression and then conducting an auxiliary regression to estimate the relationship between a given residual and various lags of itself. Whilst the BG test can be constructed to detect higher-order autocorrelation we will first illustrate the AR(1) case, in which the form of this auxiliary regression would be:

$$\hat{\varepsilon}_t = \phi + \gamma x_t + \rho_1 \hat{\varepsilon}_{t-1} + v_t \tag{7.6}$$

where ϕ is the intercept in the auxiliary regression, x is the explanatory variable from the original model, γ is the slope parameter on x and ρ is the parameter on the lagged residuals. An F version of this test can be constructed by comparing the RSS from Equation (7.6) with the RSS from a restricted version of Equation (7.6) which excludes the lagged residual:

$$\hat{\varepsilon}_t = \phi + \gamma x_t + \upsilon_t \qquad (7.7)$$

The RSS from (7.6) and (7.7) are compared using an F test of restrictions (this test is explained in Chapter 5). The degrees of freedom on this F test will be F $(r, n-k-1-r)$ where r is the order of autocorrelation encapsulated within the unrestricted auxiliary equation. In the case of a test for AR(1) autocorrelation in an estimation with one explanatory variable and n = 33, the degrees of freedom will be $F(1,30)$.

Significant differences between the RSSs in the unrestricted and restricted models will be associated with large, significant F values. So the decision rule on the BG test is: if $F > F_{crit}$ then reject H_0.

The intuition underlying this test is that if there is a systematic pattern in the residuals then there will be statistically significant associations between residuals in time t and lagged residuals. So the RSS from the auxiliary regression will increase significantly when lagged residuals are dropped in a restricted version of (7.7); F will be greater than F_{crit}.

As mentioned above, the BG test can also be tailored to pick up higher-order autocorrelation. For example if we wanted to investigate the possibility of AR(5) autocorrelation, the unrestricted auxiliary regression would be:

$$\hat{\varepsilon}_t = \phi + \gamma x_t + \rho_1 \hat{\varepsilon}_{t-1} + \rho_2 \hat{\varepsilon}_{t-2} + \rho_3 \hat{\varepsilon}_{t-3} + \rho_4 \hat{\varepsilon}_{t-4} + \rho_5 \hat{\varepsilon}_{t-5} + \upsilon_t \qquad (7.8)$$

The restricted version would be the same as for the AR(1) version, as outlined in Equation (7.7). For a sample of 33 observations with one explanatory variable, the degrees of freedom on the test would be $F(5, 26)$.

EViews will do BG tests and for our example we use EViews to test for AR(5) autocorrelation in our estimation of international aircraft emissions. The results from this EViews test are summarised in Table 7.3.

Given $p < 0.05$ we can reject the null of no autocorrelation. There is a significant problem of serial correlation in this sample and this result confirms the findings from the visual inspection and the Durbin–Watson test. The EViews BG tables also give more detailed information about the impact of lagged residuals. The results from the estimation of the auxiliary regression are summarised in Table 7.3 under 'Test equation'. Although this information does not give a very rigorous test for the detailed nature of the associations between residuals and their lags, the fact that the only significant parameter is the one on the first lag of the residuals, may suggest that the autocorrelation we are detecting in our model of aircraft emissions is AR(1)

Table 7.3 Breusch–Godfrey LM tests from EViews

F-statistic	3.92	Probability	0.01
Obs*R-squared	14.19	Probability	0.01

Test Equation:
Dependent Variable: RESID = residuals
Method: Least Squares

Variable	Coefficient	Std. Error	t-Statistic	Prob.
Intercept	−0.01	0.10	−0.10	0.92
Tourist arrivals (logged)	0.00	0.02	0.11	0.91
RESID(−1)	0.73	0.20	3.70	0.00
RESID(−2)	−0.20	0.24	−0.82	0.42
RESID(−3)	0.19	0.25	0.77	0.45
RESID(−4)	−0.17	0.26	−0.66	0.52
RESID(−5)	−0.05	0.24	−0.21	0.84

R-squared	0.43	Sum squared residuals	0.04
Adjusted R-squared	0.30	F-statistic	3.27
Durbin-Watson statistic	2.01	Prob(F-statistic)	0.02

autocorrelation. (As we will show below, the fact that a corrective procedure based around an assumption of AR(1) correlation eliminates the problem from our estimation does suggest that our tentative inference about AR(1) autocorrelation has some basis.)

Correcting autocorrelation

We have emphasised that it is important to think about the various possible reasons for the symptom of correlated residuals but assuming that the auto-correlation detected in our SRF is not a sign either of model misspecification, structural breaks and/or non-stationarity (problems which are explained in subsequent chapters), we will illustrate a classic solution to autocorrelation based around a Generalised Least Squares (GLS) procedure – as explained in Box 7.2.

Box 7.2 Generalised least squares (GLS) to correct autocorrelation

As its name suggests, GLS is a generalisation of the least squares principle and was introduced in Chapter 6 in the context of heteroscedasticity. In the context of autocorrelation, GLS is adapted to extract out the systematic patterns in the autocorrelated errors in the following way:

Taking an empirical model of the form:

$$y_t = a + \beta x_t + \varepsilon_t \tag{7.9}$$

If successive errors are correlated then:

$$\varepsilon_t = \rho\varepsilon_{t-1} + \upsilon_t \tag{7.10}$$

where υ_t is a stochastic, white noise error term with a mean of zero.

This autocorrelation will generate inefficiency in OLS: OLS will not be estimated as accurately as possible because it is not capturing the systematic pattern in the error ε. In addition, the standard errors will be estimated wrongly and so the t tests from the original regression will be incorrectly calculated.

To correct this problem we need to incorporate all the systematic information into the deterministic component of our regression model in order to create a model with a white noise error υ_t.

Using the information from Equation (7.10) we can transform our model by lagging Equation (7.9), multiplying it by ρ to give:

$$\rho y_{t-1} = \rho a + \rho\beta x_{t-1} + \rho\varepsilon_{t-1} \tag{7.11}$$

Subtracting (7.11) from (7.9) gives:

$$y_t - \rho y_{t-1} = (1 - \rho)a + \beta(x_t - \rho x_{t-1}) + (\varepsilon_t - \rho\varepsilon_{t-1}) \tag{7.12}$$

$$\text{So} \quad y_t^* = \varphi + \beta x_t^* + (\varepsilon_t - \rho\varepsilon_{t-1}) \tag{7.13}$$

where

$$y_t^* = y_t - \rho y_{t-1}, \ x_t^* = x_t - \rho x_{t-1} \text{ and } \varphi = (1 - \rho)a \tag{7.14}$$

Remember that $\varepsilon_t = \rho\varepsilon_{t-1} + \upsilon_t$ (from Equation (7.10)) which can be rearranged to show that the stochastic error in (7.13) is given by the random white noise error term, υ_t i.e. $\varepsilon_t - \rho\varepsilon_{t-1} = \upsilon_t$. All systematic influences are now captured within the deterministic portion of the model. In this case, OLS will be consistent. It will also be BLUE in small samples if x is strictly exogenous, i.e. if x exhibits no correlation with the error (Stock and Watson, 2003, p. 514). However, we will lose one degree of freedom in transforming our variables. Furthermore, the inclusion of the lagged dependent variable will create problems for linear estimation of (7.12) but these difficulties are beyond the scope of this chapter.

In a sample context we can 'clean up' the autocorrelated residuals using this approach. But to do this we need an estimate of the autocorrelation parameter $\hat{\rho}$. There are many ways to get an estimate of $\hat{\rho}$. One method is a **grid search** procedure, i.e. experimenting with different values of $\hat{\rho}$ to see which gives the best R^2. Another way is to make some assumptions about $\hat{\rho}$ – for example by using information from previous analyses. One of the most famous methods for getting an estimate of ρ is the **Cochrane–Orcutt (C–O)**

> **procedure**. This involves running the OLS regression, saving the residuals and running an auxiliary regression of the residuals on the residuals as follows:
>
> $$\hat{\varepsilon}_t = \hat{\rho}\hat{\varepsilon}_{t-1} \tag{7.15}$$
>
> The parameter on the lagged residual will give an estimate of ρ. Below, this procedure is applied to our emissions–tourism example. It is important to remember that this C–O procedure suffers from the limitations outlined above. It is also important to remember that it will only work for AR(1) autocorrelation and the procedure would have to be extended for higher orders of autocorrelation.

The Cochrane–Orcutt (C–O) two stage procedure

The C–O procedure can be performed in complex ways (e.g. by using iterative solutions to identify $\hat{\rho}$) but the simplest version, the **C–O two stage procedure**, can be used to correct the problem of autocorrelation in our estimation of (7.2) as follows:.

1. Run an OLS regression on (7.2) and save the residuals, $\hat{\varepsilon}_t$
2. Run an auxiliary regression of the residuals in period t on the residuals in period $t-1$. For our data, this auxiliary regression gave the following result:

$$\hat{\varepsilon}_i = 0.63\hat{\varepsilon}_{i-1} + \hat{v}_t \qquad \rightarrow \hat{\rho} = 0.63 \tag{7.16}$$

3. Using $\hat{\rho} = 0.63$ as identified in step (2), we transform our variables as follows:

$$y_t^* = y_t - 0.63y_{t-1} \tag{7.17a}$$

$$x_t^* = x_t - 0.63x_{t-1} \tag{7.17b}$$

4. Then we run a regression of y^* on x^*, noting that (7.14) implies a new intercept term in our transformed model; however this intercept will still be a constant (as it is an amalgam of constants itself) and so the change in the intercept will have no specific implications for our new estimation.

The results from the estimation of this transformed model (including diagnostic tests) are summarised in Table 7.4a. Overall, our corrective GLS procedure appears to have worked well and for our final regression the Breusch–Godfrey test indicates that any inefficiency in OLS estimation created by an autocorrelation problem has been eliminated by using the GLS estimator. The results from the BG test for higher-order autocorrelation (shown in Table 7.4b) indicate that, even at very low significance levels, we can retain the null of no AR(5) autocorrelation.

Table 7.4a GLS estimation of tourism arrivals and aviation emissions (Cochrane–Orcutt procedure)

Dependent Variable: y^*
Method: Least Squares
Sample (adjusted): 1972 2003
Included observations: 32 after adjustments

Variable	Coefficient	Std. Error	t-Statistic	Prob.
Intercept	0.84	0.10	8.56	0.00
x^*	0.55	0.04	12.33	0.00
R-squared	0.84	Mean dependent variable		2.06
Adjusted R-squared	0.83	F-statistic		152.06
Sum squared residuals	0.04	Prob(F-statistic)		0.00
Durbin-Watson statistic	1.82			

Table 7.4b Breusch–Godfrey LM test

F-statistic	0.21	Probability	0.95
Obs*R-squared	1.31	Probability	0.93

Test Equation:
Dependent Variable: RESID

Variable	Coefficient	Std. Error	t-Statistic	Prob.
Intercept	0.00	0.11	0.00	1.00
x^*	0.00	0.05	−0.01	1.00
RESID(−1)	0.11	0.20	0.56	0.58
RESID(−2)	−0.14	0.20	−0.67	0.51
RESID(−3)	0.12	0.21	0.57	0.57
RESID(−4)	−0.12	0.23	−0.52	0.61
RESID(−5)	−0.01	0.27	−0.04	0.97
R-squared	0.04	Mean dependent variable		0.00
Adjusted R-squared	−0.19	F-statistic		0.18
Sum squared residuals	0.04	Prob(F-statistic)		0.98
Durbin-Watson statistic	1.98			

Note that all we have done here is transform our variables to allow more efficient estimation of our parameters. We are still estimating the α, β and γ from Equation (7.2); we're just doing it more efficiently and accurately because we've incorporated information about the form of the autocorrelation into our estimation procedure.

The results from our GLS C–O estimation are broadly similar to the results from the initial OLS estimation: our t test of $H_0: \beta = 0$ against $H_1: \beta \neq 0$, gives $p = 0.00$ and so we can still safely reject H_0 at a 5% significance level. There is a statistically significant, positive association between y and x: our results suggest that a 1% rise in international tourist arrivals will be associated with a 0.55% rise in international aircraft emissions.

The F test of explanatory power also indicates that, even with very low significance levels, we can reject $H_0: \beta = 0$. For the R^2, 84% of the variability in y^* is captured by variability in x^* again confirming that the model overall has a high degree of 'explanatory' power. Using the Breusch–Godfrey test and a 5% significance level we can retain the null of no AR(5) autocorrelation in the residuals. Whilst the basic results from our GLS estimation are similar to the results from the OLS estimation, they are in fact a lot more plausible because we have adapted our technique to match the Gauss–Markov assumption of no autocorrelation in the errors.

We have identified a positive and significant relationship between international aircraft emissions and international tourist arrivals. But whilst our initial findings do suggest that controlling international tourist traffic may be crucial in moderating aviation emissions, statistically it is important to note that, whilst we have addressed the problem of autocorrelation, there may be other, more complex problems with our statistical analysis, e.g. non-stationarity. These problems are explored in subsequent chapters.

7.5 Implications and conclusions

If our empirical results are robust, then they suggest a worrying future for climate change. With increasing numbers of developing countries building prospects for growth around their tourism industries, and with rising incomes in the developed world, it seems likely that international tourist traffic will continue to rise in the future. Similarly the growth of the cheap airline industry in many OECD countries will do little to reverse the growth in international tourism. The results from this chapter suggest that these increasing flows of tourists are likely to be associated with significant increases in international aircraft emissions.

Drawing a parallel with the Prisoner's Dilemma problem outlined in the theory section, there will be no market incentive for any given individual to moderate their own international travel if others are continuing to travel. Although public awareness of environmental change has been increasing, the focus on sustainable tourism and ecotourism may do little to moderate climate change emerging from aviation because many ecotourism resorts and activities are concentrated in exotic destinations, far away from the homes of the tourist customers.

In terms of solutions to the problem, the growth of 'carbon offset' and 'carbon balancing' schemes may do something to reduce the impact of tourism on climate change – if airlines and tourists can be persuaded to compensate for negative environmental externalities generated from aviation emissions by charging and paying higher prices for air travel. As for government policy: in moderating the extent of climate change governments may have to include measures to quell the demand for international tourism. Some policy solutions include fuel taxes, tradeable emissions permits, landing charges and arrival/departure taxes. All these measures would raise the relative cost of international tourism. However, these sort of policies require international co-operation because the Prisoner's Dilemma may operate on an international scale: individual countries are unlikely unilaterally to impose new taxes and charges on their own tourism industries in the hopes of saving the environment if the most likely outcome is that tourists will just go somewhere cheaper for their annual holiday.

7.6   Further reading

Textbooks

Holden, A. (2000) *Environment and Tourism*, London: Routledge.

Opperman, M. and Chon, K-S. (1997) *Tourism in Developing Countries*, Thomson Business Press.

Stock, J. H. and Watson, M. W (2003) *Introduction to Econometrics*, Harlow: Pearson Education/Addison-Wesley.

Varian, H. (2006) *Intermediate Microeconomics* 7th edition, London: W. W. Norton & Co. Chapter 34 (on the tragedy of the commons and environmental externalities).

Academic articles and working papers

Baddeley, M. (2004) 'Are tourists willing to pay for aesthetic quality? An empirical assessment from Krabi Province, Thailand, *Tourism Economics*, vol. 10, no. 1, 45–61. Reprinted in T. Hybers (ed.) (2007), *Economics and Management of Tourism 2 – Tourism in Developing Countries*, Cheltenham: Edward Elgar, pp. 608–24.

Hardin, G. (1968) 'The Tragedy of the Commons', *Science*, vol. 162, no. 3859, 1243–7.

Newspaper articles

The Economist (2008) 'Commons sense: Why it still pays to study medieval English landholding and Sahelian nomadism', 31 July 2008.

Policy reports

Penner, J. E., Lister, D. H., Griggs, D. J., Dokken, D. J. and Mcfarland, M. (1999) *Aviation and the Global Atmosphere – Summary for policy makers*, Intergovernmental Panel on Climate Change: Cambridge: Cambridge University Press. Downloadable from www.ipcc.ch/pdf/special-reports/spm/av-en.pdf

Roe, D., Ashley, C., Page, S. and Meyer, D. (2004) *Tourism and the Poor: Analysing and Interpreting Tourism Statistics from a Poverty Perspective*, ProPoor Tourism Working Paper No. 16, March, London: Pro Poor Tourism (PPT).

Stern, N. (2006) *The Stern Review Report on the Economics of Climate Change*, Cabinet Office – HM Treasury/Cambridge University Press, Cambridge UK.

UNWTO (annual) *Tourism Market Trends*, Madrid: UN World Tourism Organisation.

7.7   Chapter exercises

1. Using the data sources outlined above, collect data on aircraft emissions and tourist arrivals and then:
    (a) Estimate an autoregressive distributed lag (ARDL) model of aircraft emissions of the following form: $y_t = \alpha + \lambda y_{t-1} + \beta_1 x_t + \beta_2 x_{t-1} + \varepsilon_t$
    (b) Test for AR(1) autocorrelation in the errors explaining which test(s) you've used and why you've used them.
    (c) Test for AR(5) autocorrelation in the errors explaining which test(s) you've used and why you've used them
    (d) What do the tests for autocorrelated residuals reveal?
    (e) Explain how and why the ARDL estimation has/hasn't worked.
2. In the discussion of autocorrelation, we outlined a number of explanations for systematic patterns. Discuss the plausibility of these explanations in the context of the relationship between aviation emissions and tourist arrivals as analysed in this chapter.

Model misspecification
Tobin's *q* and investment in the USA

Economic issues include:
- Tobin's *q* theory
- The Efficient Markets Hypothesis
- Psychology, behavioural economics and neuroeconomics

Econometric issues include:
- Identifying correct functional form
- Model misspecification errors
- Ramsey's RESET tests for model misspecfication

Data issues include:
- Measuring stock market value
- Measurement error

8.1 The issue

In this chapter, stock market valuation methods of investment appraisal are introduced and applied to US fixed asset investment data. In a simple world, business entrepreneurs use two factors of production when they are producing their goods and services: capital and labour. Fixed asset investment is about the first. As businesses invest in new plant, machinery and equipment they generate a flow of new capital goods into the stock of capital. This capital stock (when combined with labour inputs) will determine the future productive capacity both of the firm at a microeconomic level and of the macro-economy as a whole.

Some early investment theories focused on investment as the outcome of firms balancing the marginal benefits and marginal costs of buying units of new capital but these theories could not easily explain the timing of investment decisions. Also, they neglected the role of expectations and uncertainty.

This was an important omission because investment is all about planning for the future: expectations and uncertainty have crucial impacts on entrepreneurial decision-making. The problem is that expectations are not observable and so one solution is to use stock market data on market capitalisations to capture investors' expectations about the future, as explained below. This approach forms the basis of Tobin's *q* theories of investment and in this chapter we investigate variants of *q* theory to assess their empirical performance in capturing aggregate investment in the USA from 1987 to 2004.

8.2   The theory

Lots of investment theories have evolved over the years.[1] Early **accelerator theories** focussed on explaining investment as a process of capital stock adjustment, asserting that entrepreneurs invest to build up their capital stock to meet future sales demand and using past output growth to proxy future sales demand. This capital stock adjustment approach was developed in Jorgenson's influential neo-classical investment theory (Jorgenson, 1963) but, according to Jorgenson, investment is also a function of the **user cost of capital** – a measure of the opportunity costs of spending money on investment projects. The user cost includes interest costs, depreciation from wear-and-tear, and the capital gains or losses from changes in the value of capital goods. It is defined as:

$$c = r + \delta - \dot{p}_k \qquad (8.1)$$

where r = the real interest rate; δ is the depreciation rate on capital equipment and $\dot{p}_k$ captures capital appreciation from relative changes in the value of capital goods. Note that capital appreciation will reduce the opportunity costs of investment and so the sign on $\dot{p}_k$ is negative.

There are two main shortcomings with Jorgenson's theory. First, it assumes static, unchanging expectations. Second, it assumes that there are no adjustment costs but if there are no adjustment costs then the rate of investment over time will be undefined. **Tobin's *q* theory** addresses some of the limitations in Jorgenson's theory by incorporating adjustment costs into the investment decision-making process, focussing in particular on **internal adjustment costs**. Internal adjustment costs emerge from disruptions to the production process as new capital goods are 'broken-in' and workers are re-trained. With increasing

---

[1] For an analysis of the evolution of investment theory, see Baddeley (2003).

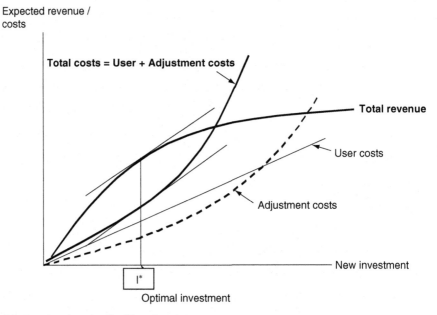

Figure 8.1   Adjustment costs and optimal investment

investment more workers are needed to 'bolt-down' new equipment and there are increasing demands on managerial time. This means that adjustment costs will be a **convex** function of new investment, i.e. adjustment costs will increase at an increasing rate as investment increases.

Figure 8.1 illustrates the basic concepts of adjustment cost theory and shows that optimal investment and maximum profits will occur at the point where expected marginal revenue balances all the marginal costs, including the adjustment costs. The *total revenue curve* shows expected revenues increasing but at a decreasing rate reflecting the diminishing marginal productivity of new investment; the slope is decreasing as new investment increases. The convexity of adjustment costs can be seen in the shape of the *adjustment costs curve*: the slope is increasing because marginal adjustment costs increase as new investment increases. The *user cost line* has a constant slope: unlike adjustment costs, the first unit of new investment is affected by the same user costs (interest, appreciation and changes in the value of capital goods) as the last unit of new investment. The *total costs curve* is the vertical sum of the user cost and adjustment cost curves and so it will be convex because the adjustment costs curve is convex. Profits from new investments will be maximised when the marginal benefits of investment (in terms of expected revenues) are balanced by the marginal costs. It is important to note that the marginal benefits of investment are marginal revenues and so are captured by the *slope* on the expected revenue curve; the marginal costs are captured by the slope on the total costs curve; when these two slopes are equal, i.e. when the lines are parallel, marginal benefits and marginal costs will be equal and profits will be maximised. This occurs at I*, which is the optimal level of investment.

The *q* theorists explain this balancing of benefits and costs using the concept of **marginal *q*** (q_M), which is the shadow price of investment – in this case the increment to total revenue expected from a unit increase in the marginal costs. In other words, it is the ratio of the marginal benefits in terms of revenue (MB) and marginal costs (MC) including user cost and marginal adjustment costs. At the point of optimal investment, MB = MC and $q_M = 1$. At this point no new investments would be profitable (apart from **replacement investment** to replace worn-out plant and equipment etc.). When MB > MC, q_M will be greater than 1 and firms should increase their capital stock by investing more: if a firm was to buy another unit of new investment then they would increase their profits (because the marginal benefits exceed the marginal costs). On the other hand, if MB < MC and $q_M < 1$, then costs exceed benefits and so the firm should decrease its investment – if it can. But disinvestment is limited by the fact that it is difficult to sell second-hand investment goods given **asset specificity** (plant and equipment is not easy to re-sell if it is designed for a very specific purpose) and/or **adverse selection** (a type of asymmetric information which occurs when buyers are reluctant to buy second-hand goods because they cannot observe the hidden attributes of these goods).

What use is q_M in practice? It is not observable because the firm is assumed to be a 'black box' – its internal workings cannot be seen i.e. a firm's managers cannot see the incremental output from each individual unit of capital, they see only the *total* output, inputs and costs. So because q_M is unobservable a proxy is needed. Average *q* (q_A) can be used as a proxy. Average q (q_A) is the ratio of total benefits (TB) expected by a firm (from its production and investment) to the total cost (TC) that would be incurred if it had to replace its entire capital stock. If TB > TC then $q_A > 1$ and net investment should take place. The capital stock will increase from inflows of new investment but, because of the diminishing marginal productivity of capital, TC will increase at a decreasing rate until TB = TC. At this point the capital stock will be at its optimal level, q_A will equal q_M and both will be equal to unity.

But profit-maximising firms operate at the margin, at least in theory, so what use is an average concept? This problem can be answered by assuming homogeneity of the capital stock and constant returns to scale, in which case marginal and average costs and benefits will be equal (Hayashi 1982). So although q_M is unobservable, q_A may be a good **proxy** and firms will respond to q_A as if they know q_M. In other words, even though q_M is unobservable, q_A will give a quantifiable measure of the incentive to invest.

How do we measure q_A? In this chapter we focus on one solution: **Tobin's q theory**. Tobin's q is the ratio of the stock market valuation of a firm (MV) to the **current replacement cost** (CRC) of its capital stock. As explained in Box 8.1, MV will be a good proxy for firms' expectations of future revenue from current investments assuming that share prices are a good signal of the profit expectations of entrepreneurs. CRC is the accounting or 'book' cost of firms' existing productive capacity; for example, if a firm's capital stock is ten sewing machines and each sewing machine costs $100 at current market prices, then the CRC = $1000. Using these measures of MV and CRC, Tobin's q is calculated as:

$$\text{Tobin's } q = \frac{MV}{CRC} \tag{8.2}$$

Box 8.1 Measuring market value and efficient markets

A share in a company is like a little piece of that company. So the market value of the firm is just a firm's **share price** multiplied by the number of issued shares. This gives a measure of the **market valuation** of an individual firm. For example, if Rolls Royce shares are trading at £5 each on the London Stock Exchange (LSE) and there are 1.8 billion shares in the company, then the market capitalisation for Rolls Royce will be £9 billion.

Most world stock exchanges report their total market capitalisations. These are calculated simply by adding together the market capitalisations for all the firms listed on a stock exchange. For example, in 2007 there were 1139 firms listed on the main market of the LSE and the total market capitalisation of these companies was over £2 trillion (trillion = a million millions). In 2007 there were more than 2600 companies listed on the New York Stock Exchange (NYSE), with a total market capitalisation of US$22.6 trillion.

Tobin's q theory is based around the **rational expectations hypothesis (REH)** and the related **efficient markets hypothesis (EMH)**. The REH is usually attributed to Muth who asserted that 'expectations, since they are informed predictions of future events, are essentially the same as the predictions of the relevant economic theory' (Muth 1961,

p. 316). The EMH incorporates the REH in hypothesising that financial markets are 'informationally efficient', i.e. they ensure that share prices listed on stock exchanges fully reflect all relevant information available to rational investors. If financial markets are informationally efficient, then share prices will fluctuate completely and instantaneously to incorporate any informative news. If new information affecting the future prospects of a firm arrives, then the relative demand and supply for the shares of that firm will adjust instantaneously via **arbitrage**. For example if there is bad news about a company and its future profitability prospects look less impressive as a consequence, then demand for shares in that company will fall and more people will try to sell its shares as rational traders will adjust their willingness to pay downwards. So the share price will fall. In this way, share prices will adjust to reflect the **fundamental value** of a firm, i.e. the discounted stream of expected future profits or dividends emerging from the firm's future production. Overall, REH and EMH together predict that share prices will provide an unbiased indicator of rational investors' expectations of future profitability.

If the efficient markets assumption is true, then it follows that the rational traders' expectations about the future value of firms will be captured by the stock **market capitalisation** of the firm. Tobin's *q* theorists argue that these stock market valuations will give an unbiased estimate of the future value of a firm's production and investment.

The ratio of total value and total costs gives a measure of average contribution of all new investment to total revenue: MV is capturing the total value and CRC is capturing the total cost and so Tobin's q measures q_A.

This theory follows Tobin's interpretation of Keynes's (1936) ideas about the role of the stock market in providing a measure of expectations about the expected future profits from new investments. (It is important to emphasise that Tobin's *q* theory is based upon just one interpretation of Keynes; some economists argue that Keynes's emphasis on crowd psychology and herd behaviour in financial markets is not consistent with Tobin's *q* theories of investment because Tobin's interpretation relies on assumptions of rational expectations and efficient markets, as also explained in Box 8.1.)

As explained above, whilst q_M is about the impacts of marginal additions to the capital stock via new investment it can be proxied by q_A. Tobin's *q* measures this average and so can be used to give investment decision rules, as outlined in Box 8.2.

So far we have concentrated on the microeconomic aspects of investor decision-making but Tobin's *q* theory can be transformed into an aggregate theory of macroeconomic investment by adopting a **representative agent hypothesis**, i.e. by assuming that all firms behave in the same way. If this is

---

Box 8.2 Incentives to invest: q_M and q_A

q_M	q_A as a proxy for q_M	Optimal choice
$q_M = \frac{MB}{MC} > 1$	$q_A = \frac{MV}{CRC} = \frac{TB}{TC} > 1$	→ increase investment
$q_M = \frac{MB}{MC} = 1$	$q_A = \frac{MV}{CRC} = \frac{TB}{TC} = 1$	→ replacement investment only
$q_M = \frac{MB}{MC} < 1$	$q_A = \frac{MV}{CRC} = \frac{TB}{TC} < 1$	→ disinvest (if possible)

---

true then we can describe the aggregate behaviour of all firms by describing the behaviour of one *representative* firm. In the macroeconomic versions of Tobin's q theory, this means that the ratio of the stock market capitalisation for all listed companies on an exchange (as explained in Box 8.1) to the overall current replacement cost of all these companies' capital stocks will give a measure of aggregate average q. In this chapter we will assess these aggregate versions of Tobin's q model of investment using US data to analyse the relationships between the rate of investment and Tobin's measure of q_A, as explained below.

8.3   The data

The dependent variable used in this analysis will be the investment rate $\frac{I}{K}$, where I is corporate investment in the US (net of replacement investment) and K is the US corporate capital stock as measured by its current replacement cost.

Tobin's q is used as an explanatory variable in our investment models. As explained above, the essence of Tobin's q is that it is a measure of q_A and so can be used as a proxy for q_M. Tobin's q model of investment rests on the assumption that stock market valuations capture the expected future profitability of companies' capital stocks and so will determine investment activity. Following Equation (8.2):

$$\text{Tobin's } q = \frac{MV}{CRC} \tag{8.2}$$

Calculating a simple version of Tobin's q is relatively straightforward, though more complex versions do incorporate adjustments for taxation and depreciation.

We collected data from the following sources:

Variable	Source	Website
Tobin's q	Smithers and Wright (2000) New York Stock Exchange	www.valuingwallstreet.com/ www.nyse.com
Investment rate (I/K)	Derived from National Income and Product (NIPA) accounts, US Bureau of Economic Analysis	www.bea.gov

The q data from Smithers and Wright (2000) are based on stock market capitalisations on the New York Stock Exchange. Similar data on stock markets and investment for the UK can be collected via the LSE (www.londonstockexchange.com) and the Office of National Statistics (ONS) (www.statistics.gov.uk).

In assessing the reliability of our data, it is important to note that we only have 18 observations and the very small size of our sample will limit the accuracy of our estimations. That said, we are forced to use a small number of observations because the data on Tobin's q is not very rich and detailed. Also, it is important to emphasise that not all firms are listed on the NYSE and so there will not be a match between the market capitalisation element of q and the investment rate. But we will assume for simplicity that stock market capitalisations act as a signal to *all* firms planning to buy some new productive capacity, whether or not they are listed on the NYSE.

Another issue to remember is that the true incentive to invest is given by q_M, an unobservable variable. As explained in Chapter 3, when data on a specific variable are unavailable (perhaps because the variable is unobservable and/or un-measurable), a proxy can be used in its place. A good proxy will be strongly correlated with the missing variable but uncorrelated with the error term of our regression. The rationale underlying Tobin's q models is that, given some assumptions, q_A will be a good **proxy** for q_M. But proxy variables may still create problems because they will introduce **measurement error** into empirical models: the proxy is not the true explanatory variable and so cannot be perfectly correlated with it. Measurement error may emerge from using proxies for other reasons (e.g. unreliable statistical collection methods). In general, if measurement error affects the explanatory variable then it may create the problem of **endogeneity** – a violation of Gauss–Markov assumptions which occurs when the explanatory variable is correlated with the error term. When the explanatory variable and error are correlated, OLS parameter estimates will pick up some of the influence of the errors and OLS

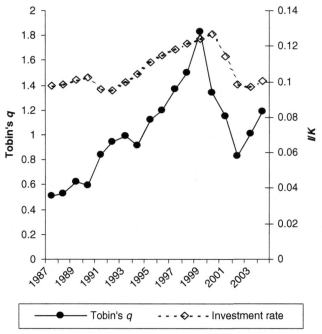

Sources: BEA, Smithers and Wright (2000).

Figure 8.2   Corporate investment and Tobin's q, USA 1987–2004

estimation will be both biased and inconsistent. Issues of endogeneity are beyond the scope of this book but see Wooldridge (2003) for a thorough analysis of these issues. Putting these complexities to one side, we will start by looking at our data for our dependent variable (I/K) and explanatory variable (q).

In Figure 8.2 the changes in the US corporate investment rate and Tobin's q are plotted to depict the broad trends between q and investment during the years 1987–2004. Figure 8.2 shows that, whilst there are some periods of volatility in Tobin's q (perhaps reflecting the dotcom boom of the early 1990s and the busts early in the new millennium), overall the series are fluctuating in similar ways. On the other hand, there are long periods in which Tobin's q is above or below 1 suggesting that entrepreneurs are taking time to adjust their capital stocks in response to changes in market valuations. (The issue of lags is not explicitly addressed in this chapter but is covered in the chapter exercises.) In analysing whether or not these patterns translate into a robust relationship between the investment rate and Tobin's q, we will run a regression of the investment rate on q, as outlined in the empirical section below.

8.4   Empirical methods and results

Does Tobin's q theory capture the empirical evidence on aggregate investment? In this chapter we will answer this question by analysing the relationship between the investment rate (I/K) and Tobin's q (q) using the following general model:

$$\frac{I_t}{K_t} = f(q_t) \tag{8.3}$$

The issue that we will investigate in this chapter is the identification of the **functional form** of the relationship between the dependent and explanatory variables. This functional form captures the nature of the mathematical relationship between the dependent and explanatory variables. We need to decide is it linear or non-linear? If it's non-linear, then what form does the non-linearity take? As explained in Box 8.3, identifying the correct functional form is important. Incorrect functional form is a type of model misspecification error and can have crucial implications for the applicability of OLS estimation.

Box 8.3 Model misspecification errors

Model misspecification bias occurs when an empirical model is constructed the wrong way. There are three main types of model misspecification error, all of which distort the relationship between observed data and their fitted values:

1. **Incorrect functional form**: for example, using OLS works well if a model is linear but if there is a non-linear relationship between the dependent and explanatory variables then OLS will be biased and inconsistent.
2. **Omitted variable bias**: this occurs when important explanatory variables have been left out of the regression. When we leave an important variable out of an empirical model (either unintentionally or because we can't measure it) then OLS estimates may be biased and inconsistent.
3. **Irrelevant variables**: a less serious form of model misspecification occurs when irrelevant variables are included. This leads to a loss of efficiency because degrees of freedom are 'wasted' in unnecessarily estimating irrelevant parameters.

What are the solutions? Hypothesis tests (such as Student's t test) will give us information about whether or not an explanatory variable is irrelevant. The first two types of model misspecification (along with measurement error) are trickier to resolve even though they can be major sources of endogeneity, as mentioned above.

> More generally, to protect against model misspecification problems, it is important to use economic theory and previous research as a guide in constructing an appropriate functional form and in selecting appropriate explanatory variables. For unmeasurable variables there are two main solutions: using a proxy (as discussed above) or using **'instrumental variable (IV)'** estimation. IV estimation is beyond the scope of this book but see Wooldridge (2003) for a thorough analysis.

We will explore a number of possible forms, including lin-log, log-log and lin-lin specifications.[2] In establishing which of these specifications is most appropriate, a good first step is to look at the scatter plot of our variables around the trend line, as shown in Figures 8.3a–c. The observations seem to be more evenly dispersed around the trend line in the lin-lin specification. However, it is difficult to form a clear impression of the patterns because the inspection of any visual plot of data is susceptible to some degree of subjectivity.

To gather some more objective information about the functional form of the relationship between investment and Tobin's q, we will estimate the following three forms of Equation (8.3):

$$\text{lin-log specification :} \quad i_t = \alpha_1 + \beta_1 \ln q_t + \varepsilon_{1t} \tag{8.4}$$

$$\text{log-log specification :} \quad \ln i_t = \alpha_2 + \beta_2 \ln q_t + \varepsilon_{2t} \tag{8.5}$$

$$\text{lin-lin specification :} \quad i_t = \alpha_3 + \beta_3 q_t + \varepsilon_{3t} \tag{8.6}$$

where $i_t = \dfrac{I_t}{K_t}$ and ε_{1t}, ε_{2t} and ε_{3t} are the stochastic error terms from (8.4), (8.5) and (8.6) respectively. From the SRFs, we will test each model for incorrect functional form using **Ramsey's RESET test**, which is explained in Box 8.4.

The EViews output tables for the estimations of the SRFs for Equations (8.4) (lin-log), (8.5) (log-log) and (8.6) (lin-lin) are summarised in Table 8.1. For the estimations of (8.4) (lin-log) and (8.5) (log-log), there are initial signs of model misspecification; the null of no AR(4) autocorrelation in the errors from the F version of the BG test is rejected at a 5% significance level. This suggests a systematic pattern in the residuals from these regressions and, as explained above, one explanation for this is some form of model misspecification error.

We also have the RR test results from EViews. To show how this RR test was calculated, using the results from the estimation of (8.4), we follow the steps outlined in Box 8.4 as follows (on page 192):

---

[2] The use of logs in specifying the functional form of empirical models was introduced in Chapter 3 Box 3.3.

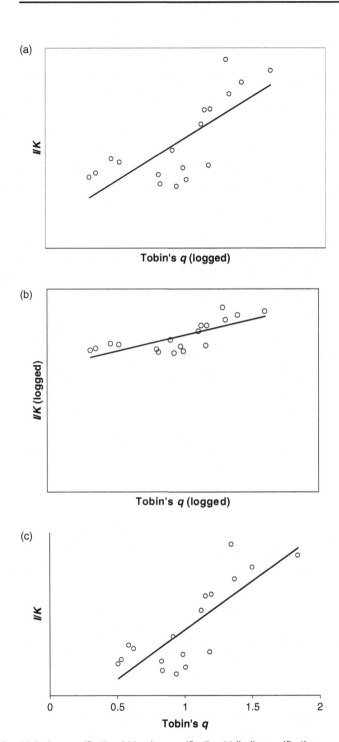

Figure 8.3   (a) lin-log specification (b) log-log specification (c) lin-lin specification

---

Box 8.4 Detecting model misspecification using Ramsey's RESET test

In Chapter 7 we explained that systematic patterns in the residuals may be a symptom of other problems one of which is **model misspecification**. So our diagnostic tests for autocorrelation, i.e. the Breusch–Godfrey (BG) test (explained in Chapter 7) will also pick up systematic patterns in the residuals emerging because of model misspecification. There are also tests designed specifically to identify problems of incorrect functional form and one of the most widely used functional form tests is Ramsey's RESET (RR) test. RR tests come in many forms; for example if you are trying to estimate a logarithmic relationship using levels, then the RR test will pick this up.

The RR test is constructed in three stages.
1. Estimate the SRF and save the fitted values.
2. Transform the fitted values to generate a variable which can capture omitted influences. The most common method is to use a quadratic transformation by squaring the fitted values, though it is possible also to include higher-order polynomial terms e.g. cubic transformations of the fitted values.
3. Run an auxiliary regression of the dependent variable on the explanatory variable and the squared fitted values.
4. Conduct hypotheses tests on the parameters for the transformed fitted values using an F test of restrictions.

For example, if our dependent variable is Y and our explanatory variable is X, then the auxiliary regression for the RR test would be:

$$\hat{Y}_i = \hat{a} + \hat{\beta}X_i + \hat{\phi}\left[\hat{Y}_i^2\right] \tag{8.7}$$

The RR test is testing the following null and alternative hypotheses:

$H_0 : \phi = 0$

$H_1 : \phi \neq 0$

The intuition underlying the Ramsey RESET test is that if the original model is complete, then including $\hat{Y}_i^2$ in the auxiliary regression will make very little difference to the goodness of fit and the F test of restrictions will not allow the rejection of H_0. On the other hand, if the original model suffers from the problem of incorrect functional form, then $\hat{Y}_i^2$ will pick up something of what is missing. Including $\hat{Y}_i^2$ will lead to a relatively large fall in the RSS relative to the RSS in the original model and the F test will allow a rejection of H_0. We will conclude that the square of the fitted value is picking up something that has been omitted from the original model.

Most econometrics packages, including EViews, will report variants of the RR test. We illustrate an example of the RR test below.

Table 8.1 Summary of EViews output tables from estimations of Equations (8.4), (8.5) and (8.6)
Sample: 1987 2004

LINLOG MODEL

Dependent Variable: Investment Rate

Variable	Coefficient	t-Statistic	Prob.
Intercept	0.11	62.37	0.00
q (logged)	0.02	4.48	0.00

R-squared	0.56	
Adjusted R-squared	0.53	
Sum squared residuals	0.000849	
F-statistic	20.05	
Prob(F-statistic)	0.00	

Breusch-Godfrey LM Tests:

F-statistic	3.88
Probability	0.03

Ramsey RESET Tests and Auxiliary Regressions:

F-statistic	8.5
Probability	0.01

Test Equation from Auxiliary Regressions:

Variable	Coefficient	t-Statistic	Prob.
C	−0.63	−2.49	0.03
q (logged)	−0.27	−2.69	0.02
FITTED^2	63.81	2.91	0.01

R-squared	0.72	
Adjusted R-squared	0.68	
Sum squared residuals	0.000542	
F-statistic	18.95	
Prob(F-statistic)	0.00	

LOGLOG MODEL

Dependent Variable: Investment Rate (logged)

Variable	Coefficient	t-Statistic	Prob.
Intercept	−2.23	−141.29	0.00
q (logged)	0.20	4.43	0.00

R-squared	0.55	
Adjusted R-squared	0.52	
Sum squared residuals	0.0714	
F-statistic	19.66	
Prob(F-statistic)	0.00	

F-statistic	3.88
Probability	0.03

F-statistic	7.9
Probability	0.01

Test Equation:

Variable	Coefficient	t-Statistic	Prob.
C	−36.83	−2.98	0.01
q (logged)	6.37	2.89	0.01
FITTED^2	6.92	2.80	0.01

R-squared	0.71	
Adjusted R-squared	0.67	
Sum squared residuals	0.0469	
F-statistic	17.98	
Prob(F-statistic)	0.00	

LINLIN MODEL

Dependent Variable: Investment Rate

Variable	Coefficient	t-Statistic	Prob.
Intercept	0.08	17.09	0.00
q	0.02	5.44	0.00

R-squared	0.65	
Adjusted R-squared	0.63	
Sum squared residuals	0.000672	
F-statistic	29.55	
Prob(F-statistic)	0.00	

F-statistic	1.92
Probability	0.17

F-statistic	1.1
Probability	0.30

Test Equation:

Variable	Coefficient	t-Statistic	Prob.
C	−0.03	−0.30	0.77
q	−0.07	−0.80	0.44
FITTED^2	18.59	1.07	0.30

R-squared	0.67	
Adjusted R-squared	0.63	
Sum squared residuals	0.000624	
F-statistic	15.47	
Prob(F-statistic)	0.00	

1. Estimate the SRF, saving the fitted values. This is the restricted model for the purposes of the RR test so $RSS_r = 0.000849$
2. Square the fitted values from step 1 to give 'FITTED^2'.
3. Run an auxiliary regression by regressing the investment rate on logged q and 'FITTED^2'. This gives us the unrestricted model for F version of the RR test and so $RSS_u = 0.000542$
4. We construct the RR version of the F test of restrictions as follows. (There is one restriction, i.e. that the parameter on 'FITTED^2' is equal to zero, so $d = 1$; $n = 18$ and $k = 1$.)

$$F(d, n - k_u - 1 - d) = \frac{(RSS_r - RSS_u)/d}{(RSS_u)/(n - k_u - 1 - d)}$$

$$= \frac{0.000849 - 0.000542}{(0.000542)/(18 - 2 - 1)} = 8.50$$

(8.8)

Following this procedure we can reject the null that the parameter on FITTED^2 is equal to zero at a 5% significance level. This is consistent with the result from a t test that the parameter on FITTED^2 is equal to zero. It is also consistent with our BG test. So we can conclude that there are significant signs of model misspecification. Similarly, you will see from Table 8.1 that there are signs of model misspecification in the estimation of (8.5) (the log-log model).

For the estimation of (8.6) (the lin-lin model) however, the F version of the RR test gives $p = 0.30$ so $p > 0.05$ and so we cannot reject the null that the parameter on FITTED^2 is equal to zero. In addition, the F version of the AR(4) BG test gives a p value of 0.17; $p > 0.05$ and so, with a 5% significance level, we do not reject the null of no autocorrelation in the errors. Again this suggests that there are no significant signs of incorrect functional form in the estimation of (8.6). We can conclude that the results from the lin-lin model seem to be relatively reliable.

The results from the estimation of the lin-lin model can be summarised as follows:

$$\hat{i}_t = \begin{array}{cc} 0.08 & +0.02q_t \\ (0.0048) & (0.0044) \\ t = 17.09 & t = 5.44 \\ p = 0.00 & p = 0.00 \end{array}$$

(8.9)

$R^2 = 0.65$	F test of explanatory power: $F(1,16) = 29.55$ $[P = 0.00]$	
RR test:	$F(1,15) = 1.14$	$[p = 0.30]$
BG test:	$F(4,12) = 1.92$	$[p = 0.17]$

Overall, the significant t test results on the parameter estimates for (8.6) (the lin-lin model) allow us to reject the nulls that the intercept and slope parameters are equal to zero. An initial inspection suggests that there is a significant positive relationship between investment and q_A, as predicted by Tobin's q theory. For our data on US investment 1987–2004, an increase in q_A is associated with increases in the investment rate. The R^2 suggests that 65% of the variability in the investment rate is captured by variability in q and the F test of explanatory power confirms that the overall goodness of fit of the model is relatively high and we can reject the null of no association between the dependent and explanatory variables. We have identified a significant association between q and the investment rate.

These results seem to confirm the theory. If our findings are robust then this suggests that, if a buoyant stock market generates rises in market capitalisation that outstrip increases in the current replacement cost of the capital stock, then this will generate rises in the investment rate. It is important however to note the shortcomings of our analysis. Empirically, we have identified a positive association between investment and q: as q rises, the investment rate (as a proportion of the capital stock) rises with it. However, as mentioned above, this finding is based on results from a very small sample. There are also problems with simple specifications of q theory. Lags are excluded even though in reality investment decisions will not be implemented instantaneously. Delays affect almost every stage of investment decision-making: there are lags between decision-making, expenditure, ordering, delivery and installation. So actual investment expenditure in the current period will reflect decisions taken some time ago. Including just current q when its lags may have more impact may have affected the reliability of our results.

Also Tobin's q models are based on assumptions of rational expectations and efficient financial markets. Are these assumptions valid? There is a growing literature asserting that stock market valuations will not reflect rational expectations of the future potential of current investments. This is because share prices reflect a range of other factors and will fluctuate in response to crowd psychology, herd behaviour, speculative bubbles, irrational exuberance and short-termism. With inefficient financial markets, market valuations will not be a reliable indicator of the future profitability prospects of current investments. This issue has been the focus of a lot of recent research and this research into inefficient markets is summarised in Box 8.5.

Box 8.5 Inefficient markets and behavioural economics

Hypotheses about efficient markets and rational agents look weak when confronted by the large number of historical examples of speculative bubbles. A **speculative bubble** occurs when an asset price deviates from its fundamental value. One of the most spectacular historical examples of a speculative bubble was **Tulipmania**, which happened during the 1630s in Holland. During this time, there was a very rare bulb that could grow into a beautiful tulip; it was called the *Semper Augustus* and, at the height of Tulipmania, it was selling for as much as a three-storey house in central Amsterdam. But when the bubble burst, within weeks the *Semper Augustus* bulb became relatively worthless. There are many more recent examples of speculative bubbles, for example the dotcom bubble of the late 1990s – the impact of which can be seen in Figure 8.2 as an upward blip in Tobin's q ratio reflecting a jump in market valuations because of speculative trading in dotcom shares. Speculative bubbles in housing and commodity markets constituted to significant instability from 2008 onwards.

Keynes (1936) was one of the first economists to focus on the irrational triggers of financial market movements, analysing the role of factors such as crowd psychology, herding and market conventions. More recently, economists such as Shiller and Shleifer have focussed on irrational forces in financial markets, developing the arguments of Federal Reserve governor Alan Greenspan (who coined the term **irrational exuberance** in response to the dotcom bubble of the late 1990s). Also, building upon the work of the George Katona, recent Nobel Prize winner Daniel Kahneman (a psychologist) and Kahneman's colleague Amos Tversky (who was an economist), behavioural economists and economic psychologists are putting to one side assumptions about rational expectations and efficient markets to concentrate on the psychology of economic and financial decision-making.

One of the more novel aspects of this literature is the research into the relationship between psychological factors and financial activity. This draws upon Jevons' sunspot theory, a nineteenth-century model of the economy focussing on the impact of cosmic rays and sunspots on the weather. Jevons argued that the consequent impacts of weather on agricultural production would spread to the macroeconomy more generally. Whilst these ideas were ridiculed at the time, the focus on weather is now being revived in a number of ways. In financial derivatives markets new instruments are being devised to hedge against weather risks using **weather derivatives**: for example natural catastrophe bonds (**cat bonds**) are instruments designed to protect agricultural firms from natural catastrophes such as hurricanes (*The Economist*, 2005).

In explaining the wider psychological impacts of the weather on financial markets, Hirschleifer and Shumway (2003) have analysed the relationships between mood, sunlight and financial trading activity and Kamstra, Kramer and Levi (2003) have identified a positive relationship between seasonal depression (a.k.a. Seasonal Affective Disorder – SAD) and subdued stock market activity.

Ideas about inefficient financial markets are also taken further in a new sub-discipline of economics called **neuroeconomics**. Neuroeconomists work with experimental psychologists, neurophysiologists and neuroanatomists using various experimental techniques to capture how and why the brain is involved in financial decision-making, particularly risk-taking and impulsive behaviour. A range of neuroeconomic techniques is outlined in Camerer, Loewenstein and Prelec (2005). Some examples of neuroeconomic techniques include functional magnetic resonance imaging (fMRI) – which involves taking detailed 'pictures' of the brain to assess oxygen flows to particular areas; single neuron experiments to monitor the neurotransmitters that operate at the synapses of neurons (e.g. dopamine); monitoring of levels of hormones such as testosterone and cortisol using saliva and blood tests; studying the behaviour of patients with lesions located in particular areas of their brains to assess whether or not such impairments affect economic behaviour; as well as psychometric testing to control for the role of various personality traits in economic decision-making etc.

Neuroeconomists investigate financial market behaviour by assessing how financial traders' brains respond when traders are making risky decisions. Ultimately, if they can show that people do not necessarily use objective information in a systematic way then rational expectations and efficient markets will no longer be at the core of theoretical analyses of financial markets. On the other hand, if the behavioural economists and neuroeconomists can show that economic and financial decision-making is associated with logical, rational cognitive responses, then we could conclude that the emphasis on rationality and market efficiency in models such as Tobin's *q* theory may be justifiable, at least as an approximation.

8.5   Implications and conclusions

In this chapter, we have analysed the impact of stock market activity on fixed asset investment by estimating Tobin's *q* model of investment in the USA 1987–2004. In terms of policy, the positive association between Tobin's *q* and investment suggests that stock market volatility will have implications for investment and capital accumulation more generally. Therefore, measures to stabilise stock markets, e.g. taxes on speculative trades (known as Tobin taxes reflecting Tobin's other research), may generate wider benefits in terms of stabilising productive activity overall. Taxes on financial transactions might moderate some of the sources of macroeconomic instability but there may be political constraints on implementing new taxes and regulations. Such policy changes are unlikely to be popular, particularly within the financial services sector, though instability in global financial markets has increased pressure to implement regulatory reforms.

Overall, Tobin's q provides a neat theoretical solution to the problem of measuring investors' expectations of the future potential of their current investment decisions. And q models capture the investment process more effectively than Jorgenson's early theory because they incorporate expectations, forward-looking behaviour and adjustment costs. However, if agents do not form rational expectations and/or if financial markets are not efficient, then the theoretical underpinnings of q models of investment will have to be rethought.

8.6   Further reading

Textbooks

Baddeley, M. C. (2003) *Investment: Theories and Analysis*, London: Palgrave Macmillan.

Keynes, J. M. (1936) *The General Theory of Employment, Interest and Money*, London: Macmillan.

NYSE (2006) *A Guide to the NYSE Market Place*, New York: New York Stock Exchange.

Shiller, R. (2001) *Irrational Exuberance*, Princeton: Princeton University Press.

Shleifer, A. (2000) *Inefficient Markets: An Introduction to Behavioral Finance*, Oxford: Oxford University Press.

Smithers, A. S. and Wright, S. (2000) *Valuing Wall Street*, New York: McGraw Hill.

Wooldridge, J. M. (2003) *Introductory Econometrics – A Modern Approach* (2nd edition), Thomson South-Western. See Chapter 9 on model misspecification and measurement error; see Chapter 15 for corrective procedures including instrumental variable (IV) estimation.

Academic articles and working papers

Camerer, C. F., Loewenstein, G. and Prelec, D. (2005) 'Neuroeconomics: how neuroscience can inform economics', *Journal of Economic Literature*, vol. 43 no. 1, 9–64.

Hayashi, F. (1982) 'Tobin's marginal q and average q: a neoclassical interpretation', *Econometrica*, vol. 50, no. 1, 213–24.

Hirschleifer, D. and Shumway, T. (2003) 'Good day sunshine: stock returns and the weather', *Journal of Finance*, vol. LVIII, no. 3, 1009–32.

Jorgenson, D. W. (1963) 'Capital theory and investment behaviour', *American Economic Review*, vol. 53, no. 2, 247–59.

Kamstra, M. J., Kramer, L. A. and Levi, M. D. (2003) 'Winter blues: a SAD stock market cycle', *American Economic Review*, vol. 93, no. 1, 324–43.

Muth, J. F. (1961) 'Rational expectations and the theory of price movements', *Econometrica*, vol. 29, no. 3, 315–55.

Policy briefs and newspaper articles

Bond, S., Klemm, A., Newton-Smith, R., Syed, M. and Vlieghe, G. (2004) 'The roles of profitability, Tobin's Q and cash flow in econometric models of company investment', *Bank of England Working Paper No. 222*, London: Bank of England.

The Economist (2005) 'Weather risk: natural hedge', 1 October 2005, p. 84.

8.7   Chapter exercises

1. In this chapter we noted that the estimation of Tobin's q models might have suffered econometrically from the exclusion of lags. Re-estimate the models from this chapter using the data sources outlined in Section 8.3 and check for signs of model misspecification. Discuss your results.

2. As explained in Section 8.3, accelerator theories of investment use past output growth as a proxy for expectations of future sales. Using the data sources outlined in Section 8.3:

   (a) Construct an empirical model of accelerator theory using output growth as an explanatory variable.

   (b) Assess your results including the diagnostic test results.

   (c) Discuss the relative empirical performance of your model and the q models from this chapter.

Part III

Time-series econometrics

In the previous parts, we have applied econometric techniques to both cross-sectional data and time-series data. Cross-sectional data has a spatial dimension and can be collected at different levels of disaggregation. It gives a 'snapshot' view from one point in time and will include observations for a number of different individuals, households, firms, regions or countries.

Conversely, time-series analysis focusses on one spatial 'entity' (e.g. a firm, a country or the world) and investigates how the behaviour of that entity changes over time. Time-series observations can be of any 'periodicity'. The most commonly used are annual, quarterly, monthly or daily. In financial markets intra-day 'high-frequency' data is also collected, e.g. to record how asset prices change even from one second to the next.

Apart from the usual econometric problems discussed in Part II, the analysis of time-series data can be complicated by lags and structural breaks. There may also be time trends – both 'deterministic' (predictable) and 'stochastic' (random). These trends will generate the problem of 'non-stationarity'.

In this part, we will investigate some of these complications. We will also introduce some econometric procedures designed specifically for the analysis of time-series data.

Structural breaks, non-stationarity and spurious regressions

Venture capital and computing investment in the USA

Economic issues include:
- The New Economy
- Investment in computing
- Venture capital funding

Econometric issues include:
- Structural breaks
- Unit roots, non-stationarity and spurious regressions

Data issues include:
- Measuring the New Economy

9.1　The issue

In this chapter we will look at the relationship between computing investment and venture capital financing in the New Economy. Computing investment has been essential to the growth of the New Economy: Yang and Brynjolfsson (2001) argue that computerisation is the most pervasive technological change this era. IT (information technology) investments promoted improved macroeconomic performance, culminating from large increases in productivity and growth in the 1990s onwards, particularly in the US. Increasing GDP growth was accompanied by reduced volatility in GDP. This is because IT innovations played a key role in promoting greater flexibility; for example, innovations such as price comparison sites (e.g. dealtime.com and kelkoo.com) increased micro-economic flexibility via increased price transparency.

The New Economy grew rapidly from the 1990s onwards and its growth was enabled by venture capital injections. Venture capital is of particular importance because young entrepreneurs are responsible for a substantial proportion of the innovative New Economy investments. These entrepreneurs do not have profits retained from existing production. So venture capital funds are important in providing them finance for their new investments.

In this chapter we will explore the relationship between New Economy investment and venture capital funding. We will focus in particular on IT in the New Economy by examining the relationships between venture capital funds and investment in computing software in the US 1980–2004. We will also use this data set to illustrate the econometric implications of structural breaks, non-stationary variables and spurious regressions.

9.2   The theory

These days it seems that everyone's talking about the New Economy. But what is it? There is no universally accepted definition of the New Economy but the term is generally used to refer to the development of new high-tech knowledge-based industries, particularly those associated with IT. The New Economy also includes industries associated with biotechnology (biotech) but the IT sector has been particularly influential.

The growth of the New Economy and particularly the development of the Internet, have made physical location and resources less important. This is because one of the key characteristics of the technological changes in IT are that they are **knowledge-driven** and therefore **aspatial**. They are knowledge-driven because brain-power, research and innovation play a more important role than they do in traditional industries, for which physical location and local resources (e.g. plentiful labour) are important. Knowledge-driven technologies and industries are also aspatial because they do not rely on physical assets fixed in particular locations. This means that knowledge-driven industries can transcend national/regional boundaries more easily. For example, computing innovations such as email and the Internet mean that geographical divisions are not as important as they once were. Developments in the New Economy have progressed in tandem with the process of globalisation; for example, different people in different parts of the world can communicate and trade almost instantaneously because of IT innovations particularly those based on Internet and mobile technologies. So these technologies have had enormous implications for global economic activity and trade.

What is the history of the IT Revolution? Widespread computerisation of economic activity began in 1971 when Intel marketed its first microprocessor chip, allowing the development of powerful personal computers (PCs). During the 1970s, news of these innovations spread and new IT-related products and services evolved, starting with basic computerisation of business activities (e.g. word-processing, spreadsheet and accounting packages). Computerisation eventually affected almost every aspect of modern economic life with the development of innovations associated with computer networking and the Internet, mobile phone technologies and computer-based financial innovations (for example Electronic Funds Transfer at Point of Sale (EFTPOS), and Automated Clearing House (ACH) systems).

This diffusion of computer technologies is described via **Moore's Law**: the power of microprocessors doubles every 18 months. Moore's Law operates because technological developments have allowed an increasing number of transistors to be built into each individual microprocessor increasing their power: the transistor count in the average microprocessor rose from just above 1,000 transistors in 1971 to close on 100 million transistors in 2001. This exponential growth in electronic transistors translated into a rapid growth of computing power, in turn fostering rapid falls in the cost of computing equipment. These falls in computing costs allowed technological changes from the IT sector to spread rapidly through the economy, particularly for innovations that overlap industries. For example, recent innovators in the high-tech sector have been developing **mobile wallets**, which allow people to store and use money via their mobile phones. Mobile wallets link together IT technologies from the computing and telecommunications industry and from the financial sector.

Computing innovations have had significant impacts on the broader economy. The US Department of Commerce estimates that high-tech industry accounted for more than one third of GDP growth between 1995 and 1999. Gordon (2000) and Whelan (2002) also provide evidence about the impacts of the IT Revolution on increasing trend growth rates in real GDP and productivity. In addition, Landefeld and Fraumeni (2000) estimate that, between 1995 and 1999, the contribution of high-tech products to real GDP growth was 24%; they also observe that difficulties measuring the impacts of high-tech investments mean that this is likely to be an under estimate.

IT developments have affected productivity, real wages and unemployment too. Plants using computer-aided manufacturing paid workers two-thirds more than traditional plants in the same industry (Dunne, 1991). Output growth in the computing industries has been associated with declines in UK unemployment (Baddeley, 2008). The IT Revolution promoted increasing international trade in computers, semi-conductors and other high-tech goods and household wealth increased in parallel: US household wealth doubled in the 1990s, reflecting increases in share prices – particularly in the IT sector – in turn fostering income growth and growing consumer confidence (Landefeld & Fraumeni, 2000).

However, not all commentators agree about the revolutionary impact of the IT Revolution. Many assert that the IT Revolution is not a unique event, and it is neither a new phenomenon nor qualitatively different from other techno-logical revolutions, e.g. those that accompanied the Industrial Revolution. Some of the pessimism about the IT Revolution emerged because com-puterisation's contribution to productivity and economic growth was not immediately obvious. This was the essence of **Solow's Computer Paradox** (SCP): many people had expected computerisation to boost labour and capital productivity a lot more quickly – but between the 1970s and the 1990s, productivity actually *slowed* despite widespread computerisation. Solow (1987) famously observed that computerisation can be seen everywhere, except in the productivity statistics. But productivity gains did eventually emerge, suggesting that the SCP may have reflected lags in investment decision-making, slow diffusion of innovations, substantial adjustment costs involved in adopting innovative technologies and/or problems of measurement. Specifically, measurement problems will occur because computerisation involves intangible investments (e.g. in computing skills, R&D etc.) and focusses on the provision of services rather than the production of goods; conventional productivity statistics do not effectively capture these factors.

Even so, these benefits did not last forever. Following the NASDAQ crash in mid 2001 surplus computers stockpiled because access to cheap finance had encouraged an unsustainable over-investment in computing resources (Cecchetti, 2002). But IT innovations may have made economies naturally more resilient and flexible, for example new innovations in inventory control allowed firms to respond relatively quickly to changes in economic conditions; for example, Cecchetti (2002) observes that the 2000–2001 slowdown in the US was remarkably subdued and short-lived because computerisation had increased macroeconomic flexibility. Economies were also far more resilient in the aftermath of the September 2001 terrorist attacks than was initially predicted. US Bureau of Economic Analysis (BEA) data show that although US annual real GDP growth slowed to 1.7% in the last quarter of 2001, in the first quarter of 2002, it recovered to 5.6%. Hopeful commentators might also predict that the flexibility engendered by computerisation of economic activity may also moderate the recessionary impacts of the 2007/8 credit crunch.

What are the limits to growth in the New Economy? Have economies had their New Economy 'burst' or can we expect technological progress to continue at its current pace? Will new technologies continue to develop and spread? According to some observers, the rise and fall of the dot coms and the accompanying boom–bust investment cycle suggests that perhaps the processes of invention and innovation will falter until the next technological revolution. Furthermore, some economists believe that technological developments are a key factor in *explaining* the ups and downs of business cycles. Schumpeter (1939) analysed technological booms associated with the telephone, railways and electrification and his ideas can be extended to investment in the New Economy. Schumpeter argued that innovative industries emerge from a process of 'creative destruction' with oligopolistic firms competing technologically (rather than via price competition) and creating cyclical instability as a consequence. The clumping of innovations leads to 'bursts' of entrepreneurship; bandwagon effects encourage herds of entrepreneurs to copy innovative entrepreneurs in exploiting new innovations. But as more and more entrepreneurs try to exploit the diffusion of technological innovations, profits will be eroded. Financing new innovations will become more and more difficult, contributing to an ebbing of confidence in innovative industries. So downswings are the inevitable consequence of the innovative phases that generate the upswing.

A key factor affecting technological cycles is the availability of finance. The process of investing in new types of plant, machinery and equipment ensures that technological innovation diffuses through the economy allowing people and businesses to learn about new innovations. But, even if an entrepreneur has a brilliant idea, the success or failure of his/her business venture will still depend upon whether or not funds are available to finance the costs of establishing a new business. All fixed investments, whether innovative or not, depend on finance so innovative activity will slow as financing constraints emerge.

In innovative phases, specific types of funding may be necessary. One way to fund investment is via retained profits from existing production but the established firms that are likely to have these retained profits may initially be resistant to technological change. The technological leaders are more likely to be young entrepreneurs with great new ideas but no existing business to provide them with retained profits for new investments. Famous examples of businesses started by young entrepreneurs include Mark Zuckerberg (who founded Facebook) and Larry Page and Sergey Brin (who founded Google) – all were under 26 years old when they founded their businesses. Without a fund of retained profits young entrepreneurs often have to rely on specific types of financial backing including **venture capital funds** or **angel investors**.

Venture capital funds represent a pool of funds managed for a group of financial investors. Angel investors are individuals providing finance from their own resources. Venture capitalists and angel investors will provide financial backing for new businesses and, in return, will either charge interest or retain equity in the entrepreneur's firm (i.e. they will own some proportion of the firm's assets). The interest rate charged on lending will usually be relatively high – reflecting the fact that the lending is very risky. On the other hand, the maximum returns may also be very high: angel investors and venture capitalists often have a large number of firms on their books but the success of just one of those firms may deliver a profit large enough to cover the failure of a number of the other firms that they're backing.

In this chapter we will explore the links between computing investment and venture capital funding. We choose computing investment because computerisation is an essential aspect of the growth of the New Economy. We focus on venture capital funds because innovative entrepreneurs do not usually have their own sources of funds to finance investment projects and the success or failure of innovations will therefore depend upon whether or not venture capitalists are prepared to fund innovative production. In our empirical analysis, we will not specifically address the impact of angel investment because data on angel investors are scare and venture capital funds play a more significant role.

So the theoretical model that we will estimate in this chapter is:

$$ci_t = \alpha + \beta vc_t + \gamma Time_t + \varepsilon_t \tag{9.1}$$

where ci_t is the natural log of computing investment; vc_t is the natural log of venture capital funds and $Time$ is a **deterministic trend**. Deterministic trend variables are included to capture stable proportionate increases in a variable over time, e.g. reflecting factors such as technological progress and GDP growth.

For the parameters, α is the intercept parameter, β is the elasticity of computing investment with respect to venture capital funding, γ is the parameter on the deterministic trend and ε_t is the error term. Our variables are logged because we are interested in the elasticity of computing investment with respect to venture capital funding.

9.3   The data

In this analysis, we are examining the links between computing investment and venture capital funding. How do we measure this relationship between computing investment and venture capital financing? Our data sources are:

Variable	Source	Website
Computing Investment (software)	Bureau of Economic Analysis (BEA), US National Income and Product Accounts (NIPA)	www.bea.gov/national/ nipaweb/
Venture capital disbursements (software)	National Science Foundation (NSF), Science and Engineering Indicators 2006	www.nsf.gov/statistics

The BEA data is expressed in real terms – as a quantity index. We transform the venture capital data into real terms by deflating venture capital disbursements using the US GDP deflator from the IMF's *World Economic Outlook Database* (www.imf.org/external/pubs/ft/weo/2008/01/weodata).

Figure 9.1 plots computing investment and venture capital disbursements over the period 1980 to 2004. This figure captures the changing patterns in computing investment and venture capital disbursements. Until about 1994, there was no clear association between computing investment and venture capital: growth in venture capital was relatively stagnant until about 1995 suggesting that computing investment was propelled by other factors during this early period. From 1995 onwards a positive association between computing investment and venture capital emerged alongside considerable volatility in venture capital disbursements. Venture capital disbursements shot up during the 1999–2001 dotcom bubble but collapsed again with the dotcom crash in 2001. This instability did not strongly impact on computing investment, perhaps because the long lags on investment decisions enabled a smoothing of the path of computing investment.

There are two key features to the patterns depicted in Figure 9.1: firstly, the relationship between computing investment and venture capital does not have a stable form; and secondly, both series of data are exhibiting some instability over time: they do not have a stable mean and variance. These

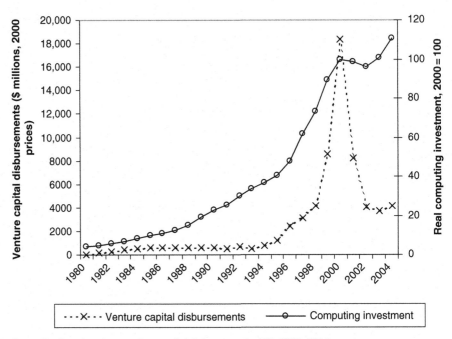

Figure 9.1   Computing investment vs. venture capital disbursements, USA 1980–2004

features will complicate our econometric analysis and will be explored further in Section 9.4.

Before beginning an econometric analysis, it is important to examine some of the limitations of the data set. The growth of high-tech industry is a relatively recent development and for many countries the range of detailed data on hign-tech production and investment is limited, although more efforts have been made recently to collect and standardise data particularly in the USA. The BEA computing investment data are provided in real terms (as a quantity index). Whilst quantity measures do, in theory at least, abstract from price effects, they will not capture the substantial improvements in computing quality that have occurred over time (e.g. via the operation of Moore's Law). Ideally, hedonic price measures are needed effectively to capture these quality improvements but hedonic price measures for IT are not yet widely available.[1]

We have focussed specifically on computing investments in software because the BEA data on computing investments in other categories is not disaggregated in the same way as the NSF data on venture capital disbursements into computing. This may introduce a selection bias into our analysis

---

[1] See Chapter 5 for an explanation of hedonic pricing methodologies.

and our results from an analysis of software investment may not be representative of all computing investment.

Also, we have only 25 observations and so our analysis might suffer from the consequences of micronumerosity (i.e. a small sample size), particularly as micronumerosity will reduce the accuracy of our estimation and compromise the power of our hypothesis tests.

Finally, as mentioned above, we may have reason to be concerned about the stability of our data series; for example, the large fluctuations in venture capital disbursements may have implications for the reliability of our results. In assessing this issue, in this chapter we emphasise the impacts of structural breaks and non-stationarity on the stability of our data and these problems are defined and assessed in more detail in Section 9.4.

9.4   Empirical methods and results

When we run a regression on Equation (9.1), we get the following estimated equation for computing investment (standard errors are in brackets):

$$ci_t = \quad 2.12 \qquad\qquad + 0.074vc_t \quad + 0.133\,Time \quad + \hat{\varepsilon}_t$$

$$\begin{array}{llll}
 & (0.107) & (0.0401) & (0.00779) \\
 & t = 19.9 & t = 1.82 & t = 17.0 \\
 & p = 0.000 & p = 0.082 & p = 0.000 \\
R^2 = 0.987 & \bar{R}^2 = 0.986 & \text{DW} = 0.256
\end{array}$$

$$(9.2)$$

On first inspection at least, our results look good: our adjusted R^2 is high suggesting that about 98% of the variability in computing investment is captured by variability in venture capital disbursements. If we test the H_0: $\beta = 0$, we find that β, the coefficient capturing the elasticity of computing investment spending with respect to venture capital disbursements, is significantly different from 0 at a 10% significance level though not at a 5% significance level.

But there are signs of a problem as can be seen from an inspection of the actual versus fitted values for computing investment – plotted in Figure 9.2.

The vertical distances between the actual and fitted values are the residuals and these are are exhibiting wave-like patterns. In the early period there is a run of negative residuals but from 1990 until about 2001 there is a long run of mostly positive residuals. As explained in Chapter 7, wave-like patterns are a sign of positive autocorrelation and the presence of this

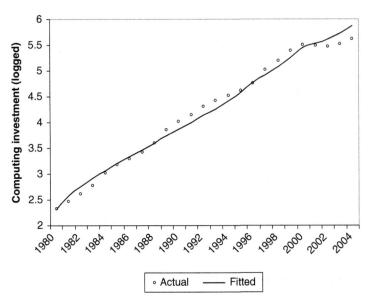

Figure 9.2   Actual vs. fitted computing investment, 1980–2004

problem is confirmed by the DW statistic $\hat{d} = 0.256 < d_L(n = 25, k = 2) = 1.21$.[2] It is important to remember that the DW statistic is not the most powerful autocorrelation test but it is routinely reported in many econometrics packages and does provide a quick 'at a glance' indicator of potential problems before more rigorous investigations proceed. Also, as explained in Chapter 7, finding autocorrelation may indicate that an econometric model suffers from more serious problems such as, for example, structural breaks and non-stationary variables, as explained below.

Structural breaks

One of the explanations for this residual correlation may be that there is a structural break in the relationship between computing investment and venture capital disbursements. Structural breaks can be captured using a Chow test for a structural break and the methodology underlying this test is explained in Box 9.1.

---

[2] See Chapter 7 for an explanation of the DW test.

Box 9.1 Structural breaks, parameter instability and Chow tests

One of the assumptions made when running a regression is that parameters are stable over the entire period sampled. This may not be a valid assumption because **structural breaks** are common in a lot of econometric analysis.

To illustrate: Figure 9.3 below shows two sets of observations over time – the dotted lines depict the lines of best fit just for the sub-sets of observations. Clearly, the slope and intercept for these two sub-samples of data are different. The solid line depicts what would happen if you tried to treat these two sub-sets of observations as identical, i.e. if you were to assume that the slope and intercept parameters were the same for both sub-sets. In this case, vertical distances between the dots and crosses and straight line would be relatively large and this would be picked up in a relatively high residual sum of squares (RSS).

If there have been structural shifts in the parameters of the model then we can test for these using **Chow's structural break test**. Whilst we show how to do this 'by hand', most statistical packages, including EViews, are programmed to calculate Chow tests.

Calculating the Chow structural break test

Constructing the Chow test involves running a series of regressions to capture shifts across two (or more) subperiods of data to allow a comparison of the unrestricted RSS (when you allow the parameters to shift across your sample) with the restricted RSS (when you force the parameters to be the same across your sample). When you impose a restriction upon a

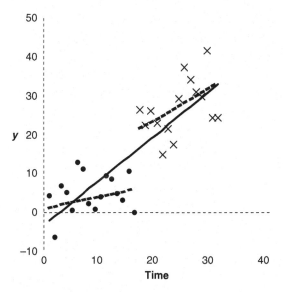

Figure 9.3 Parameter shifts across a sample

model, the RSS will necessarily increase and this can be measured using an adaptation of the F test of restrictions explained in Chapter 5.

To illustrate, if we are regressing y on x:

$$y_t = a + \theta x_t + \varepsilon_t \tag{9.3}$$

We will be testing the following hypotheses:

$$
\begin{aligned}
H_0 &: a_1 = a_2; \theta_1 = \theta_2 \\
H_0 &: a_1 \neq a_2; \theta_1 \neq \theta_2
\end{aligned}
\tag{9.4}
$$

where subscript 1 denotes Period 1 and subscript 2 denotes Period 2.

We estimate the restricted model over the whole sample of data – thereby forcing the parameters to be the same throughout. This restricted regression gives the RSS_r. There are as many restrictions as there are parameters in the theoretical model, i.e. two in this case (one intercept parameter and one slope parameter).

The next step is to see what happens to the RSS if we allow the parameters to change – by estimating two separate regressions for the sub-samples of data and calculating the unrestricted RSS as the sum of the RSSs from the sub-sample regressions, i.e. $RSS_u = RSS_1 + RSS_2$. The RSS_r and RSS_u are then incorporated into the following formula:

$$F(k, n_1 + n_2 - 2k - 2) = \frac{(RSS_r - RSS_u)/k}{RSS_u/(n_1 + n_2 - 2k - 2)} \tag{9.5}$$

The degrees of freedom in the numerator are the number of restrictions imposed in the restricted model: in this case it will be $k+1$ – the number of parameters in our model. For model (9.3) we estimate one intercept and one slope parameter.

The degrees of freedom in the denominator capture the degrees of freedom in the unrestricted model. In this case we've had to estimate Equation (9.3) twice – once for the early period and once for the later period. There are $(n_1 + n_2)$ observations but $2(k+1)$ degrees of freedom will be lost because each set of parameters is estimated twice and this leaves $n_1 + n_2 - 2k - 2$ degrees of freedom in the denominator.

If the F value from the Chow test is relatively large (i.e. if $F > F_{crit}$) then this suggests that the RSS increases significantly when we force the parameters to be the same over the entire period; the goodness of fit has declined. This would suggest that the assumption of parameter stability is not a valid assumption and so H_0 would be rejected. On the other hand, if $F < F_{crit}$, then imposing the restriction of parameter stability has not made much difference to the goodness of fit and has not increased the RSS significantly. This would suggest that the restriction of parameter stability, i.e. that the parameters are the same across both sub-samples, is mirrored in the data and it would be valid to retain H_0.

If a break is identified, how can it be modelled? Dummy variables may be useful. As explained in Chapter 5, dummy variables can be used to capture effects that can only be categorised and cannot be measured in the ordinary way. In Chapter 5, we discussed their use in the context of seasonal effects but dummies can also be used to capture the impacts of other non-measurable forms of change, for example structural breaks. Using dummies to capture breaks in Equation (9.4), if we want to control for simple shifts in the intercept, then we can introduce an **additive dummy** variable taking the value 1 after the break and the value zero before it. This will shift the intercept for periods after the break by an amount captured by the estimated parameter γ on the dummy variable D:

$$y_t = (a + \gamma D) + \theta \cdot x_t + \varepsilon_t \tag{9.6}$$

Note that before the break $D = 0$ and so the additive dummy disappears from the equation, and we are left with our original specification.

Shifts in slope can be captured using a **multiplicative dummy**; in this case constructed by multiplying D by the explanatory variable x to give:

$$u_t = (a + \gamma D) + (\theta + \varphi D) \cdot x_t + \varepsilon_t \tag{9.7}$$

where φ captures the shift in slope when $D = 1$.

Constructing models that include these additive and multiplicative dummy variables can also give us an alternative to the conventional Chow test for a structural break if we conduct an F test of restrictions to test $H_0: \gamma = \varphi = 0$. The restricted model would exclude the dummies, the unrestricted model would include them. If the F test of restrictions indicates that RSS_r is not significantly greater than RSS_u, then we would conclude that parameters on the additive and multiplicative dummies are jointly equal to zero. We would not reject our H_0 above and this would be exactly equivalent to not rejecting the $H_0: a_1 = a_2; \theta_1 = \theta_2$ from Equation (9.3).

One problem for structural break tests is in identifying the timing of breaks. Relatively sophisticated methods exist to 'endogenously' identify the timing of a break by testing all possibilities for the start of the break. At a more elementary level, a good understanding of the underlying economic/political trends will help to inform hypotheses about the timing of breaks. Also, structural break tests can be designed to capture more than one break and this issue is explored in the chapter exercises.

Using the methodology outlined in Box 9.1, we can perform a structural break test on our model as follows:

Step 1: Estimate the model over the entire period 1980–2004 to get RSS_r. For this estimation the parameters are restricted to be the same over the entire period. For this dataset, EViews gives $RSS_r = 0.3618$.

Step 2: Estimate the model separately over two sub-periods (1980–1994 and 1995–2004) to give $RSS_u = RSS_1 + RSS_2$. For this data set, EViews gives: $RSS_u = RSS_1 + RSS_2 = 0.0279 + 0.0225 = 0.0504$.

Step 3: For the degrees of freedom, we are imposing three restrictions (i.e. that the intercept, the slope on the venture capital variable and the slope on the time trend are the same in the second period as in the first period) so we have three degrees of freedom in our numerator. In our unrestricted model we have used observations for the whole period of data ($n_1 + n_2 = 15 + 10 = 25$) and we have estimated two sets of parameters – one set for the first period and another set for the second period so $2(k+1) = 6$ and the remaining degrees of freedom in the denominator is 19.

Step 4: Incorporating these numbers into our formula for the F test of restrictions gives:

$$F(k, n_1 + n_2 - 2k - 2) = \frac{(RSS_r - RSS_u)/k + 1}{RSS_u/(n_1 + n_2 - 2k - 2)}$$

$$= \frac{(0.3618 - 0.0504)/3}{0.0504/19} = 39.13$$

EViews will calculate this test automatically and you can verify this result using EViews as follows: in the *Equation* output box, pull down *Stability Tests* from the *View* menu, pull across to *Chow Breakpoint test*, then input 1995. Click on *OK* and you have your Chow test result of $F = 39.13$ $[p = 0.000]$.

Given this result, we reject the null that the parameters are stable throughout the period: even at very low significance levels there is evidence of a significant shift in the parameters of our model. This is unsurprising given the patterns from Figure 9.1: these show that there is a far stronger correlation in venture capital disbursements after 1995 than before 1995.

Non-stationarity

As noted above, our initial regression indicated that there are systematic patterns in our residuals i.e. there is residual autocorrelation in our model. Above we have explored the possibility that this residual autocorrelation reflects a structural break in the relationship between computing investment and venture capital. Another possibility is that our variables have unstable properties: it is possible that we have **non-stationary** variables and a symptom of non-stationarity is autocorrelation in the residuals. Non-stationarity in variables will also mean that the variances of our variables will be unbounded, compromising OLS estimation. Non-stationarity may also generate a **spurious regression,** i.e. a regression with a misleadingly high degree of explanatory power. For example, if two variables, by coincidence, are exhibiting common upward trends, then the covariance between them will be high and $\hat{\beta}_{OLS}$ – the OLS estimate of the slope parameter – will be inflated accordingly. A detailed explanation of non-stationarity is provided in Box 9.2.

Box 9.2 Unit roots and non-stationarity

For our regressions to be estimated accurately and reliably the variables used must be well behaved, i.e. the variables must be stable over time with constant means, variances and **autocovariances** (the autocovariance is the covariance of a variable between itself and its own lagged values). Usually, OLS estimation procedures will only work properly if all the variables (dependent and explanatory) are stationary.

A non-stationary variable is a variable with a changing mean, variance or autocovariance. Non-stationarity is caused by trends in variables and there are two broad types of trends: **deterministic trends** and **stochastic trends**. A deterministic trend is a systematic, stable upward movement in a variable and can be captured using a deterministic time trend variable.

A stochastic trend emerges as a consequence of randomness in variables. Stochastic trends can be illustrated using some simple stochastic processes: the unit root processes. There are various types of unit root processes but two common forms are **random walks** and **random walks with drift**. If we are looking at the relationship between a variable y_t and its own lagged value y_{t-1}:

$$y_t = \rho y_{t-1} + \varepsilon_t \tag{9.8}$$

y will have a unit root if $\rho = 1$, i.e. if the parameter on the lag is exactly equal to one. In other words, if we have a unit root process then:

$$y_t = y_{t-1} + \varepsilon_t \tag{9.9}$$

For this simple form of unit root process subtracting y_{t-1} from both sides gives:

$$\Delta y_t = \varepsilon_t \tag{9.10}$$

Thus, when $\rho = 1$ Δy_t follows a completely random pattern, i.e. its movements will be determined by ε_t: y will be changing or 'walking' in a random way. For this reason this form of non-stationarity is called a **random walk**. This is a simple example of a stochastic trend because the trends in y are generated by the stochastic, random element, i.e. ε_t.

A more complex unit root process is the **random walk with drift** where a 'drift' or intercept term a is affecting the random walk process:

$$y_t = a + y_{t-1} + \varepsilon_t \tag{9.11}$$

To illustrate how non-stationarity emerges with the random walk with drift, assume that we start in period 1 with $y = y_0$. If y is a random walk with drift then it will evolve in the following way:

$$y_1 = a + y_0 + \varepsilon_1 \tag{9.12}$$

$$y_2 = a + y_1 + \varepsilon_2 = a + (a + y_0 + \varepsilon_1) + \varepsilon_2 = 2a + y_0 + \varepsilon_1 + \varepsilon_2 \tag{9.13}$$

So it follows that:

$$y_3 = a + y_2 + \varepsilon_3 = 3a + y_0 + \varepsilon_1 + \varepsilon_2 + \varepsilon_3 \tag{9.14}$$

In Equations (9.6)–(9.8) the drift terms and errors are adding up because of the unit root. Past errors and drift terms are always being multiplied by 1 and so their impact will never diminish. This means that the mean of y will increase over time because of the build-up of drift terms a. The variance will also be increasing over time because of the build-up of random error terms ε_t.

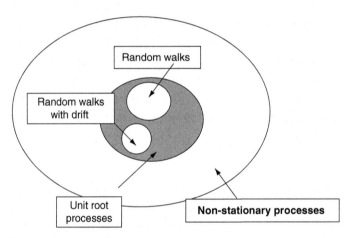

Figure 9.4   Venn diagram of non-stationary processes

It is easy to confuse the different types of non-stationarity and so in Figure 9.4 the various possibilities for stochastic trends are depicted using a Venn diagram. This shows that random walks and random walks with drift are subsets of unit root processes and unit root processes are a subset of non-stationary processes. So in some cases, non-stationarity, unit roots and random walks are all the same thing. (Note that we have not shown deterministic trends in the diagram, although these are also in the set of non-stationary processes.)

Why is non-stationarity a problem? It is a problem because, when non-stationary variables are regressed on non-stationary variables, this can create a spurious regression, i.e. a model that has a misleadingly high degree of explanatory power.[3] Looking at Figure 9.1 you will notice that computing investment and venture capital disbursements show trend increases over time. This may be because there is a causal relationship between these two variables but perhaps these variables are rising together by coincidence e.g. because the general economy is in a boom phase or because these variables are rising with GDP growth. Either way, the fact that the variables are exhibiting common trends means that they will be highly correlated: when we regress one of these non-stationary variables on the other the covariance between them is high so we will get a high R^2, but not necessarily because we've detected any real relationship between the variables. Ice-cream sales also exhibit a common upward trend and so we'd also get a high R^2 if we regressed computing investment on ice-cream sales but of course there can be no (obvious) meaningful causal relationship between ice-cream and computing investment.

As mentioned above, one classic sign of a spurious regression is a systematic pattern in the residuals: there may be strong correlations between variables exhibiting common time trends but the model as a whole will be misspecified and the systematic pattern in the residuals will capture divergences in the upward trends for the dependent versus explanatory variables. So a high R^2 and a significant autocorrelation test together can be a sign that non-stationarity in the variables is generating a spurious result. Engle and Granger used this insight to construct the **Engle–Granger rule of thumb** and they observe that when $R^2 > DW$ this may be a sign of a spurious regression reflecting non-stationarity in the variables. This is just a simple rule of thumb and, as with using the DW for a quick indicator of autocorrelation, more rigorous investigations should follow, as explained below.

What can we say about the evidence for a spurious regression in our estimation of (9.2)? Our results reveal that $R^2 = 0.984 > DW = 0.256$. So, using the Engle–Granger rule of thumb, we can conclude that there may be signs of a spurious regression. Therefore we should carefully explore the possibility that we are using non-stationary variables, e.g. by using the Dickey–Fuller (DF) and Augmented Dickey–Fuller (ADF) unit root tests outlined in Box 9.3.

The DF and ADF tests for non-stationarity can easily be found using EViews by clicking on the variable name. Then pull down *Unit Root Test* from the *View* menu and click the appropriate boxes depending on whether you want to test that the level, first difference or second difference of the

---

[3] A key exception to this occurs when non-stationary variables are cointegrated: i.e. when a linear combination of the non-stationary variables is stationary. For more on cointegration and related issues, see Chapter 10.

Box 9.3 Testing for non-stationarity

Given the possibility of non-stationarity in time-series data, it is important to test for non-stationarity in all variables (dependent and explanatory) before running a regression. The most famous tests for non-stationarity are the Dickey–Fuller (DF) and Augmented Dickey–Fuller (ADF) unit root tests (there are other tests too). Both the DF and ADF test involve testing the H_0 that a variable has a unit root. From Box 9.2:

$$y_t = \rho y_{t-1} + \varepsilon_t \tag{9.8}$$

and a unit root process occurs when $\rho = 1$. A simple example of a unit root process is:

$$y_t = y_{t-1} + \varepsilon_t \tag{9.9}$$

In constructing DF/ADF tests, non-stationarity in y will affect the accuracy of a straightforward regression of (9.3). For this reason the DF/ADF tests are reformulated from (9.3) by subtracting y_{t-1} from both sides to give:

$$\Delta y_t = \delta y_{t-1} + \varepsilon_t \quad \text{where } \delta = \rho - 1 \tag{9.15}$$

The following hypotheses are then assessed using a one-tailed test: $H_0 : \rho = 1, \delta = 0$, $H_1 : \rho < 1, \delta < 0$. The H_0 is that the variable is stationary and the H_1 is that the variable is non-stationary. The DF/ADF tests involve constructing a τ (tau) test statistic calculated as:

$$\hat{\tau} = \frac{\hat{\delta}}{se(\hat{\delta})} \tag{9.16}$$

Whilst this looks like the formula for the conventional t test, it is important to remember that the potential non-stationarity in the variables generates a bias in small samples and affects the distribution of Student's t test statistic. For this reason special Dickey–Fuller tables must be used to construct decision rules for the DF and ADF tests. Using the special DF tables, the decision rule is:

if $|\hat{\tau}| > |\tau_{crit}|$ then reject H_0 but if $|\hat{\tau}| < |\tau_{crit}|$ then do not reject H_0.

The DF test can be constructed using different specifications to control for other forms of trend apart from the stochastic trend generated by the unit root process. Other specifications incorporate intercepts to capture drift and/or time trend variables to capture deterministic trends. The three key specifications are of a simple random walk as described above (with no trend, no intercept), a random walk with drift (including an intercept term to capture the drift) and random walk with drift and trend (including an intercept term and a time trend to capture a deterministic trend). The DF Tables include three sets of critical values to cover these three groups of specification. The appropriate specification to use will depend on the characteristics of a given variable and the simplest way to judge the appropriate specification of the DF test involves inspecting plots of the variable over time, though model comparison tests will provide a more objective measure, as explained below.

What about econometric problems with the DF test? When the DF test is characterised by autocorrelation in the residuals then the results are unreliable and so ADF tests must be used instead. The ADF test is much the same as the DF test but lagged Δys are included as well, to 'mop-up' any autocorrelation in the DF test. The simplest form of ADF test is an ADF(1) which incorporates one lag on Δy_{t-1}:

$$\Delta y_t = \delta y_{t-1} + \phi \Delta y_{t-1} + \varepsilon_t \tag{9.17}$$

It is important to remember that we will still be constructing the test statistic using (9.6) and using the accompanying decision rule as outlined above. The variable Δy_{t-1} has been included just to resolve the autocorrelation problem. For the ADF tests, the DF tables are used and, as for DF tests, the ADF test can be expanded to control for drifts and deterministic trends.

In this example, we have included only one lag on the dependent variable in order to keep things simple. But in reality, as many lagged variables as are necessary to eliminate the autocorrelation should be included in the ADF tests. Deciding how many lags to include in the ADF tests will depend on how many lags are needed to remove significant auto-correlation in the residuals of the DF/ADF tests. In practice, econometrics packages will automatically report the best specification by using some general model comparison tests to identify the relative explanatory power of the various forms of the test. Some of the model comparison tests used include Akaike's Information Criterion and the Schwartz Information Criterion. A detailed explanation of these model comparison tests is beyond the scope of this book but in essence they are based around the RSS and so are capturing the residual variance of the different specifications.

variable has a unit root. You will also have to make a choice about whether to include either just an intercept or an intercept plus trend (as explained in Box 9.3, an inspection of a time-plot of the variable is a simple way to decide which of the specifications is appropriate). Then click on *OK* and EViews will report the results from the best specification of the DF/ADF test (and the judgement about the best specification is made using model comparison tests, also explained in Box 9.3).

For the variables in our model, Figure 9.1 suggests that both variables are drifting upwards over time at an increasing rate. We control for these factors by including an intercept and a deterministic trend in our specifications of the

DF/ADF tests. For ci, the ADF(1) test includes one lag on Δci_t giving the following estimated equation:

$$\Delta ci_t \ = 0.641 \qquad -0.262 ci_{t-1} \quad + 0.791 \Delta ci_{t-1} \quad + 0.0373\,Time \quad + \hat{\varepsilon}_t$$

$$t = 2.461 \qquad \tau = -2.087 \quad t = 3.457 \qquad t = 1.931$$

$$p = 0.0236 \quad p = 0.051 \quad\ p = 0.0026 \qquad p = 0.0686$$

$$R^2 = 0.537 \ \ \bar{R}^2 = 0.464 \qquad\qquad\qquad DW = 1.810 \qquad\qquad (9.18)$$

As explained in Box 9.3, for the test on computing investment, we are focussing on the parameter estimates on ci_{t-1} . EViews has selected ADF(1) as the best specification of the DF/ADF test. Using a 5% significance level (remembering that special of tables must be used, as explained in Box 9.3), $p = 0.051 > 0.05$ so we do not reject H_0 and can conclude that ci is non-stationary and does have a unit root, though this decision is borderline. The fact that the parameters on the intercept and drift terms are significantly different from zero at a 10% significance level suggests that there is some evidence supporting the existence of a drift and deterministic trend in our specification of this unit root test.

We get similar results for vc and both sets of results are summarised in Table 9.1. The key difference between the test of ci and the test on vc is that EViews selects ADF(4) as the best specification for testing vc; this is an ADF test with 4 lags on Δci_t. The probability value for this ADF(4) test is $p = 0.12$ and so $p > 0.05$. We do not reject H_0 and we conclude that vc is also a non-stationary unit root process.

What do we do if we have non-stationary variables? Unless the variables are cointegrated (a relatively complex issue that will be introduced in Chapter 10) then we must use the variables in stationary form. Non-stationarity can be eliminated by differencing the variables and to establish whether or not these first differences are themselves stationary they are tested for a unit root using the DF/ADF tests. If the first differences are also non-stationary then they should be differenced again to give the second differences which again should tested for unit roots $etc.$ etc: this process continues for as long as it takes to reject the H_0 of a unit root. The number of times that the variables must be differenced to make it stationary is the **order of integration** of the variable, with the order of integration indicated by the notation $I(q)$, where q is the order of integration.

From Table 9.1, we can see that both our variables ci and vc are stationary in first differences, i.e. Δci_t and Δvc_t are I(0); ci_t and vc_t are I(1) and so a regression on first differences should remove the non-stationarity and should give a non-spurious regression result.

Table 9.1 Unit root tests (with constant and linear trend)

	Lag length	$\hat{\tau}$	Probability value	5% critical value from DF tables	Inference
Computing investment – logged (ci)					
Level	1	−2.09	0.53	−3.62	Do not reject $H_0 \rightarrow$ non-stationary
First difference	5	−4.16	0.02	−3.69	Reject $H_0 \rightarrow$ stationary
Venture capital disbursements – logged (vc)					
Level	4	−3.16	0.12	−3.66	Do not reject $H_0 \rightarrow$ non-stationary
First difference	0	−4.00	0.02	−3.62	Reject $H_0 \rightarrow$ stationary

This all suggests, not necessarily that venture capital is unimportant to computing investment, but that the determinants of computing investment are more complex than we initially postulated. So we cannot trust the results from our initial regression summarised in Equation (9.2). The next step would be to ensure that we include stationary versions of our variables in the model – see chapter exercises.

Structural breaks and non-stationarity

So far we have treated structural breaks and non-stationarity as separate issues but it is possible that both problems are occurring in the same data set. It is also possible that the presence of one of these problems will reduce the power of tests for the other; for example, the presence of structural breaks will reduce the power of the DF/ADF tests because if a break is not controlled for then the DF/ADF tests will pick up its influence.

For our investigation of the links between computing investment and venture capital we have shown that there is significant evidence of a structural break. There is also significant evidence of a unit root in the computing investment and venture capital variables. In estimating our model we can incorporate both possibilities. Table 9.2 shows the results from a regression on the first differences of computing investment and venture capital (as we showed above, these first differences are the stationary, I(0) forms of our variables). We have also incorporated additive and multiplicative dummies to control for parameter shifts from 1995 onwards (using dummies to capture parameter shifts is explained in Box 9.1).

The results from this final estimation are a lot more promising than our earlier regressions. There are no immediate signs of a spurious regression because DW > R^2. We have also conducted a BG test for residual autocorrelation

Table 9.2 Summary of EViews printout
Estimation on I(0) variables, with structural break in 1995

Dependent Variable: ΔLCI
Method: Least Squares
Sample (adjusted): 1981 2004

Variable	Coefficient	Std. Error	t-Statistic	Prob.
Intercept	0.157	0.016	9.832	0.000
ΔVC	−0.002	0.032	−0.070	0.945
D	−0.068	0.024	−2.862	0.010
$D.\Delta VC$	0.127	0.045	2.809	0.011
R-squared	0.500	F-statistic		6.657
Adjusted R-squared	0.425	Prob(F-statistic)		0.003
Durbin-Watson statistic	1.456			

(the methodology for the BG test is explained in Chapter 7) giving $F = 1.925$ [$p = 0.175$]; so with $p > 0.05$ we can retain the H_0 of no autocorrelation at a 5% significance level (and in fact at any significance level up to 17.5%).

The parameter estimates also confirm our initial judgements about the relationships between computing investment and venture capital as outlined in Section 9.3: there is a clear association between computing investment and venture capital only from 1995 onwards and this is reflected in the statistically significant parameter estimate on the additive dummy D and the multiplicative dummy $D \cdot vc_t$.

9.5   Implications and conclusions

Our empirical analysis has shown that the relationship between computing investment and venture capital funding is affected by structural breaks and non-stationary variables. So we tested and corrected for non-stationarity and controlled for structural breaks. Our preferred estimation suggested that parameter shifts affected the interaction between growth in computing investment and venture capital funding. Our results indicate firstly, that there is a significant upward shift in computing investment from 1995 onwards and secondly, that growth in computing investment was associated with growth in venture capital funding from 1995 onwards but not before. Growth in venture capital funding only had a significant impact on growth in computing investment from 1995 onwards. This latter finding may suggest that it takes time to build up momentum in the financing of innovative investments – perhaps because venture capitalists need clear evidence that an innovative burst will be sustained before they are prepared to commit their money to risky innovative ventures.

In terms of policy implications, if our finding about delays in the provision of venture capital funds is robust, then it suggests that governments could play a role in ensuring that funds are available to subsidise innovative new industries (e.g. see UNCTAD, 2008). This may be particularly important for computing innovations given the evidence about the economic benefits of computerisation. Also, the considerable volatility in venture capital funding, as captured by the spike in venture capital disbursements in Figure 9.1, suggests that trends in private venture capital disbursements can be unstable, e.g. as shown during the 1999–2001 period of the dotcom bubble and subsequent bust. Volatility in private venture capital financing has the potential to create significant instability in the macroeconomy and so financial policies could be implemented to manage this instability. Overall, governments may have a role to play both in supporting innovative investment and in managing the volatility that emerges via the private financing of innovative investments.

9.6   Further reading

Text books

Schumpeter, J. A. (1939) *Business Cycles: A Theoretical, Historical and Statistical Analysis of the Capitalist Process*, New York: McGraw-Hill.

Thomas, R. L. (1997) *Modern Econometrics – An Introduction*, Harlow: Addison-Wesley, Chapters 13 and 14.

Academic articles and working papers

Baddeley, M. (2008) 'Structural shifts in UK unemployment: the twin impacts of financial deregulation and computerisation', *Bulletin of Economic Research*, vol. 60, no. 2 (April), 123–57.

Cecchetti, S. G. (2002) *The New Economy and Challenges for Macroeconomic Policy*, National Bureau of Economic Research Working Paper No. 8935, National Bureau of Economic Research.

Gordon, R. J. (2000) 'Does the "New Economy" measure up to the great inventions of the past?', *Journal of Economic Perspectives*, vol. 14, 49–74.

Whelan, K. (2002) 'Computers, obsolescence and productivity', *Review of Economics and Statistics*, vol. 84, no. 3, 445–61.

Yang, S. and Brynjolfsson, E. (2001) 'Intangible Assets and Growth Accounting: Evidence from Computer Investments', Massachusetts Institute of Technology, downloaded from http://ebusiness.mit.edu/erik/itg01-05-30.pdf.

Policy briefs and newspaper articles

Dunne, T. (1991) *Technology Usage in US Manufacturing Industries*, Washington D.C.: US Census Economic Studies.

Landefeld, J. S. and Fraumeni, B. M. (2000) 'Measuring the New Economy', US Bureau of Economic Analysis Advisory Committee Meeting.

Solow, R. M. (1987) 'We'd better watch out', *New York Times Book Review*, 12 July 1987, 36.

UNCTAD (2008) *Science and Technology for Development: the New Paradigm of ICT*, Geneva and New York: United Nations.

9.7   Chapter exercises

1. Using the methodology outlined in Box 9.1 and the data sources outlined in Section 9.3, extend the Chow testing methodology to construct your own test for two structural breaks, i.e. a first break in 1995 and a second break in 2000. (Hint: this will involve an unrestricted model estimated for three separate subperiods rather than two.) Verify the results of your test using EViews.

2. In the final version of our computing investment model we ran regressions on a hybrid model that simultaneously addressed problems of non-stationarity and parameter instability. Estimate a computing investment model that incorporates only stationary variables (i.e. estimate a model that does not control for structural breaks). Discuss your results commenting in particular on whether the regression on stationary variables has, by itself, resolved the problems identified in the initial estimations of Equation (9.2).

Error correction models

Consumption and the multiplier in the UK

Economic issues include:
- Marginal and average propensities to consume
- The multiplier
- Permanent income hypothesis and life-cycle hypothesis

Econometric issues include:
- Autoregressive distributed lag (ARDL) models
- Error correction models (ECMs) and cointegration
- Granger causality tests

Data issues include:
- Using lags

10.1 The issue

When income rises do we spend more or save more? This question most famously excited the interest of the British economist, John Maynard Keynes (1883–1946) during the depression years of the 1930s, but it is of equal importance today. Consumption is the single largest element in household spending and has significant implications for demand and the subsequent health of the economy. Recognition of this role of household spending was evident in the flurry of newspaper articles in late 2001 and early 2002, when many commentators feared the world was headed for recession, if not a complete depression. 'The shoppers who saved the nation' was a typical headline in 2005: journalists who had previously expressed shock at the high debt held at stores and on credit cards by the average household, now applauded the fact they were continuing to spend and thereby maintaining the multiplier effects that might ward off the nation's – and indeed the world's – slide into recession. Policy-makers struggled to estimate precisely the extent to which an extra dollar's spending would trickle through the economy to keep the country's producers, manufacturers and retailers afloat.

What explains these rises in consumption? Across the OECD, spending patterns have been changing in response firstly to the loosening of consumer credit controls following financial deregulation, and secondly to the more fluid flows of foreign finance encouraged by globalisation. But if too much money is being pumped into consumption in the current period then it means that not enough will be saved to spend on investment in future productive capacity.

In this chapter we explore one of the factors affecting consumption by analysing the relationships between income and consumption. We examine two important theoretical consumption models: the Keynesian consumption function and Friedman's consumption function. In the empirical estimations, we analyse these models empirically for the UK 1979 to 2005. We use the hypothesis of a stable average propensity to consume (APC) to construct an error correction model (ECM) – an empirical specification that enables us simultaneously to capture long-run equilibrium and short-run 'out-of-equilibrium' dynamics.

10.2   The theory

In analysing consumption theory we start with Keynes's analysis of consumption (Keynes, 1936, 1937). The **marginal propensity to consume** (MPC) lies at the core of Keynes's analysis and reflects specific assumptions about human nature and about our psychological motivations. Keynes asserted that:

... the prevailing psychological law seems to be that when aggregate income increases, consumption-expenditure will also increase but to a somewhat lesser extent. (*Keynes, 1937, p. 219*)

That is, we will spend more when our income rises, but not by as much as our increase in income. Technically speaking, the marginal propensity to consume is positive but less than 1: consumption rises as income rises but by a lesser proportion. The MPC is central to Keynes's macroeconomic analysis because it drives the **multiplier effect**. Multiplier effects emerge because various spillover effects are generated by each spending transaction. As we spend more on consumer goods, shops employ more sales staff to cope with the increased demand; factories employ more staff to meet the increased demand from the shops; suppliers boost their production capacity to cope with the increased demand for their inputs. More truck drivers and perhaps more trucks are needed to ferry the goods from supplier to factory to warehouse to shop. And so on. Sales assistants, factory workers and truck drivers will each have more income to spend spurring more and more consumption spending. Via these multiplier effects, household consumption decisions permeate through to all the corners of the economy.

We can analyse the impact of these multiplier effects mathematically. Assuming a closed economy with no trade and no government, the simplest form of the multiplier is:

$$\text{Multiplier} = \frac{1}{1 - MPC} \tag{10.1}$$

For example, if the estimate of MPC was 0.8, this means that a £1 increase in income will produce a £0.80 increase in spending for each individual and the multiplier will be 5:

$$\text{Multiplier} = \frac{1}{1 - 0.8} = 5 \tag{10.2}$$

This captures the fact that each 80% increase in household spending trickles down through all the various sectors of the economy generating £5 of total income per £1 of initial income.

This can be shown with a simple arithmetic example. Let's assume that everyone has the same MPC of 0.8, i.e. they spend 80% of their current income on consumption. To keep it simple, we will also assume that the prices are net of production costs such as the price of raw materials etc. As shown in Table 10.1, imagine that Bob gets an extra £10 in his pay-packet and spends 80% of it (i.e. £8) buying beer from Sally. So Sally's income has increased by £8. Sally uses 80% of this £8 (i.e. £6.40) to buy some cherries from Sanjeev. Sanjeev uses 80% of his income of £6.40 (i.e. £5.12) to buy pencils from Joshua. Joshua uses 80% of his £5.12 income to buy chocolate from Maya. Maya buys

Table 10.1 Illustrating the multiplier effect

	Bob	Sally	Sanjeev	Joshua	Maya	Lee	Abdul	Theo	Total
MPC	0.8	0.8	0.8	0.8	0.8	0.8	0.8	0.8	
Income	£10	£8	£6.40	£5.12	£4.10	£3.28	£2.62	£2.10	£41.62
Consumption	£8	£6.40	£5.12	£4.10	£3.28	£2.62	£2.10	£1.68	£33.3

£3.28 of bread from Lee; Lee buys £2.62 of nuts from Abdul; Abdul buys £2.10 of milk from Theo. And so the process continues until the increments to further spending become too small to measure. From the table you can see that the initial £10 that Bob earned has been multiplied up to generate a total extra income of more than £40 for them all.

This is an example of a geometric progression – a type of mathematical series which determines how an initial value (of £10 in this case) increases over time and it can be summarised as:

$$\sum_{n=1}^{\infty} (£10 \times 0.8^n) = (£10 \times 0.8^0) + (£10 \times 0.8^1) + (£10 \times 0.8^2) \cdots (£10 \times 0.8^n)$$

$$= £10 + (£10 \times 0.8) + (£10 \times 0.8 \times 0.8) + (£10 \times 0.8 \times 0.8 \times 0.8) + \cdots etc.$$

$$(10.3)$$

If this process were to continue *ad infinitum* (i.e. beyond Theo's spending) until, for the last person, income earned is negligible, everyone together would have earned a total of £50, i.e.:

$$Multiplier = \frac{1}{1 - MPC} = \frac{1}{1 - 0.8} = 5 \qquad (10.4)$$

Research into the relationship between the MPC and the multiplier has taken many forms, with writers focussing on different countries, different periods of history, different occupational groups, and even different forms of incomes; for example, most studies measure income by using measures of aggregate income, but some have narrowed the focus down to look specifically at income effects that are created by rising equity markets, or rising house prices. An eclectic sample of these is shown in Table 10.2 to illustrate the importance of context: the MPC will vary geographically and across occupations.

Each diverse sample noted in Table 10.2 reveals an interesting insight. The 1951 study by Jan Tinbergen compared the multiplier effects created by the spending habits of different occupational groups – and found that manual workers created more spillover benefits than farmers for example. Tinbergen also compared the MPC of different countries. More recently, researchers at the Bank of England examined consumption patterns of different countries, focussing only on the behaviour of people who owned shares, but looking at income in aggregate measures rather than equity income (Norman *et al.*, 2002). They found that as the value of share portfolios increased, greater multiplier effects were generated; for example, American households generate greater multiplier effects through their spending patterns than German or French households because they hold more equity.

Table 10.2 Differing estimates of MPC and the multiplier

Studies included:	Estimated MPC	Implied Multiplier
National occupational groups (Tinbergen, 1951)		
manual workers	0.83	5.88
'brain workers'	0.82	5.56
agricultural workers	0.70	4.76
farmers	0.44	1.78
Countries (aggregate income) (Tinbergen, 1951)		
Germany	0.42	1.72
Britain	0.52	2.08
Sweden	0.60	2.50
Poland	0.71	3.44
United States	0.75	4.00
Countries – equities income (*Source:* Norman et al., 2002)		
United States	0.80	5.0
Germany	0.50	2.0
France	0.60	2.5

But how does the empirical evidence fit Keynes's theory? The shift-from-thrift arguments outlined above imply that the **average propensity to consume** (APC) will fall as income rises. This can be shown as follows:

$$APC = \frac{C}{Y} = \frac{\alpha + \beta Y}{Y} = \frac{\alpha}{Y} + \beta \tag{10.5}$$

where β is the MPC (and is assumed to be a constant) and α is autonomous consumption; both α and β are constants and so the APC should fall as Y rises because as Y is increasing, $\frac{\alpha}{Y}$ will necessarily get smaller as Y gets larger (given that α is a constant).

There has been substantial empirical debate about whether or not it is defensible to assume a falling APC. Historical evidence from Kuznets (1946) shows that, historically, the APC has been stable and this does appear to undermine Keynes's specification of the consumption function. Also, theoretical critics of Keynes's theory argued that Keynesian consumers are a bit simple-minded. Their decision to spend or save depends only on their current income: if income rises one week, they will spend more; if it falls the next week, they will spend less. Lags may be important, as explained in Box 10.1. Also, can we really aggregate to an entire nation made up of diverse peoples, of different ages and tastes for example, from such a simplistic vision of a household?

Box 10.1 Using lags

In the Keynesian model of consumption, current consumption is expressed as a function of current income. In practice this means (for example) that consumption in 1980 is determined by income in 1980; consumption in 1981 is set against 1981's income and so on. The implicit assumption here is that people can observe a change in their real disposable incomes and respond very quickly – there is no lag between an increase in wages (or a fall in taxes, or inflation) and corresponding increases in consumption expenditure. This implies either that people are responding to current income or that, even though current consumption is not a direct function of current income, current income is acting as a proxy for future expected income.

Generally there may be many reasons to expect lagged effects i.e. that a change in the explanatory variable in one year will take time to feed through to a change in the dependent variable. For example, lags are particularly important in agricultural markets. When the price of wool increases (P), we expect farmers will not be able to increase their supply of wool (S) for at least one year (assuming they had no wool stockpiled from previous years and so needed to breed more sheep). In this case, the model specification should be $S_t = a + \beta P_{t-1} + \varepsilon_t$. If the lag was as long as two years, we would write the equation as $S_t = a + \beta_1 P_{t-1} + \beta_2 P_{t-2} + \varepsilon_t$.

More complex lag structures exist, ranging from the relatively straight-forward **distributed-lag** specification where the lag effect is spread out over a number of time periods e.g. $S_t = a + \beta_0 P_t + \beta_1 P_{t-1} + \beta_2 P_{t-2} + \beta_3 P_{t-3} + \varepsilon$; to more complex models such as Median and Mean lag models, and models incorporating partial adjustment and adaptive expectations, such as the Koyck model.[1]

Choosing which lag structure to use depends on the reason a delay is expected. Lags may be *institutional* (e.g. students need time to finish their degrees before they can respond to new employment opportunities; homeowners need to sit out fixed duration mortgage contracts before they can respond to cuts in interest rates); *technological* (sheep still take at least half a year to grow a new woollen coat and a year to reproduce themselves); or *psychological* (habit and addiction make us slow to change; as does the belief that something is a 'one-off' and will not be repeated). More generally, technological progress may reduce lags by speeding up production and distribution processes. The development of new technologies and use of flexible employment or financial contracts has hastened the rate with which we can respond to unexpected events. It may also be that we can learn from past experiences (and economic research!).

---

[1] See Thomas (1997) for more detail on complex lag structures.

Keynesian theory is a demand-led theory built in a world of excess capacity, where the economy is below full employment. Other theories, such as Friedman's and Modigliani's focus more on the supply-side and on future expectations of future income (rather than current income) as determinants of current consumption. These ideas underlie more sophisticated postulates about human behaviour, including the argument that people's spending decisions in the present are based on their expectations about the future generating **consumption smoothing**. Milton Friedman argues that it is not current income that determines how you spend or save, but your expected **permanent income**. If we get a wage rise but expect it to be short-term, lasting only a year for example, it may not be sensible just to increase our spending. Rather, we might save the extra money, seeing it as a one-off bonus. But if we expect a permanent wage rise, then we would increase our spending accordingly. This is the essence of the **permanent income hypothesis** (PIH).

Friedman's model is describing microeconomic decisions and applying them to a macroeconomic context so it is a **micro-founded** macroeconomic theory. Micro-founded theories are built around the representative agents hypothesis (first introduced in Chapter 8). This hypothesis asserts that if we describe the behaviour of one representative household then, assuming that all households behave in the same way as the representative agent (at least on average), this representative behaviour captures aggregate macroeconomic behaviour too.

Another consumption-smoothing theory of consumption is the **life-cycle theory**, formulated by Franco Modigliani. He suggests that rather than follow the reflex response implied by Keynes, we intelligently calculate our expected income stream over our entire lives, and spend in each year that amount which would enable us to 'break even' in our (predicted) year of death. So we spend more than we earn when we are young (e.g. when we are students), less than we earn when we are older and more again when we retire.

More recently, behavioural economists have investigated whether or not the consumption-smoothing approaches are consistent with real-world behaviour. At a microeconomic level, **Veblen effects** may operate: we may consume something because we see our neighbours consuming it. Past experiences and past expectations will have an impact; consumption may reflect ingrained habits rather than sensible choices. People may have relatively short time horizons and their preferences may shift over time. This will mean that consumption behaviour is not necessarily rational and sensible in the ways envisaged by Friedman and Modigliani.

None of the theories outlined in this theory section can offer a single, perfect, explanation. Modigliani's life-cycle consumers may find that no matter how accurate are their forecasts of tomorrow's income, the bank will not grant them the loan they need today and so **liquidity constraints** will mean that people don't have the necessary cash that they need to buy something that they want today because they cannot borrow money.

In this chapter, we investigate these issues in analysing the relationships between consumption and income in the UK 1979 to 2005. We will analyse two specifications of the consumption function: the Keynesian consumption function and Friedman's PIH consumption function.

10.3   The data

The data used in this chapter is published by the UK's Office of National Statistics (ONS). Consumption and income incorporated in real terms using the following data sources:

Variable	Source	Website
Final Consumption Expenditure – current prices (RPQM) deflated using the RPI (CZBH)	UK ONS, *Economic Trends Annual Supplement (ETAS)*	www.statistics.gov.uk
Real household disposable income (OSXS)	UK ONS, *Economic Trends Annual Supplement (ETAS)*	www.statistics.gov.uk

In assessing the relationships between consumption and income we will examine evidence for some of the theoretical predictions outlined in Section 10.2. As mentioned above, Kuznets (1946) presented evidence showing that the APC was stable over time and this result is inconsistent with Keynes's specification of the consumption function. In reassessing Kuznets's evidence about a stable APC we can inspect the raw data: Figure 10.1 plots consumption and real disposable income over time revealing a relatively steady relationship between the two, though there are some short-term fluctuations.

Figure 10.2 plots the APC over time using annual data and whilst there are episodes where the APC has been relatively high or relatively low, overall it does seem to be steady at around 0.70, again suggesting that the APC is stable.

Together our data show that Kuznets's early finding is being mirrored in recent data. This stable pattern suggests that changes in income are being matched by equivalent changes in consumption.

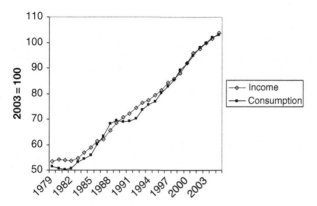

Figure 10.1   Real consumption and real disposable income – UK 1979–2005

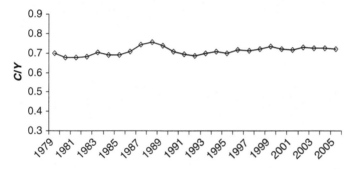

Figure 10.2   Aggregate average propensity to consume (APC), UK 1979–2005

In the following empirical section we will assess the Keynesian consumption function and Friedman's consumption function, keeping in mind that a stable APC would be more consistent with the latter functional form. We will also use the evidence about a stable APC to build an error correction model (ECM) of the relationship between consumption and income, as will be explained below.

10.4   Empirical methods and results

In this section we will estimate Keynes's consumption function and Friedman's consumption function. Our empirical models will be as follows.

Keynesian consumption function

To recap on the key theoretical postulates, Keynes (1936) assumed a stable marginal propensity to consume and so the Keynesian empirical model is of this form:

$$C_t = \alpha + \beta Y_t + \varepsilon_t \qquad (10.6)$$

where $0 < \beta < 1$

As shown above in Equation (10.5), this mathematical relationship implies a stable MPC. It also implies that the APC is declining.

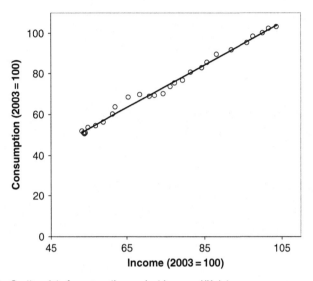

Figure 10.3   Scatter plot of consumption against income, UK data

To capture the patterns between consumption and income, we show a scatter plot in Figure 10.3. This scatter plot reveals a relatively steady positive relationship between consumption and income and the trend line captures a linear pattern consistent with the Keynesian specification of the consumption function. However there is some evidence that the relationship is not completely robust: some of the observations on consumption (those associated with low to middling levels of income) are relatively far away from the trend line.

Friedman's permanent income hypothesis (PIH)

As explained in Section 10.2 Friedman's permanent income hypothesis is based around rational, forward-looking consumption-smoothing behaviour. Friedman constructs a consumption function around a multiplicative function form as follows:

$$C_t = \alpha Y_t^P v_t \qquad (10.7)$$

where Y^P is permanent income and v_t is a stochastic error term with a mean of zero. Permanent income is assumed, on average, equal to total income. (Shocks to consumption are assumed to be random with a mean of zero.) With this multiplicative form of consumption function, the elasticity is unitary and the APC will be constant: as Y goes up, C goes up by a proportional amount and so the APC is unchanging.[2] Here we have a model that is non-linear in the variables but by taking logs we get the following model (which is linear in the parameters, thus satisfying one of the Gauss–Markov assumptions explained in chapter 1):

$$c_t = \ln \alpha + \beta y_t + \varepsilon_t \qquad (10.8)$$

where c is logged consumption, y is logged income and $\varepsilon = \ln(v)$. To be consistent with (10.7) and the unitary long-run elasticity explained above, we assume that $\beta = 1$.

Before estimating the models, we establish the orders of integration of each variable using Augmented Dickey–Fuller tests (as explained in Chapter 9 – see Table 10.3).

Table 10.3 Augmented Dickey–Fuller unit root tests

	Levels			First Difference		
	t-Statistic	Prob.*	Critical value 5% level	t-Statistic	Prob.*	Critical value 5% level
Consumption (C)	1.34	1.00	−2.98	−3.38	0.02	−2.99
Income (Y)	2.21	1.00	−2.98	−3.32	0.02	−2.99
Logged consumption (c)	−1.13	0.68	−3.02	−4.06	0.01	−3.02
Logged income (y)	0.55	0.99	−2.98	−3.54	0.02	−2.99
Error Correction Term (EC)	−3.27	0.03	−2.99	n/a	n/a	n/a

Using a 5% significance level, these tests indicate that consumption, income, logged consumption and logged income are I(1). We have also constructed an error correction term variable. The meaning and usefulness of this variable will be explained below but note for the moment just that this error correction term is I(0). (We have also tested the variables for structural breaks and have found no significant evidence of breaks at a 5% significance level.)

The EViews output from the estimation of (10.6) (the Keynesian consumption function) is summarised in Table 10.4. Note that this estimation (and the

---

[2] This is also consistent with Modigliani's life-cycle hypothesis, which also predicts a constant APC.

Table 10.4 EViews output: Keynesian consumption function

Dependent Variable: Consumption (C)
Sample: 1979 2005
Included observations: 27

Variable	Coefficient	Std. Error	t-Statistic	Prob.
Intercept	−5.21	1.69	−3.08	0.01
Income (Y)	0.90	0.16	5.57	0.00
Time	0.30	0.34	0.89	0.38
R-squared	0.99	F-statistic		1432.91
Adjusted R-squared	0.99	Prob(F-statistic)		0.00
DW	0.75			

Diagnostic Tests
Breusch-Godfrey Serial Correlation LM Test:

	F-statistic	10.20	Probability	0.00

Ramsey RESET Test:

	F-statistic	0.47	Probability	0.50

subsequent ones too) include a deterministic trend term ('Time') to capture systematic upward trends over time. (Deterministic trends were explained in Chapter 9.)

An initial inspection of these results from the estimation of the Keynesian consumption function suggest that the null that the parameter on income is equal to zero can be rejected at a 5% significance level. Also, the F test of explanatory power indicates that the null of no association between the dependent variable and explanatory variable can be rejected at a 5% significance level. However, these results are unlikely to be reliable; the Breusch–Godfrey test (conducted here as an AR(4) version) indicates that the null of no autocorrelation in the errors must be rejected with a 5% significance level.

From Chapter 9 (and our unit root test results as summarised in Table 10.3), you will probably guess that non-stationarity in our variables is generating spurious regression results; and adopting the Engle–Granger Rule of Thumb (explained in Chapter 9) we can provisionally infer that there is evidence of a spurious regression because $R^2 > $ DW. So non-stationarity in our variables is creating a problem but (as also explained in Chapter 9) this can be resolved by differencing our variables.[3]

---

[3] The other possibility is model misspecification error from omitted variable bias. See chapter 8 for further discussions of model misspecification.

Table 10.5 EViews output: Friedman's permanent income model

Dependent Variable: Consumption (logged) (c)
Sample: 1979 2005
Included observations: 27

Variable	Coefficient	Std. Error	t-Statistic	Prob.
Intercept	9.33	0.79	11.76	0.00
Income (logged) (y)	0.83	0.25	3.39	0.00
Time	0.01	0.01	0.95	0.35
R-squared	0.99	F-statistic		1176.22
Adjusted R-squared	0.99	Prob(F-statistic)		0.00

Diagnostic tests
Breusch-Godfrey LM Test:

	F-statistic	5.73	Probability	0.00

Ramsey RESET Test:

	F-statistic	0.70	Probability	0.41

Turning to our second hypothesis, the EViews output from the estimation of equation (10.8) (Friedman's permanent income consumption function) is summarised in Table 10.5.

On initial inspection, these results are similar to the results from the estimation of the Keynesian consumption function: the R^2 is high and there is a highly significant relationship between logged consumption and logged income. But examining these results more carefully reveals that the Breusch–Godfrey LM test is significant, again indicating problems of non-stationarity, spurious regression and/or omitted variable bias.

As explained in Chapter 9, when our variables are non-stationary we should difference them until we have identified a stationary transformation of our original variable. The unit root tests summarised in Table 10.3 suggest that our consumption and income variables are I(1). In the last chapter we discussed the implications of using I(1) variables but in this chapter we introduce the possibility of **cointegration**. Cointegration occurs when a linear combination of non-stationary variables is stationary. For example, the I(1) variables consumption and income will be cointegrated if a linear combination of them is I(0). With cointegration, OLS estimators exhibit the property of **super consistency**. This means that as the sample size increases the sampling distribution of the OLS estimators collapses more rapidly onto the true parameter value.[4]

---

[4] The problem for our analysis is that we have a small sample and so it may not be valid to claim on these (relatively) large sample properties but we will nonetheless show the procedures involved.

We test for cointegration by doing a unit test on the residuals from our ARDL: this is called an **Engle–Granger test** and involves applying the DF/ADF testing methodology to the residuals and the null will be that there is a unit root in the errors. The Engle–Granger test on the model reported in Table 10.5 gives $\hat{\tau} = -4.280(\text{p} = 0.003)$ and so we can reject the null of a unit root and conclude that our residuals are stationary. This suggests that logged consumption and logged income are cointegrated.

Cointegration is important to the construction of error correction models. For our example, the error correction term (ECT) is a linear combination of consumption (logged) and income (logged) because it is constructed as follows:

$$ECT_t = \ln\left[\frac{C_t}{Y_y}\right] = c_t - y_t \tag{10.9}$$

The unit root tests noted in Table 10.3 indicated that the null of a unit root in ECM could be rejected with a 5% significance level so ECT is I(0) even though c_t and y_t are themselves I(1). So there is some evidence that our consumption and income are cointegrated. We can use the information to construct an **error correction model** (ECM) as we explain below.

Autoregressive distributed lag (ARDL) and error correction models (ECMs)

An **error correction model** incorporates some assumption about a long-run equilibrium relationship between two variables. The first step in constructing an ECM is to gather some information about the long-run patterns. The evidence outlined above suggests that there *is* a stable long-run equilibrium relationship between C and Y, i.e. there is a constant APC. We will use this insight to construct an ECM using the constant APC to capture the long-run equilibrium path. A constant APC implies that (at least in the long-run) the elasticity of C with respect to Y is unitary (i.e. equal to 1). This is what will ensure a constant APC: with a unitary elasticity, a 1% rise in income will be matched by a 1% rise in consumption and so overall APC (the ratio of consumption to income) will remain constant.

Long-run elasticities can be calculated from autoregressive distributed lag (ARDL) models. Autoregressive (AR) means that the variable is related to past lags of itself; as explained in Box 10.1 a distributed lag (DL) is a lag structure in which the impact of the explanatory variables is distributed over more than one period. An ARDL model combines lags on both the dependent and explanatory variable(s). In the case of consumption functions, this means that a simple ARDL (1,1), i.e. an ARDL with one lag each on the dependent and explanatory variables, will look like this:

$$c_t = \alpha + \lambda c_{t-1} + \beta_1 y_t + \beta_2 y_{t-1} + \varepsilon_t \qquad (10.10)$$

For an explanation of the relationships between long-run elasticities, ARDLs and ECMs, see Box 10.2.

Box 10.2 The link between an ARDL and an ECM

An Error Correction Model (ECM) is a restricted version of an Autoregressive Distributed Lag (ARDL) model incorporating some assumption about a constant long-run relationship between a dependent variable and its explanatory variable(s). In this case we are looking at a very simple sort of ECM incorporating a unitary long-run elasticity (of 1) between income and consumption. (Note that a unitary elasticity does not imply that income and consumption are the same, just that they *change* in the same way.)

We can show how the ARDL can be restricted to give an ECM by starting with our ARDL (1,1) specification:

$$c_t = a + \lambda c_{t-1} + \beta_1 y_t + \beta_2 y_{t-1} + \varepsilon_t \qquad (10.10)$$

Adapting the ECM methodology outlined in Thomas (1997) to derive the restricted ECM version of the ARDL model first we need to 're-parameterise' (10.10) by subtracting c_{t-1} from both sides:

$$c_t - c_{t-1} = \Delta c_t = a + \beta_1 y_t + \beta_2 y_{t-1} + (\lambda - 1)c_{t-1} + \varepsilon_t \qquad (10.11)$$

Then we add and subtract $\beta_1 y_{t-1}$ from the right-hand side to give:

$$\Delta c_t = a + \beta_1 \Delta y_t + (\beta_1 + \beta_2)y_{t-1} + (\lambda - 1)c_{t-1} + \varepsilon_t \qquad (10.12)$$

Now that the ARDL has been re-parameterised, we can impose a restriction that the long-run elasticity is equal to one. As we've explained above, the stable APC justifies imposing a unitary long-run elasticity on the ARDL because for the APC to remain stable the elasticity of consumption with respect to income must be unitary. We can get an expression for the long-run elasticity by constructing a long-run model in which $c_t = c_{t-1} = c^*$ and $y_t = y_{t-1} = y^*$, which when incorporated into (10.10) gives:

$$c^* = a + \lambda c^* + \beta_1 y^* + \beta_2 y^* \qquad (10.13)$$

Rearranging this to collect c^* on the righthand side and y^* on the left-hand side gives:

$$c^* = \frac{a}{1 - \lambda} + \left[\frac{\beta_1 + \beta_2}{1 - \lambda}\right] y^* \qquad (10.14)$$

The parameter on y^* is the long-run elasticity (LRE) which is equal to:

$$LRE = \frac{\beta_1 + \beta_2}{(1 - \lambda)} \qquad (10.15)$$

if $LRE = 1$, then

$$\beta_1 + \beta_2 = 1 - \lambda \qquad (10.16)$$

If this is true then the parameter on c_{t-1} in (10.12) will be equal but of opposite sign to the parameter on y_{t-1} and so we can restrict our ARDL to give:

$$\Delta c_t = a + \beta_1 \Delta y_t + (1 - \lambda) y_{t-1} + (\lambda - 1) c_{t-1} + \varepsilon_t \qquad (10.17)$$

Collecting together c_{t-1} and y_{t-1} whilst remembering that their parameters are equal but opposite sign gives:

$$\Delta c_t = a + \beta_1 \Delta y_t + (\lambda - 1)[c_{t-1} - y_{t-1}] + \varepsilon_t \qquad (10.18)$$

This is the error correction model (ECM) specification. Note that as the variables are in natural logs so Δc_t is the growth rate in consumption and Δy_t is the growth rate in income. On the long-run equilibrium path (given $LRE = 1$), consumption and income will rise in proportion and will grow at the same rate. But if the consumption should move above the long-run equilibrium path, then the lagged error correction term ($ECT_{t-1} = c_{t-1} - y_{t-1}$) will be above average and, assuming $(\lambda - 1) < 0$, then growth in consumption will be negatively related to excessive consumption growth in the previous period. In other words, growth in consumption above the long-run equilibrium path (described by a constant APC) will be 'corrected' by a fall in consumption growth in the subsequent period; given the negative parameter on the error correction term, consumption growth will fall in the subsequent period.

Overall, one of the interesting things about ECMs is that they have a clear intuition that fits into the concepts of equilibrium that are so common in economics. We can illustrate this link between long-run equilibrium and short-run disequilibrium dynamics using the consumption example. We're approximately regressing consumption growth on income growth and whilst these variables are moving in proportion, the economy will be on its long-run equilibrium path of the constant APC. In disequilibrium however, if consumption grows relatively rapidly in comparison with income growth, then the negative effect of the EC term will pull consumption growth down in the next period. On the other hand if consumption is growing too slowly relative to income, then consumption will be below its long-run equilibrium path. Again the negative sign on the ECT parameter will pull growth in consumption in the opposite direction; and in the subsequent period consumption will grow more rapidly. In other words, the system will adjust to errors away from long-run equilibrium. Thus the ECT term captures corrections to consumption in disequilibrium and ensures that consumption and income return to the long-run equilibrium path given by a constant APC.

In estimating ARDL and ECM models, it is important to conduct **Granger Causality** tests. Granger causality tests involve establishing whether or not a variable 'Granger causes' another variable; a variable Granger causes another if it 'leads' the other variable and F tests of restrictions are used to assess the contribution of lags on one variable to the variability in the other. If lags on x_t capture a significant proportion of the variability in y_t then x_t 'Granger causes' y_t; if lags on y_t capture a significant proportion of the variability in x_t, then y_t Granger causes x_t; if a significant proportion of the variability in both variables are captured by lags on the other variable, then they Granger cause each other and this suggests that there may be simultaneity (i.e. feedback effects). If there is no correlation at all between the variables and the lags, then neither variable 'Granger causes' the other. Granger causality may mean very little in terms of a real causal link between variables; as emphasised in earlier chapters, in statistical analysis correlation does not imply causation and this is particularly true for regression analysis in economics because people's expectations compli- cate the timing of events – for example, Christmas cards do not cause Christmas, they merely 'Granger cause' Christmas.

As explained in Box 10.2, when we impose the restriction of a constant APC and therefore a unitary long-run elasticity of consumption with respect to income, then the unrestricted ARDL model is transformed into a restricted ECM. The EViews output from the estimation of these models is summarised in Table 10.6.

Note that there is less evidence of a spurious regression in these regressions that in the earlier regressions and, using the Breusch–Godfrey test we can retain the null of no autocorrelation at a 10% significance level, though we would have to reject this null at 5% (The DW test cannot be used in this case because it is invalidated by the presence of a lagged dependent variable.) The results have improved because, as explained in Chapter 9, spurious regressions are the outcome of non-stationary variables and for the ARDL and ECM specifications we have used the following stationary variables: Δc (the first difference in logged consumption – approximately equal to consumption growth), Δy (the first difference in logged income – approximately income growth) and EC (the error correction term). As noted above and shown in Table 10.3 we can reject the H_0 of a unit root for all these variables at a 5% significance level and so all the variables in our regression are I(0), i.e. are stationary.

We can also test the statistical merit of the ECM transformation incorpor- ating a long-run elasticity of 1 using an F test of restrictions. As explained in Chapter 5, the intuition underlying these tests is that if the parameters in a model are restricted, then the restricted RSS will increase: if it increases by a small amount then this suggests that the restriction is mirrored in the real

Table 10.6a EViews output: ARDL Model

Dependent Variable: logged consumption (c_t)
Sample (adjusted): 1980 2005
Included observations: 26 after adjustments

Variable	Coefficient	Std. Error	t-Statistic	Prob.
Intercept	4.27	1.58	2.70	0.01
logged consumption lagged c_{t-1}	0.74	0.18	4.11	0.00
logged income (y_t)	0.45	0.36	1.25	0.23
logged income, lagged (y_{t-1})	−0.81	0.25	−3.24	0.00
Time	0.02	0.01	3.12	0.01

R-squared	0.99	F-statistic		1124.22
Adjusted R-squared	0.99	Prob(F-statistic)		0.00
Sum squared residuals	0.006339			

Diagnostic tests
Breusch-Godfrey Serial Correlation LM Test:

	F-statistic	2.53	Probability	0.08

Ramsey RESET Test:

	F-statistic	2.21	Probability	0.15

Table 10.6b EViews output: error correction model (ECM)

Dependent Variable: Change in logged consumption (Δc_t)
Sample (adjusted): 1980 2005
Included observations: 26 after adjustments

Variable	Coefficient	Std. Error	t-Statistic	Prob.
Intercept	3.33	1.81	1.84	0.08
Change in logged income (Δy_t)	1.03	0.36	2.88	0.01
Time	0.00	0.00	1.17	0.25
ECT(−1)	−0.38	0.21	−1.84	0.08

R-squared	0.28	F-statistic		2.88
Adjusted R-squared	0.18	Prob(F-statistic)		0.06
Sum squared residuals	0.009068			

Diagnostic tests
Breusch-Godfrey LM Test:

	F-statistic	2.49	Probability	0.08

Ramsey RESET Test:

	F-statistic	0.75	Probability	0.40

data, we therefore infer that the restriction has empirical support and we do not reject it. However if the RSS increases significantly when we restrict a model, then we infer that the restriction does not fit the data well and so we reject the restriction. Here we will use the F test of restrictions to test the following null:

$$H_0 : \frac{\beta_1 + \beta_2}{(1 - \lambda)} = 1$$

$$\therefore \beta_1 + \beta_2 = 1 - \lambda$$

The ECM is the restricted model (it incorporates the restriction that the long-run elasticity is unitary); the ARDL is the unrestricted model. This gives the following working for the F test of restrictions:

$$F(1, 21) = \frac{(RSS_r - RSS_u)/d}{(RSS_u)/(n - k_u - 1)} = \frac{(0.009068 - 0.006339)/1}{0.006339/(26 - 4 - 1)} = 9.04$$

At a 5% significance level, $F_{crit}(1,21) = 4.32$, and since $F > F_{crit}$, we reject H_0 and conclude that our results unfortunately *do not* confirm the ECM incorporating a unitary long-run elasticity.

Overall, we have outlined some of the mechanics involved in constructing ARDL and ECM specifications of the relationship between consumption and income. We found some evidence that logged consumption and logged income are cointegrated but the imposition of a unitary long-run elasticity was not justified at a 5% significance level. This is a disappointing finding and may reflect our small sample size so one solution might be to collect more data and hope for more reliable results with a larger sample. Also whilst it is possible that another assumption about the elasticity could generate a more robust ECM, this would not be consistent with the constant APC identified by Kuznets and adopted by Friedman and Modigliani. For the data here, our main evidence about a constant APC came from a visual inspection of our data; graphs and charts cannot give us definitive answers about the precise magnitude of parameters and in this sense the finding from the F test of restrictions is more objective. There are however other ways of testing particular assumptions about long-run elasticities (see Thomas, 1997) and further investigations could focus on uncovering more evidence about the long-run relationship between consumption and income.

Another issue to keep in mind is that, whilst the diagnostic test results allowed us to retain a null of no autocorrelation in the errors at a 5% significance level, this finding was borderline and the autocorrelation in the residuals may be a sign of omitted variable bias, in which case our OLS estimations will be biased and inconsistent. So further investigations could focus on analysing the influence of other factors apart from income; it is important to remember that consumption will also be affected by other variables, for example by interest rates, liquidity constraints and wealth.

10.5   Implications and conclusions

The policy implications and strategies that stem from the analysis of consumption functions focus on government initiatives to stimulate consumer demand by lowering tax and interest rates, and/or by employing large numbers of people on infrastructure and other public works projects. On these grounds, UK Prime Minister Gordon Brown and US Presidents Kennedy, Clinton and Bush could all be described as Keynesian policy makers even though they are not from the same political party. President Bush's tax cuts in late 2001 and, in 2008, expansionary policies across the OECD introduced as recession-fighting tools, were – political motivations aside – an attempt to keep households spending their money, in the hope this would prevent the economy from stalling or, worse, free-falling, in the aftermath of numerous financial and political shocks. Also, the low spending in Japanese households from the 1990s onwards had been considered partly to blame for Japan's failure to lift itself out of economic slump. Unless households buy more, factories cannot increase their production, and the economy cannot grow. Consumption is by far the largest component of aggregate demand in most national economies and policy-makers need to be able to estimate its determinants reasonably accurately in order to predict the likely impact on the economy as a whole.

10.6   Further reading

Textbooks

Friedman, M. (1957) *A Theory of the Consumption Function*, Princeton: Princeton University Press.

Griffiths, A. and Wall, S. (1997) *Applied Economics, An Introductory Course* (7th edition), Harlow: Longman, Chapter 13, pp. 312–17.

Keynes, J. M. (1936) *General Theory of Employment, Interest and Money*, London: Macmillan. Chapters 8–10.

Mankiw, G. (2006) *Macroeconomics* (5th edition), New York: Worth, Chapter 10.

Thomas, R. L. (1997) *Modern Econometrics – An Introduction*, Harlow: Addison-Wesley. Chapter 11 (on lag structure); Chapter 15 (on ECMs), Chapter 16 (Granger causality tests).

Tinbergen, J. (1951) *Business Cycles in the United Kingdom, 1870–1914*, Amsterdam: North-Holland.

Academic articles

Keynes, J. M. (1937) 'The general theory of employment', *Quarterly Journal of Economics*, vol. 51, 209–23.

Kuznets, S. (1946) *National Product Since 1869* (assisted by L. Epstein and E. Zenks), New York: National Bureau of Economic Research, 1946.

Tinbergen, J. (1942) 'Does Consumption Lag Behind Incomes?' *Review of Economic Statistics*, vol. 24, No. 1, 1–8.

Policy briefs and newspaper articles

The Economist (2005), 'How to tame the thrift shift', 22 September 2005.

Norman, B., Sebastia-Barriel, M. and Weeden, O. (2002), 'Equity, wealth and consumption – the experience of Germany, France and Italy in an international context', *Bank of England Quarterly Journal*, vol. 42, Spring, 78–85.

10.7   Chapter exercises

1. In this chapter, we have estimated an error correction model (ECM) using logs of consumption and income. Estimate a linear ECM model of consumption following the procedures outlined in this chapter, i.e.:
   (a) Test consumption and income for unit roots and establish the order of integration of these variables;
   (b) Generate an EC variable and use unit root tests to establish its order of integration;
   (c) Estimate the ECM and discuss your results. Does the ECM modelling strategy work when the variables are in levels?
   (d) What are the policy implications of Keynesian consumption theories?
2. In this chapter we explained the importance of Granger causality tests. Conduct some Granger causality tests on logged consumption and logged income to establish whether these variables Granger cause each other. Discuss the implications of your findings for the estimation of the ARDL and ECM models in this chapter.

Part IV

Advanced topics

In this section, we introduce some relatively advanced econometric topics: panel estimation and logit/probit.

In the previous sections we have treated cross-sectional data and time-series data as separate but it is possible to combine these data sets, either by pooling or via panel estimation. We illustrate these techniques in the chapter on marriage and divorce.

Until now, we have focussed on linear estimation techniques. With 'binary' dependent variables, we estimate the *probability* of finding a particular characteristic. Linear estimation techniques may not work well when estimating probabilities. So, in the chapter on war and poverty, we introduce some non-linear techniques for the estimation of probabilities: logit and probit.

CHAPTER

Panel estimation
Divorce and income

Economic issues include:
- Rational choice theory
- Economics and happiness

Econometric issues include:
- Heterogeneity bias
- Pooling and panel estimation

Data issues include:
- Combining cross-sectional and time-series data

11.1   The issue

Economic analysis is not confined to the study of money and finance. Some economists use their tools for 'theoretical imperialism' – i.e. to analyse issues affecting human happiness and welfare that are usually the focus of socio-logical and/or psychological analysis. How is such an economic approach justified? Economic imperialists take the basic economic principle of balan-cing benefits and costs and apply it to some of the decisions that people make every day, e.g. choices about drug use, criminal behaviour, decisions to get married and/or divorced etc. The idea is that people engage in certain beha-viours, even ostensibly anti-social or destructive behaviours, because the benefits outweigh the costs. This is the essence of the rational choice theory made famous by Gary Becker.

Other economists have also used economic tools to illuminate social issues and problems. In this chapter we illustrate how economics and econometrics can be used to illuminate an area of family life that has been the focus of many analyses by economists: marriage and divorce. In this chapter, we focus on divorce data from 45 US states over the period 2002–4 so our data set has both a spatial/geographical dimension and a temporal dimension. When cross-sectional and time-series data are combined, particular techniques may be needed and in this chapter we illustrate **panel estimation** techniques – techniques designed simultaneously to capture both a spatial dimension and a temporal dimension.

11.2   The theory

Gary Becker popularised (and won the Nobel prize) for **rational choice theory** – an approach that applies economic principles to a wide range of social and psychological behaviours. Becker asserts that we are economisers not only when it comes to incomes and money but in other areas of our lives too. So economic theory can be helpful in understanding relationship decisions as well as financial and economic decisions.

In *A Treatise on the Family* (1991), Becker applies rational choice principles to family life asserting that decisions about marriage and divorce reflect a rational, maximising approach to life. People marry and divorce when they perceive that the overall benefits from entering into or breaking the marriage contract outweigh the costs.

Some economists confront these rational choice principles in arguing that people are not maximisers: anti-social and self-destructive behaviours may be the product of a complex range of motivations, including behaviours that are associated with irrational and/or ill-informed decision-making. For example, Daniel Kahneman (another Nobel laureate) and Amos Tversky approached socio-economic problems from the opposite direction: they argued that the psychological underpinnings of people's life experiences are as important as an economic analysis of the benefits and costs and their ideas triggered the development of hedonic psychology, as outlined in Box 11.1.

Rowthorn (1999) analyses marital decisions using a hybrid approach. He uses economic principles to draw parallels between economic investments and relationship-specific investments (such as marriage) requiring mutual levels of trust, describing marriage as a joint project in which the two partners pool and share resources and assets: marriage has an important economic dimension. But Rowthorn, captures some of the insights of the hedonic psychologists when he observes that **contagion effects** will operate – attitudes and expectations will influence the likelihood of divorce. So it is not only about benefits and costs; it is also about social and psychological factors too.

Box 11.1 Economics and happiness

Kahneman and Tversky (1979) introduced psychological factors into modern economic analysis via **prospect theory**. Prospect theory is not based on strict assumptions of rational and consistent behaviour. Instead it assumes that people operating in a risky world will assess the likely prospects of a range of different behaviours. Rather than balancing benefits and costs in a symmetric and systematic way, people will prefer avoiding losses to making gains, and happiness will be affected by changing situations not the status quo.

Tversky and Kahneman (1986) also argue that people are not necessarily very good at judging the probabilities of various events and will often misjudge future prospects, with statistical errors emerging because of **cognitive biases** such as anchoring effects and framing effects. **Anchoring effects** operate when people's decisions and choices reflect what they have experienced already: if they are happy with a given situation then they will anchor their expectations of the future to what they are currently experiencing. **Framing effects** focus on the psychological context of people's reported perceptions of personal issues: when researchers asked students two questions: "Are you happy?" "Did you have a date last night?" the students' answers were affected both by which question is asked first and by how things had gone the night before. For a good introduction to some of the main findings from this research into prospect theory and other research into aspects of behavioural economics see Lunn (2008).

Kahneman and Tversky's research propelled a whole new approach to economics – **hedonic psychology** – the psychology of well-being.[1] In one sense hedonic psychology is a modern development of **utilitarianism** – a moral doctrine, associated with the English economist and philosopher Jeremy Bentham, asserting that actions should be assessed according to their impact on utility i.e. on pleasure, satisfaction and happiness. The hedonic psychologists argue that we are not necessarily strictly rational in our decision-making and our subjective judgements of our own satisfaction, e.g. in the context of decisions such as to marry or divorce, may not necessarily tie in with monetary measures. So economics should be extended to analyse not only monetary measures of utility but also measures of **experienced happiness**: our own experiences of psychological well-being are as important as monetary measures of benefits and costs. Because the hedonic psychologists focus on experienced happiness, their empirical analyses tend to concentrate on survey data and related reports of individuals' reported levels of happiness.

These ideas are applied to the assessment of marriage and divorce by focussing on the insight that it is *change* that affects people's perceptions of their own welfare. People will judge their own happiness against a benchmark of what they've experienced in the past. For married couples, their experience of marriage and divorce is determined by the recent past.

---

[1] See Kahneman, Diener and Schwarz (2003) for a collection of papers from hedonic psychology.

> Happiness peaks at the point of marriage but falls rapidly until after (on average) two years of marriage it stabilises at a level equivalent (and sometimes below) pre-marital happiness levels (Layard 2005). Stutzer and Frey (2006) develop these ideas analysing marriage using German survey evidence: their analysis suggests that happy singles are more likely to select into marriage and unhappy people are likely to self-select into divorce. These findings remain preliminary because most economists have only recently developed an interest in analysing social and psychological issues; the evidence is relatively sparse. But a large volume of research is in progress from which we can anticipate fascinating new insights.

Economists have also analysed broader issues relating to marriage and divorce. Wilson and Oswald (2005) analyse the relationships between marriage and health (both physical and psychological) identifying health gains from being married. Edland (2005) focusses on the impact of marital decisions on labour mobility and migration and hypothesises that females will move to urban areas because they are attracted by the higher incomes of the richer urban men. Gautier, Svarer and Teulings (2005) assert that singles are more likely to pay higher property prices in cities because of better marriage markets in cities.

In this chapter we will build on Rowthorn's idea that marriage is a joint economic contract by exploring the relationship between divorce and economic conditions. We assume that when disposable incomes are relatively low, people will experience financial pressures and these will increase the economic and psychological costs of partnership thereby increasing the likelihood of divorce. Hypotheses about a negative association between income and divorce are emerging in the academic literature and in the mainstream press – for example Burgess, Propper and Aassve (2003) examine the relationships between income and divorce finding negative correlations for men; and *The Economist* has highlighted debates about the impact of recessions on divorce (*The Economist*, 2008). In this chapter we investigate these assertions by analysing the associations between divorce rates and personal income across the different states of the USA over the period 2002–2004.

11.3   Data

The theoretical hypothesis outlined in Section 11.2 is that macroeconomic conditions affect divorce rates and we assess this hypothesis using divorce statistics for 45 US states over the period 2002 to 2004. Our data comes from the following sources:

Variable	Source	Website
Divorce rate per 1000 inhabitants, by state	US National Center for Health Statistics (NCHS)	www.cdc.gov/nchs/data/nvss/ divorce90_04.pdf
Personal disposable income per capita, by state	US Bureau of Economic Analysis (BEA)	www.bea.gov/regional/spi/ drill.cfm

The divorce rate is measured using data on the divorces from household health surveys conducted and analysed by the NCHS. Income is measured as average annual personal disposable income (PDI) per capita by state, collected from the BEA's regional income and product accounts.[2]

In assessing our data, the key limitations will be that PDI does not completely capture the full range of macroeconomic conditions affecting marital pressures – for example mortgage and housing markets are likely to have an impact on the stability of relationships particularly if the family home is threatened by repossession. Also, our data is focussing closely on macroeconomic factors and this abstracts from the social and psychological pressures on family life.

Given these caveats, we show a scatter plot of divorce rates and PDI in Figure 11.1. This preliminary assessment of the data reveals that there is a negative association between divorce rates and personal income, confirming our hypothesis that difficult economic conditions are associated with higher divorce rates, though there is also a lot of variability across the data set.

11.4   Empirical methods and results

In exploring the relationship between incomes and divorce across the US states more thoroughly, we will estimate the following model:

$$d_{i,t} = \alpha + \beta y_{i,t} + u_{i,t} \tag{11.1}$$

d is the divorce rate and y is PDI per capita. Note that we have two subscripts on each variable. This is because we have two dimensions to our data set: we have data for i individual states (45 states in the sample) over t different time periods (3 years in this analysis). The intercept term is included to capture all

---

[2] For the UK, similar data are available via the ONS; for statistics on marriage and divorce see the ONS's *General Household Survey* results which can be found at www.statistics.gov.uk/ghs/.

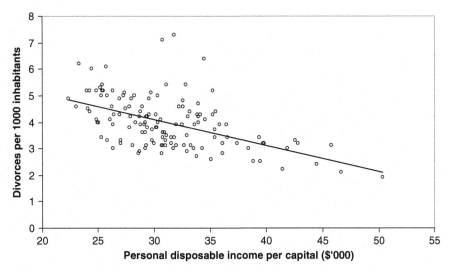

Figure 11.1   Scatter plot of divorce rates vs. personal income, USA 2002–4

the constant factors that might affect the divorce rate, for example social conventions and attitudes.

There are two econometric approaches to combining cross-sectional and time-series observations: pooling and panel estimation.

Pooled estimation

Pooling is the simple combining of cross-sectional and time-series data without adjustment. A pooled regression would be a regression on our 135 pairs of observations (45 states × 3 years) without making any allowance for factors specific to each individual state. If we were to look at just one year of data, we'd have just 45 observations but with 3 years of data we have 135 observations. This may increase the accuracy of our estimation because if we have a problem of micronumerosity (which, as explained in Chapter 5, is the technical term to describe a sample with few degrees of freedom, i.e. a sample in which the number of observations is small relative to the number of parameters to be estimated) then OLS estimates will not be so precise. The standard errors on the OLS parameter estimates will be larger and confidence intervals will be wider.

For some samples of data it may be appropriate just to pool the observations in this simple way. If the samples are randomly selected from each point in time, then there will be no systematic cross-sectional specific effects to affect the parameter estimates – for example, if we were taking three different

Table 11.1 EViews output from the pooled estimation

Dependent Variable: Divorce rate
Method: Least Squares
Sample: 1 135

Variable	Coefficient	Std. Error	t-Statistic	Prob.
Intercept	7.055	0.445	15.854	0.000
PDI per capita	−0.099	0.014	−7.004	0.000
R-squared	0.269			
Adjusted R-squared	0.264 Prob(F-statistic)			0.000
Sum squared residuals	94.061			
Durbin-Watson statistic	0.536			

Breusch-Godfrey Serial Correlation LM Test:
F-statistic	77.393	Probability		0.000

random samples of 1000 households three times across three years from a population of 30 million households, then it is very unlikely that the same households would be selected more than once; the households sampled in each year would be different and so household-specific effects are unlikely to be important. In this case simple pooling will be valid.

We run a simple pooling regression on our data set and the results are shown in Table 11.1.

These results do capture a strong association between divorce rates and PDI: for a t test of the null that the parameter on logged income is equal to zero, we can reject the null at a 5% significance level ($p < 0.05$). The R^2 indicates that variability in PDI captures 26.9% of the variability in divorce rates and the F test of explanatory power confirms that the overall goodness of fit is relatively high.

However, looking at the results more carefully there are signs that OLS may not be working well because Gauss–Markov assumptions are violated. For example the DW statistic is low and close to zero suggesting that autocorrelation may be a problem and this is confirmed by the results from the BG test – which indicates that the null of no autocorrelation must be rejected even at very low significance levels.

So what is happening with this data set? The autocorrelation problem may be emerging because in our data set we have ordered our data set so that the three years of data for each state follow from each other. We might expect that each state is affected by some factors that are constant but specific to an individual state, but do not affect the other states. These state-specific constant factors will not vary over time and the BG and DW tests are picking up the correlations between these state-specific constant factors over the three consecutive years of data for each state.

This illustrates the essential problem of a simple pooling procedure: pooling is only valid if all the parameters of the model are constant across space. So a simple pooling of our data procedure is unlikely to be valid for our sample because we have some **fixed effects** i.e. state-specific effects which are time invariant but unobservable. Unless we control for these fixed effects we will generate biases in our estimation and to show how these biases are created when we ignore region-specific fixed effects we start with our empirical model from (11.1):

$$d_{i,t} = \alpha + \beta y_{i,t} + u_{i,t} \tag{11.1}$$

We extend this model by including a deterministic time trend (T) as follows:

$$d_{i,t} = \alpha + \beta y_{i,t} + \phi T_t + u_{i,t} \tag{11.2}$$

(This time trend is constant across the states hence there is no subscript i.) If we ignore the state-specific fixed effects then these will be left in the error term as follows:

$$u_{i,t} = a_i + \varepsilon_{i,t} \tag{11.3}$$

where a_i is the fixed effect specific to each state i.

Putting (11.2) and (11.3) together we have:

$$d_{i,t} = \alpha + \beta y_{i,t} + \phi T_t + (a_i + \varepsilon_{i,t}) \tag{11.4}$$

The problem with this model is that the state-specific effects have been left in the error term of the model even though they may be exerting a systematic influence on the divorce rate; the error term is meant to capture truly random factors. To illustrate what is happening by linking into some of the theoretical ideas outlined above: if Rowthorn's contagion effects are operating, then variations in attitudes and expectations across the states may mean that divorce is regarded as being more socially acceptable in some states than others and the a_i for each individual state will capture these (and other) differences across the states. But if a_i is left in the error then the deterministic part of the model won't properly capture all systematic influences.

If these fixed effects are ignored then this generates **heterogeneity bias**. Heterogeneity bias occurs because the time invariant fixed effects influencing individual cross-sectional units have have been left out of the deterministic part of the model so in essence heterogeneity bias is a form of omitted variable bias. As explained in Chapter 8, omitted variable bias is a potentially serious type of model misspecification. At the least it will generate autocorrelated errors, again because an important systematic influence has been left out of the deterministic part of the empirical model and is being captured in the error term. For our analysis, heterogeneity bias explains our significant DW and BG tests. More seriously, if there is a correlation between the state-specific effects a_i and the explanatory variable(s) then heterogeneity bias will create the problem of endogeneity (also introduced in Chapter 8), i.e. the explanatory variable and error will be correlated and OLS estimators will be biased and inconsistent. So simple pooling in the presence of heterogeneity bias is likely severely to compromise the efficiency of OLS estimation.

Panel estimation

In the presence of cross-section specific fixed effects, before drawing any firm conclusions from our estimations it will be important either to capture or to remove the fixed effects and thus eliminate potential heterogeneity bias. One solution to heterogeneity bias is to use panel estimation techniques. These allow us to combine the advantages of pooling as outlined above (i.e. efficiency gains from reducing micronumerosity) with techniques to control for heterogeneity bias.

We outline two ways of removing time constant cross-section specific effects – the difference estimator and fixed effects estimation. A further method, the random effects estimator model, is beyond the scope of this book but see Wooldridge (2003) for a detailed explanation.

The difference estimator

The difference estimator eliminates the heterogeneity bias by differencing it away over time as follows. Starting with (Equation (11.4)):

$$d_{i,t} = \alpha + \beta y_{i,t} + \phi T_t + (a_i + \varepsilon_{i,t}) \tag{11.4}$$

Lag (11.4) by one time period to give:

$$d_{i,t-1} = \alpha + \beta y_{i,t-1} + \phi T_{t-1} + (a_i + \varepsilon_{i,t-1}) \tag{11.5}$$

Then subtract (11.5) from (11.4) Remembering that $\Delta T_t = 1$, a_i is constant over time and so $\Delta a_i = 0$, this gives:

$$\Delta d_{i,t} = \beta \Delta y_{i,t} + \phi + \Delta \varepsilon_{i,t} \tag{11.6}$$

The a_i has been differenced away and subtracted out, removing the potential source of heterogeneity bias. Note that the parameter ϕ has become our new intercept in the differenced model because $\Delta T_t = 1$.

The difference estimator has removed the heterogeneity bias but suffers from the following limitations:

- we may want to retain levels information in our model e.g. if we are more interested in the levels variables rather than changes;
- by differencing our explanatory variables we reduce their variability, we will not have such a strong source of explained variance and this lower 'explanatory' power will be associated with a lower R^2;
- by differencing our model we lose degrees of freedom and the accuracy of our estimation will decline accordingly;
- in differencing the error term we may create problems with our errors, e.g in Equation (11.6) our error is a **moving average** $(\Delta\varepsilon_{i,t} = \varepsilon_{i,t} - \varepsilon_{i,t-1})$ i.e. it is an average of successive values of ε_i.

The fixed effects estimator

Another approach to dealing with cross-section specific effects in panel estimation is to use the **fixed effects estimator**, which involves a **within transformation**: i.e. the observations within each cross-sectional subgroup are **demeaned** to remove the unobservable fixed effects (see also Wooldridge 2003). To illustrate these concepts, demeaning involves subtracting the mean for each subgroup from each observation in that subgroup. For our chapter example, if we want to demean the Florida observations on d and y, then we subtract the mean for Florida over the period 2002–4 from each of the Florida observations.

We can show how and why the demeaning procedure works by starting again with Equations (11.1) and (11.3):

$$d_{i,t} = \alpha + \beta y_{i,t} + (a_i + \varepsilon_{i,t}) \tag{11.1}$$

$$u_{i,t} = a_i + \varepsilon_{i,t} \tag{11.3}$$

Taking the mean for d for each subgroup i gives

$$\bar{d}_i = \bar{\alpha} + \beta\bar{y}_i + \bar{a}_i + E(\varepsilon_i) \tag{11.7}$$

Demeaning involves subtracting this subgroup mean from each observation to give:

$$d_{i,t} - \bar{d}_i = (\alpha - \bar{\alpha}) + \beta(y_{i,t} - \bar{y}_i) + (a_i - \bar{a}_i) + \varepsilon_{i,t} - E(\varepsilon_i) \tag{11.8}$$

This can be simplified because the mean of a constant is just that constant and the mean of the error is zero i.e. $\bar{a}_i = a_i$, $\bar{\alpha} = \alpha$ and $E(\varepsilon_i) = 0$ giving:

$$(d_{i,t} - \bar{d}_i) = \beta(y_{i,t} - \bar{y}_i) + \varepsilon_{i,t} \tag{11.9}$$

In this way, the fixed effects have been demeaned away.

A directly equivalent procedure to demeaning is to use dummy variables to control for the cross-section specific fixed effects. A dummy variable can be used to bring the a_i out of the error ($u_{i,t}$) into the parameter estimate on the dummy variable. If we create a dummy variable D_i for each cross-sectional unit i, then we have:

$$d_{i,t} = \alpha + \beta y_{i,t} + \sum_{i=1}^{44} a_i D_i + \varepsilon_{i,t} \qquad (11.10)$$

To illustrate – we create a dummy variable for Florida called D_{Florida}, which is equal to one for the three years of Florida data and equal to zero for all observations referring to other states. When $D_{\text{Florida}} = 1$ all the other D_is are zero, we have the following:

$$\begin{aligned} d_{\text{Florida},t} &= \alpha + \beta y_{\text{Florida},t} + a_{\text{Florida}} D_{\text{Florida}} + \varepsilon_{\text{Florida},t} \\ &= (\alpha + a_{\text{Florida}}) + \beta y_{\text{Florida},t} + \varepsilon_{\text{Florida},t} \end{aligned} \qquad (11.11)$$

In this way, the parameter on each dummy variable will pick up the a_i for each cross-section – e.g. the parameter on Florida's dummy has shifted the intercept to capture the cross-sectional fixed effects that apply only to Florida. This gives the same result as demeaning.

For our data set we create similar dummy variables for all the 45 states in our sample and include all the state-specific dummies in our model to capture state-specific effects. We use Alabama as the reference category i.e. Alabama is the state to which the conventional intercept refers.[3]

Alternatively we could have dropped the intercept because the dummy variables will be capturing all the constant factors for each state but dropping the intercept complicates interpretation of adjusted R^2. We couldn't do both (i.e. include the Alabama dummy as well as the conventional intercept) because this would create perfect multicollinearity and we'd be in a dummy variable trap (as explained in Chapter 5).

The fixed effects estimation with dummy variables is reported in Table 11.2.

This estimation procedure has worked relatively well; the R^2 is high and the F test of explanatory power allows rejection of the null that the parameters on the explanatory variables are jointly equal to zero even at low significance levels.

In testing for individual significance, the parameter on PDI is still significantly different from zero even at low significance levels. The t tests on the parameters on the state dummies are, at 10% significance levels and lower,

---

[3] See Chapter 5 for an introductory explanation of dummy variables and reference categories.

Table 11.2 EViews output from fixed effects estimation using dummy variables

Dependent Variable: DIVORCE
Method: Least Squares
Sample: 1 135

Variable	Coefficient	Std. Error	t-Statistic	Prob.		Coefficient	Std. Error	t-Statistic	Prob.
Intercept	7.675	0.310	24.767	0.000					
PDI per capita	-0.094	0.011	-8.392	0.000					
Dummy variables					Dummy variables				
Alaska	-0.308	0.135	-2.273	0.025	Nevada	2.305	0.132	17.453	0.000
Arizona	-0.827	0.116	-7.141	0.000	New Hampshire	-0.272	0.149	-1.823	0.072
Arkansas	0.738	0.118	6.262	0.000	New Jersey	-0.670	0.193	-3.476	0.001
Colorado	0.009	0.145	0.063	0.950	New Mexico	-0.567	0.117	-4.867	0.000
Connecticut	-0.353	0.224	-1.575	0.119	New York	-1.021	0.161	-6.325	0.000
Delaware	-0.771	0.142	-5.424	0.000	North Carolina	-0.711	0.117	-6.085	0.000
District of Columbia	-1.095	0.258	-4.243	0.000	North Dakota	-2.023	0.117	-17.337	0.000
Florida	0.203	0.125	1.626	0.108	Ohio	-1.088	0.121	-8.974	0.000
Idaho	-0.054	0.116	-0.471	0.639	Oregon	-0.542	0.121	-4.494	0.000
Illinois	-1.743	0.142	-12.296	0.000	Pennsylvania	-1.575	0.131	-12.002	0.000
Iowa	-2.029	0.119	-17.074	0.000	Rhode Island	-1.479	0.135	-10.954	0.000
Kansas	-1.454	0.121	-11.991	0.000	South Carolina	-1.917	0.116	-16.583	0.000
Kentucky	-0.183	0.116	-1.582	0.117	South Dakota	-1.807	0.119	-15.246	0.000
Maine	-0.515	0.118	-4.354	0.000	Tennessee	0.003	0.117	0.024	0.981
Maryland	-0.833	0.172	-4.852	0.000	Texas	-1.106	0.121	-9.171	0.000
Massachusetts	-1.512	0.189	-8.008	0.000	Utah	-1.218	0.116	-10.475	0.000
Michigan	-1.190	0.125	-9.496	0.000	Vermont	-0.763	0.124	-6.176	0.000
Minnesota	-1.449	0.146	-9.920	0.000	Virginia	-0.409	0.144	-2.842	0.006
Mississippi	-0.821	0.122	-6.748	0.000	Washington	-0.068	0.140	-0.482	0.631
Missouri	-1.017	0.119	-8.536	0.000	West Virginia	-0.227	0.118	-1.925	0.058
Montana	-1.284	0.115	-11.124	0.000	Wisconsin	-1.672	0.125	-13.415	0.000
Nebraska	-1.325	0.124	-10.708	0.000	Wyoming	0.777	0.136	5.695	0.000

R-squared	0.986		Sum squared residuals	1.779			F-statistic		141.162
Adjusted R-squared	0.979		Durbin-Watson statistic	2.871			Prob(F-statistic)		0.000

significantly different from zero for all states except Colorado, Connecticut, Florida, Idaho, Kentucky, Tennessee and Washington State. However, the significance of the parameters on the fixed effects dummies for Florida, Connecticut and Kentucky is borderline – these parameters are significantly different from zero at significance levels just about 10%. An F test of joint restrictions for the remaining four states with fixed effects parameters more clearly insignificantly different from zero confirms the t test results: the null that the parameters on the dummy variables for those four states are equal to zero is not rejected even at high significance levels – $F(4,88) = 0.195 \; [p = 0.941]$.

For the 41 remaining states, the statistical significance of the state-specific fixed effects suggests that divorce rates are affected by factors specific to each state as well as by PDI. Some state-specific factors that might be captured by these fixed effect dummies include financial constraints, mortgage defaults and repossessions, unemployment (assuming that it is relatively constant over short time spans) and possibly a number of non-economic factors, such as psychological health and social factors.

11.5   Implications and conclusions

In terms of econometric techniques, this chapter has shown that econometric results can be affected profoundly by whether or not the correct techniques have been used. For example, as illustrated in this chapter, a naïve pooling of the data on divorce rates and PDI may generate misleading conclusions and panel estimation techniques will more efficiently control for time invariant fixed effects.

If our empirical findings about the negative association between divorce and PDI across the US states between 2001 and 2004 are robust, then this suggests that government policies to improve economic performance may have some positive social effects in moderating family breakdown. However, the fact that cross-section specific fixed effects are also significant suggests, unsurprisingly, that other factors are important. Other economic factors such as financial instability and unemployment will affect divorce rates too, but whilst economic factors may have some impact on social phenomena such as divorce, psychological characteristics, social attitudes and expectations will play a central role. In the future, interdisciplinary research involving not only appropriate econometric techniques but also more suitable, disaggregated sources of data (e.g. survey data used to capture the likelihood of divorce at a household level) may more effectively capture the complex effects of economic, social and psychological factors on divorce rates.

11.6   Further reading

Books

Becker, G. (1991) *A Treatise on the Family*, Cambridge MA: Harvard University Press.

Kahneman, D., Diener, E. and Schwarz, N. (2003) *Well-Being: Foundations of Hedonic Psychology*, New York: Russell Sage Foundation.

Layard, R. (2005) *Happiness: Lessons from a New Science*, London: Allen Lane/Penguin.

Lunn, P. (2008) *Basic Instincts: Human Nature and the New Economics*, London: Marshall Cavendish Business.

Wooldridge, J. M. (2003) *Introductory Econometrics – A Modern Approach* (2nd edition), Thomson South-Western, Chapters 7 and 14.

Academic articles and working papers

Burgess, S., Propper, C. and Aassve, A. (2003) 'The role of income in marriage and divorce transitions among young Americans', *Population Economics*, vol. 16, no. 3, 455–75.

Edlund L. (2005) 'Sex and the City', *Scandinavian Journal of Economics*, vol. 107, no. 1, 25–44.

Gautier, P. A., Svarer, M. and Teulings, C. N. (2005) 'Marriage and the City', *CEPR Discussion Paper No. 4939*, Centre for Economic Policy Research, London.

Kahneman, D. and Tversky, A. (1979) 'Prospect theory – an analysis of decision under risk', *Econometrica*, vol. 47, no. 2, 263–92.

Rowthorn, R. (1999) 'Marriage and trust: some lessons from economics', *Cambridge Journal of Economics*, vol. 23, no. 5, 661–91.

Stutzer, A. and Frey, B. S. (2006) 'Does marriage make people happy, or do happy people get married?' *Journal of Socio-Economics*, vol. 35, no. 2, 326–47.

Tversky, A. and Kahneman, D. (1986) 'Rational choice and the framing of decisions', *Journal of Business*, vol. 59, no. 4, 251–78.

Wilson, C. M. and Oswald, A. J. (2005) 'How does marriage affect physical and psychological health, a survey of longitudinal evidence', Institute for the Study of Labour Discussion Paper, IZA Discussion Paper No. 1619.

Newspaper articles

The Economist (2008) 'Divorce and economic growth: negatively correlated', 24 July 2008.

11.7   Chapter exercises

1. Using the data sources outlined in Section 11.3, use the difference estimator to analyse the relationship between the divorce rate and personal disposable income per capita across the US states. Interpret your findings. How do your results differ from the results reported in this chapter?

2. Using the data sources outlined in Section 11.3, perform a 'within trans-formation' by subtracting the relevant cross-sectional means away from each observation (e.g. for the Florida observations, subtract the Florida mean). Confirm that this demeaning procedure gives the same result as for fixed effects estimation.

Binary dependent variables
War and poverty

Economic issues include:
- Conflict and inequality
- Institutions and development

Econometric issues include:
- Binary dependent variable estimation
- Logit and probit

Data issues include:
- The Gini coefficient

12.1 The issue

Poverty and armed conflict are the norm for a large proportion of the world's poor. In moderating the socio-economic impacts of these conflicts, the military as an institution plays a complex role. It may bestow some benefits in countries with institutions that are otherwise underdeveloped and perhaps it is not surprising that a well-organised and powerful public institution, when engaged in peaceful activity, should have positive impacts in countries with otherwise underdeveloped institutions. A lot of empirical work has been done, following Benoit (1978), to show that defence spending necessitated by real or potential armed conflicts encourages the development of human skills and essential infrastructure within poor economies, thus alleviating poverty. Benoit's study led to a range of further studies, some of which questioned Benoit's methodology and findings, and others which investigated the relationship between defence and economic growth using different methodologies.[1]

---

[1] For example, see Sandler and Hartley (1995, pp. 200–20) for a discussion of the relationship between economic growth, development and military expenditure.

Whilst the military as an institution may have a positive impact in peacetime, what about the direct impacts of war and conflict? What are its causes and consequences? In this chapter we will start to illuminate these questions by assessing evidence about the relationship between the incidence of war and relative poverty. To do this we will estimate the probability of conflict in a binary response model i.e. in a model in which the dependent variable takes one of two discrete values: 0 or 1. OLS estimation is not the most effective estimation method for binary response models and special binary estimation techniques are usually needed. In this chapter, we will introduce some relatively simple binary estimation techniques: Logit and Probit.

12.2   The theory

Given the destruction of life and resources that accompanies violent conflict, why would a government want to go to war? Analyses of the political and strategic motivations affecting governments' decisions to engage in armed conflict (or not) have been analysed by Nobel laureate Thomas Schelling (1958, 1960) using game theory concepts, as is explained in Box 12.1

In this chapter we will focus on one of the explanations for civil war – the political control of social unrest amongst poorer groups, and we will analyse the probability of war using poverty as an explanatory variable.

In assessing the specific impact of poverty and inequality on the probability of war, a range of issues must be considered. Many armed conflicts are the product of local socio-economic conditions rather than territorial motivations. Poverty and discrimination can be particularly prevalent in **dual economies**: economies characterised by a sharp divide between a globalised, industrialised urban sector and a poorer, more traditional, rural sector. In dual economies, political and economic leaders may have incentives to protect their economic and financial interests using violent techniques, increasing susceptibility to civil war. This hypothesis forms the basis of **greed and grievance theory**. In greed and grievance theory poverty and underdevelopment contribute to social unrest, generating feelings of political insecurity amongst the local elite groups. Rich elites have an incentive to use violent methods to protect their political and economic interests and so respond by increasing security expenditure on both the police and defence forces thus fostering the conditions for armed conflict. So according to the greed and grievance theorists, the probability of conflict is positively

---

Box 12.1 Game theory and the strategy of conflict

In *The Strategy of Conflict* (1960), Thomas Schelling uses game theory concepts to analyse military strategies (see also Schelling, 1958). As explained in Chapter 7, game theory is used to examine the bargaining behaviour of a small number of players devising their own strategies based on the potential strategies of the other players. Schelling argues that conflict situations can often be described as strategic bargaining situations: countries are concerned not so much with the application of force as with the exploitation of *potential* force. For example, during the Cold War, the US and USSR accumulated arms including nuclear weapons to prevent not encourage conflict. So it could be argued that the Arms Race was about deterrence not conflict. Schelling uses these ideas to devise the concept of **limited war**, i.e. strategic manoeuvres that can stabilise conflicts without resulting in actual armed engagement. Limited war will result in wasteful expenditures: nations will accumulate weapons just because they expect other countries to do so, generating a spiralling of armament accumulation, yet these weapons are accumulated in the hope that they will never be used. War breaks out when the strategies fail so actual conflict emerges from failed bargains. These ideas have been extended more recently, e.g. by Jackson and Morelli (2005), who argue that asymmetric information and **political bias** (i.e. bias away from democracy) increase the probability that peace bargains fail.

In this chapter we are concentrating on a specific type of armed conflict, i.e. civil war in developing countries. In this situation military strategies are moulded by a different set of goals and constraints, partly reflecting the fact that civil wars are not often games played between two equally powerful players. Nonetheless the concepts of game theory can still be applied and the strategy of deterrence can be a useful one for incumbent governments if a visible military presence acts as a deterrent to civil uprisings.

---

related to the extent of poverty and socio-economic tensions within poor countries (Collier and Hoeffler, 2004). Interactions between poverty and conflict will have other consequences too – for example undermining financial stability and financial wellbeing (Baddeley, 2008).

In this chapter we will develop some of these ideas by simplifying greed and grievance theory and concentrating on one dimension of the relationship between poverty and conflict: the impact of relative poverty on the probability of armed conflict. It is important to note that feedback effects will probably exist between poverty and conflict because the causality may run both ways – conflict may generate poverty e.g. if military expenditure crowds out social expenditure. If vicious circles are operating to increase poverty and armed conflict, feeding into each other, reinforcing destabilising political, socio-economic and financial effects then the simple unidirectional model estimated in this chapter is unlikely to pick up all the interactions. This reverse causality will be manifested as **simultaneity** in the relationship between war and poverty, creating endogeneity (first introduced in Chapter 8). This may bias our OLS results. One solution would be to use **simultaneous equation estimation** – i.e. estimating more than one regression equation at a time. However, these techniques are beyond the scope of this book though further details can be found in Wooldridge (2003). In this chapter we will keep things simple by illustrating the principles of binary estimation assuming that there is no simultaneity.

12.3   The data

As explained above, we are examining the impact of poverty on the probability of armed conflict. To do this, we have collected two sets of data: data on armed conflict and data on poverty. As explained in the theory section, there will be many more factors affecting the probability of war but here we are deliberately focussing on a simple model so that we can illustrate binary estimation techniques as clearly as possible.

Data on conflict

Overall, measuring conflict is not straightforward and there are a lot of data available – on the types of conflict (civil versus international) and the length/severity of conflicts. Conflict data are collected by a number of institutions including the Stockholm International Peace Research Institute (www.sipri.org/), the US Arms Control and Disarmament Agency (http://dosfan.lib.uic.edu/acda/) and Uppsala Conflict Database (www.ucdp.uu.se/database). Data from the Uppsala Universitet Conflict Database are captured in Figure 12.1 and show that, numerically, the incidence of war and conflict has subsided over the period 1992 to 2003, with the number of conflicts decreasing from 36 in 1992 to 29 in 2003. The severity of conflicts was also diminishing over this period with 16 full-scale wars in 1992 decreasing to 5 in 2003.

Using World Bank data to sort the countries identified in the Uppsala database into income groups reveals that, between 1992 and 2003, 64% of low income countries (LICs); 37% of lower middle income countries (LMICs); 8%

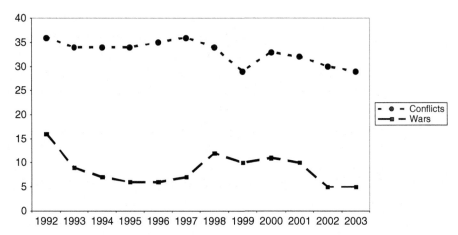

Figure 12.1 Conflicts and wars, 1992–2003

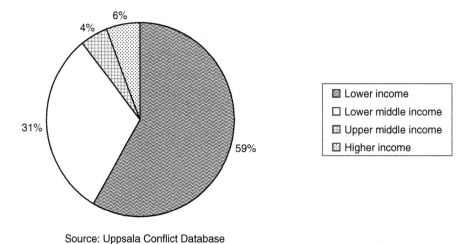

Source: Uppsala Conflict Database

Figure 12.2 Involvement in armed conflict, by income category

of upper middle income countries (UMICs) and 7% of upper income coun-tries (UICs) were involved in conflicts.

As a proportion of total numbers of conflicts, the incidence of conflict in each of these income categories is shown in Figure 12.2: of the 67 countries engaged in conflict during the period 1992 to 2003, 59% were low income countries; only 6% were the high income countries. So conflict is most common in the poorest countries and this finding adds weight to our broad hypothesis that there is a positive relationship between poverty and the incidence of war/armed conflict so it is the poorest countries that are likely to experience the devastating consequences.

Data on poverty and development

There are also many measures of poverty. As discussed in Chapters 2 and 4, data on levels of development, poverty and inequality are collected by a number of UN agencies and by other organisations such as the CIA. These include the UN Development Program (UNDP http://www.undp.org/) and the organisations within the World Bank group including the International Bank for Reconstruction and Development (IBRD) and the International Development Association (IDA). The World Bank co-ordinates these data collection tasks in collating a comprehensive collection of data on the international patterns of poverty and development, covering the various facets of poverty both absolute and relative.

As explained in Chapter 2, **absolute poverty** captures the proportion of a population earning below the national/international poverty lines – where poverty lines are defined in terms of basic needs (such as for food, shelter, health care etc.) and broad indicators of human welfare can be captured by looking at life expectancy, literacy, infant mortality etc.

In this chapter we will examine the relationships between war and relative poverty. **Relative poverty** is about inequalities in the distribution of income (or wealth). In a population in which everyone has access to plentiful food, shelter etc. there may still be relative poverty if the richest groups have a lot more than the poorest groups.

Relative poverty can be measured by examining the proportion of economic activity taking place amongst the richest versus poorest groups in a population and the commonest way to do this is to calculate the Gini index, as explained in Box 12.2.

We use some of these data sources to analyse the impact of poverty on conflict across a sample of 50 countries. We construct our dependent variable (W = War) as follows: for a given country, if intrastate conflicts were active i.e. if there were 25 or more deaths from civil conflicts in at least one of the years between 2004 and 2006, then $W = 1$; if not, then $W = 0$.

We use the Gini index to capture relative poverty, our explanatory variable. Unfortunately, annual data on Gini indexes are not readily available so we are forced to use different years of data for different countries; however, it is probably justifiable to assume that the extent of relative poverty does not change very rapidly within a given country, so we use the latest Gini coefficient available over the period 2000–4. We have used the period preceding 2004–6 for measuring poverty because our simple starting hypothesis is that poverty generates civil unrest, i.e. relative poverty is our leading

---

Box 12.2 Measuring inequality: Gini coefficients and Lorenz curves

The **Gini coefficient** was developed by an Italian statistician, Corrado Gini in 1912 as a measure of relative poverty. We use the Gini coefficient and index to capture income inequality but it can also be used to measure inequality in the wealth distribution.

An essential building block in calculating the Gini coefficient is the **Lorenz curve**. The Lorenz curve traces out the cumulative proportions of income earned by cumulative proportions of the population, as shown in Figure 12.3. The Lorenz curve is 'benchmarked' against the perfect equality case, i.e. when each percentile of the population earns an equivalent percentile of the national income – as captured by the 45 degree line.

The Gini coefficient measures the difference between the perfect equality scenario and the Lorenz curve and it is calculated using the areas under the 45 degree line. If the area between the line of perfect equality and Lorenz curve is A, and the area underneath the Lorenz curve is B, then the Gini coefficient is calculated as A/(A+B) and will take a value between 0 and 1, where 0 indicates perfect equality (everyone has the same income) and 1 indicates perfect inequality (one person has all the income).

If the Lorenz curve is not very far from the 45 degree line (i.e. in a situation of relative equality e.g. when the richest 1% would earn not much more than 1% of the national income), then the area A will be small and the Gini coefficient will be close to zero. On the other hand, if there is a lot of inequality, then the Lorenz curve will be bent away from the 45 degree line and the area A will be large: for example, in a relatively (economically) unequal population the richest 10% might earn 90% of the national income and in this case the Gini coefficient will be closer to 1. The **Gini index** is just the Gini coefficient as a percentage, i.e. is calculated by multiplying the Gini coefficient by 100.

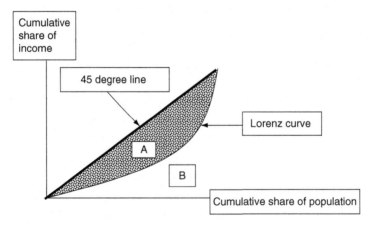

Figure 12.3 Calculating the Gini coefficient

variable. Data on the Gini index is published frequently in the UNDP's *Human Development Report* (and other UN publications) but here we have used the CIA's *World Factbook* because this publication provides more detailed information about the year to which their data applies.

To summarise, the data sources are as follows:

Variable	Source	Website
$W = War$ ($W = 1$ if > 25 deaths in civil conflicts, 2004–6)	Uppsala Conflict Database (UCDP)	www.ucdp.uu.se/database
$G = Gini$ *coefficient*	CIA World Factbook	www.cia.gov/library/publications/the-world-factbook/

Given the patterns described in Figures 12.1 and 12.2 it would be easy to conclude that there is a causal link but it is important to remember that correlation does not equal causation so whilst here we are investigating the role of poverty in creating conflict there are other possibilities, e.g. either that conflict is creating the poverty and/or some third variable is the fundamental cause of both.

12.4   Empirical methods and results

In this chapter, one of our aims is to illustrate binary estimation techniques and so we will draw a sharp dividing line – using a very simple measure of conflict, just to capture whether or not it happened in a given country over the period 2004 to 2006, as explained above. More specifically, we are trying to capture $P_i = \Pr(W = 1|G_i)$ – which is the probability of war conditioned on the degree of inequality, i.e. dependent on G. The function that we're estimating is:

$$P_i = \Pr(W = 1|G_i) = F(Z_i) \text{ where } Z = \alpha + \beta G_i + \varepsilon_i \qquad (12.1)$$

The function outlined in Equation (12.1) describes a **binary response model**, i.e. our dependent variable is a binary variable – it covers just two mutually exclusive and exhaustive possibilities so it takes one of two possible values: 0 or 1. Binary variables are essentially dummy variables but the key difference in comparison with the dependent variables in previous chapters is that they are being used on the left-hand side as a dependent variable rather than on the right-hand side as an explanatory variable.

Binary response models enable us to estimate the probability of war given the extent of relative poverty, i.e. the probability that $W = 1$ conditioned on

Table 12.1 EViews output from estimation of the linear probability model

Dependent Variable: W
Method: Least Squares
Sample: 1 50

Variable	Coefficient	Std. Error	t-Statistic	Prob.
Intercept	−0.414	0.366	−1.133	0.263
G	0.0182	0.0092	1.983	0.053
R-squared	0.08	Mean dependent variable		0.30
F-statistic	3.93			
Prob(F-statistic)	0.05			

G: $\Pr(W = 1|G)$. This latter part is important: if all we want to estimate is the probability of conflict and we aren't interested in the specific impact of poverty then we need nothing more than a calculator: the overall probability of conflict in this sample is 30%: i.e. 15 of the 50 countries in our sample have a $W = 1$; and 35 of these countries have $W = 0$ so the probability of peace is 70%.

$F(Z_i)$ in Equation (12.1) is a **link function** i.e. it links the binary variable to a linear functional form. The simplest thing that we can do is to use the **linear probability model** i.e. estimate the probability of war using OLS. In this case the link function and the estimated function would both be linear and:

$$P_i = \Pr(W = 1|G_i) = \alpha + \beta G_i + \varepsilon_i \tag{12.2}$$

In Table 12.1 we have summarised the EViews output table for the OLS estimation of the LPM. These results suggest that there is a statistically significant relationship between W and G: the t test on the poverty parameter is significantly different from zero at a 10% significance level ($p = 0.053$) and we can reject the null that the parameter on G is zero. This finding is confirmed by the F test of explanatory power. However, R^2 is not much more than zero (for reasons explained below).

We should anyway be cautious in our interpretation because we have imposed a linear world onto the estimation of non-linear probabilities and, potentially, we have misspecified our model. To explain: OLS is a linear technique – it involves estimating a *line* of best fit. In using OLS, we have implicitly assumed that there is a constant relationship between the probability of war and the extent of inequality. Lines are unbounded functions with a constant slope – they extend up and down without limit. But probabilities aren't linear: they are bounded by the values 1 (i.e. a certain outcome) and 0 (i.e. an impossible outcome). As OLS estimates are not similarly bounded, OLS estimation is not always the best technique to use with binary dependent variables (though it may work well as an approximation for certain data sets).

There are some complications with the use of the LPM to estimated probabilities. Firstly, in using a linear link function, it is possible that we will predict probabilities for a given values of the explanatory variable that are more than 1 or less than zero – either of which would be nonsensical results. Secondly, the error variances in the LPM will be heteroscedastic though this problem can be addressed using variants of the weighting procedures outlined in Chapter 6.

Given these limitations of the LPM we may prefer to use a non-linear link function. As explained in Box 12.3, we can express the probability of war as a non-linear function of Z_i even though Z itself is a linear function of our explanatory variable G. This will ensure that our estimates of the probability of war will be bounded between 0 and 1.

Box 12.3 Logit and Probit

For binary variables, the probabilities of each outcome sum to 1 as the two possible events are mutually exclusive and exhaustive; there is either war or peace so the probability of one is 1 minus the probability of the other. When estimating probabilities the LPM has a number of limitations, one of which is the assumption of a constant slope on the explanatory variables. There are two non-linear functions that are commonly used to overcome this problem: logit and probit. For both these functions, the marginal effects of the explanatory variables on P_i will change as the explanatory variables change – the marginal effects are not constant.[2]

Logit

Logit is the log of the odds ratio, where the **odds ratio** is $P_i/(1 - P_i)$. The log of the odds ratio will be linear:

$$\log\left(\frac{P_i}{1 - P_i}\right) = \log[P_i] - \log[1 - P_i] = a + \beta G_i + \varepsilon_i \tag{12.3a}$$

$$\text{where } P_i = \frac{\exp(a + \beta G_i + \varepsilon_i)}{1 + \exp(a + \beta G_i + \varepsilon_i)} \tag{12.3b}$$

Mathematically it can be shown that the logit will have the 'sigmoid' shape depicted in Figure 12.4 – the slope is not constant and the function flattens as it asymptotically approaches the bounds of 0 and 1:

---

[2] Mathematically, this change in marginal effect is captured by differentiating P_i with respect to G_i; the derivative will itself be a function of G, i.e. will be changing as G changes. See Wooldridge (2003).

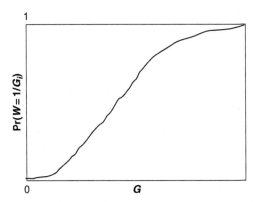

Figure 12.4   Logit function

Probit

Probit is the cumulative density function from the standard normal distribution. This means that it is capturing what happens to P_i as X_i increases – P_i for a given X_i is measured by taking the area underneath the standard normal distribution up to X_i. Mathematically, it is derived by integrating the standard normal distribution to give the cumulative density function. The shape of the probit function is broadly similar to the shape of the logit function. See Wooldridge (2003) for further details.

As explained above, the key advantage of using logit and probit is that they are non-linear functions and so the marginal effects of the explanatory variables on P_i are not constant. As they are non-linear functions, logit and probit cannot be estimated using linear estimation techniques. Instead they can be estimated using Maximum Likelihood Estimation (MLE). MLE involves identifying values of the unknown parameters (the constant and slope) that maximise the likelihood function capturing the probability of getting the values of the variables observed in the sample of data. A detailed explanation is beyond the scope of this book but see Wooldridge (2003) and Thomas (1997) for further details.

Log likelihood function

MLE is based around assessing the likelihood of the dependent variable conditional upon a link function and so measuring the empirical 'fit' of a model involves assessing the log of the likelihood function derived via MLE. For the model in this chapter, the **log likelihood function** is given by:

$$L = \sum_{i=1}^{15} \{W_i \cdot \ln(P_i)\} + \sum_{i=16}^{50} \{(1 - W_i) \cdot \ln(1 - P_i)\} \tag{12.4}$$

For logit and probit the log likelihood function will always be negative because the probabilities are bounded between 0 and 1 and so the logs of the probabilities will be negative. If the likelihood function is relatively close to zero then the empirical model is working relatively well.

The most restricted version of the log-likelihood function contains only the intercept. The restricted log likelihood function for the example in this chapter can easily be calculated as follows:

1. The probability of war ($W = 1$) is given by $P_i = 0.30$, $\ln(0.30) = -1.204$. The probability of peace ($W = 0$) is given by $(1 - P_i) = 0.70$ and $\ln(0.70) = -0.357$.
2. For 15 of our observations $W = 1$ and adding these together gives 15×-1.204
3. For 35 of our observations $W = 0$ and adding these together gives 35×-0.357
4. The restricted log likelihood function is calculated by applying Equation (12.4) as follows:

$$L = \sum_{i=1}^{15} \{W_i \cdot \ln(P_i)\} + \sum_{i=16}^{50} \{(1 - W_i) \cdot (1 - P_i)\} \tag{12.5}$$
$$= \{15 \times -1.204\} + \{35 \times -0.357\} = -30.55$$

Likelihood ratio (LR) test

We can use a restricted log-likelihood function to assess the contribution of our explanatory variables by comparing the log likelihoods in restricted and unrestricted models. Thus the LR test is like a non-linear equivalent of the F test of restrictions and it is calculated using the following formula:

$$LR = 2(L_u - L_r) \tag{12.6}$$

This test follows a χ^2 distribution with df $= d$ where d is the number of restrictions embedded within the restricted model.

As explained in Box 12.3 two non-linear techniques commonly used to estimate probabilities are logit and probit. In capturing W as a non-linear function of G, we have used logit estimation. We have selected logit because it has a clear conceptual basis. However, probit is also very commonly used and we have designed a chapter exercise around probit estimation; for the empirical model in this chapter, the results from logit and probit estimations are very similar. The output from the EViews estimation of the logit model is summarised in Table 12.2.

For our EViews output table, the sample statistics provided are z scores calculated from standard normal distributions. This is because, as explained in Box 12.3, logit estimation requires MLE techniques – asymptotic techniques that assume a large sample. As Student's t distribution is a small sample approximation of the standard normal distribution, t statistics are not reported.

Table 12.2 EViews output from estimation of the logit model

Dependent Variable: W
Sample: 1 50

Variable	Coefficient	Std. Error	t-Statistic	Prob.
Intercept	−4.46	1.95	−2.29	0.02
G	0.09	0.05	1.92	0.05

Log likelihood	−28.63	LR statistic (1 df)	3.84
Restr. log likelihood	−30.54	Probability (LR stat)	0.05
Obs with Dep = 0	35	Total observations	50
Obs with Dep = 1	15		

Note that the parameter estimate on G (0.09) is capturing the average marginal effect. It's important to re-emphasise that for logit (and probit) estimation the slopes are varying and the marginal effects will be conditional upon a particular value of the explanatory variable. The observed responsiveness for any given observation will be conditional upon the magnitude of the explanatory variable.

These results from the logit estimation are similar to the results from the estimation of the LPM; the null that the parameter on the Gini coefficient is equal to zero can be rejected at a 10% significance level. EViews does not provide R^2 for logit and probit estimations because R^2 is not particularly meaningful: it captures the goodness of fit in linear estimation and we are using logit – a non-linear estimation technique. As explained in Box 12.3, for non-linear models the log likelihood function is more meaningful than R^2 in measuring the relative 'fit' of the model. As shown in Box 12.3, calculating the log likelihood function involves summing together the log likelihoods across the sample and for the estimation of Equation (12.7) the restricted log likelihood is −30.55. This restricted log likelihood incorporates the restriction that the parameters on an explanatory variable are jointly equal to zero and so this statistic can also be calculated using EViews by regressing W just on the constant term. Notice also that this restricted log likelihood is approximately equal to the natural log of the estimated intercept in the LPM (see Table 12.1).

We can calculate the relative contribution of G to the model by comparing log likelihoods from the restricted and unrestricted versions (where the unrestricted model is the model including all the explanatory variables as well as the constant) using a Likelihood Ratio test as explained in Box 12.3.

Applying the LR test to our example this gives the following (the probability value is from EViews):

$$LR = 2(L_{UR} - L_R) = 2 \times (-28.63 + 30.55) = 3.84 \ [p = 0.05] \qquad (12.7)$$

With $p>0.05$ we can reject the null that the slope parameter on G is insignificantly different from zero at a 5% significance level. We can conclude that there is a statistically significant relationship between W and G and this confirms the findings from our Z test – in this sample of data there is a positive association between conflict and poverty.

How do these results differ from our LPM estimated using OLS? With the logit estimation, the estimates of the probability of war are bounded between 1 and 0 for all possible values of G. This is because the slope parameter, which captures the marginal effect of G on P_i, is not constant but is itself a function of G_i. At extreme values of G_i the change in the probability of war for a given change in G_i is very small but, for average values of G_i, the change in the probability of war for a given change in G_i is relatively large. These changes in the marginal effects are what ensure that the logistic function has the sigmoid shape described in Box 12.3.

The results from the estimation of the logit function seem plausible. But further investigations are needed to establish the directions of causality and possible simultaneity. There may also be other variables that are important, for example financial instability. A more thorough investigation of these issues would require a combination of techniques, for example logit/probit techniques to capture probabilities, combined with simultaneous equation estimation techniques to capture simultaneity. As mentioned above, simultaneous estimation is beyond the scope of this chapter but refer to Wooldridge (2003) for further guidance.

12.5   Implications and conclusions

The results from this chapter suggest that there is a positive relationship between poverty and conflict. If further studies establish that this positive association is robust, then strategies to promote peace should concentrate (amongst other things) upon ensuring a more equitable distribution of income and resources within economies.

More detailed analyses would have to take into account a range of other variables and in understanding conflict in poor countries it is important not only to examine the causes of war but also the consequences. Feedback effects may affect the relationship between poverty and conflict: just as poverty encourages conflict so conflict will exacerbate poverty. Collier and Hoeffler (2004) observe that conflicts will encourage opportunistic behaviour and weaken the institutions that usually provide low cost services and/or facilitate the smooth operation of the market mechanism, thus exacerbating poverty. This explains why conflict and inequality are so common in poor countries with abundant natural resources such as diamonds and oil (Collier, 2008).

During civil war, the ratio of military expenditure to GDP rises sharply, 'crowding out' social expenditures that could be used to promote broadly based development. So the poorest groups will suffer the most if economic decisions reflect military and political goals. Overall there will be the potential for a significant peace dividend when conflicts end not only in terms of economic growth but also in terms of a less impoverished society.

There may be other implications too: if arms are being imported (as they often are), then this may create external problems of balance of payments crisis and excessive foreign debt burdens. These will contribute to financial instability and will retard/reverse the evolution of modern financial institutions, creating substantial and prolonged constraints on the availability of finance.

12.6   Further reading

Textbooks and monographs

Collier, P. (2008) *The Bottom Billion*, Oxford: Oxford University Press.

Sandler, T. and Hartley, K. (1995) *The Economics of Defense*, New York: Cambridge University Press.

Schelling, T. (1960) *The Strategy of Conflict*, Cambridge, MA: Harvard University Press.

Thomas, R. L. (1997) *Modern Econometrics – An Introduction*, Harlow: Addison-Wesley, pp. 469–77.

Wooldridge, J. M. (2003) *Introductory Econometrics* (2nd edition), Thomson South-Western, Chapters 7 and 17.

Academic articles and working papers

Baddeley, M. C. (2008) 'Poverty, armed conflict and financial instability', *Cambridge Working Papers in Economics No. 0857, Faculty of Economics*, University of Cambridge.

Benoit, E. (1978) 'Growth and defense in developing countries', *Economic Development and Cultural Change*, vol. 26, 271–80.

Collier, P. and Hoeffler, A. (2004) 'Greed and grievance in civil wars', *Oxford Economic Papers*, vol. 56, 563–95.

Fitzgerald, E. V. K. (1997) 'Paying for the war: macroeconomic stabilization in poor countries under conflict conditions', *Oxford Development Studies*, 25(1), 43–65.

Schelling, T. (1958) 'The strategy of conflict – prospectus for a reorientation of Game Theory', *The Journal of Conflict Resolution*, vol. 2, no. 3 (September), 203–64.

Policy briefs

Jackson, M. O. and Morelli, M. (2005) 'War, Transfers, and Political Bias', http://economics.sbs. ohio-state.edu/morelli/warbias4.pdf.

UN *Millennium Development Goals Report 2007*, Geneva: United Nations.

UNDP, *Human Development Report*, Geneva: United Nations, various years.

World Bank, *World Development Report*, World Bank, Washington, various years.

12.7   Chapter exercises

1. Estimate a Probit version of Equation (12.1) using the data provided. Briefly explain the method and check your results against the results from this chapter.

2. In this chapter, we have focussed on only one of the potential determinants of conflict, i.e. poverty. Using the data sources cited in this chapter:

   (a) Collect your own data focussing on the variables that you think might be important determinants of armed conflict.

   (b) Construct an empirical model of conflict.

   (c) Estimate your model using binary estimation techniques.

   (d) Interpret your results and assess the policy implications.

Index

Printed in the United States
by Baker & Taylor Publisher Services